SOCIAL HAPPINESS
Theory into policy and practice

Neil Thin

First published in Great Britain in 2012 by

The Policy Press
University of Bristol
Fourth Floor
Beacon House
Queen's Road
Bristol BS8 1QU
UK

Tel +44 (0)117 331 4054
Fax +44 (0)117 331 4093
e-mail tpp-info@bristol.ac.uk
www.policypress.co.uk

North American office:
The Policy Press
c/o The University of Chicago Press
1427 East 60th Street
Chicago, IL 60637, USA
t: +1 773 702 7700
f: +1 773-702-9756
e:sales@press.uchicago.edu
www.press.uchicago.edu

British Library Cataloguing in Publication Data
A catalogue record for this book is available from the British Library.

Library of Congress Cataloging-in-Publication Data
A catalog record for this book has been requested.

ISBN 978 1 84742 919 3 paperback
ISBN 978 1 84742 920 9 hardcover

The right of Neil Thin to be identified as author of this work has been asserted
by him in accordance with the 1988 Copyright, Designs and Patents Act.

The statements and opinions contained within this publication are solely those
of the author and not of The University of Bristol or The Policy Press. The
University of Bristol and The Policy Press disclaim responsibility for any injury
to persons or property resulting from any material published in this publication.

The Policy Press works to counter discrimination on grounds of gender, race,
disability, age and sexuality.

Cover design by Qube Design Associates, Bristol
Front cover: image kindly supplied by wistock.com
Printed and bound in Great Britain by TJ International,
Padstow
The Policy Press uses environmentally responsible print
partners.

MIX
Paper from
responsible sources
FSC® C013056

This book is dedicated to my wife, Christine, and our three moderately happy children, Sandy, Flora and Tommy.

Contents

List of tables and boxes

Tables

Boxes

About the author

Neil Thin is a Senior Lecturer and Director of Undergraduate Teaching in the School of Social and Political Science at the University of Edinburgh. He lectures and researches on happiness, social planning, poverty, education, human rights, and sustainable development. Since the early 1980s he has been continuously active in international development cooperation as an adviser, trainer, planner, and policy evaluator at all levels from project work with local NGOs to policy analysis for global agencies such as the World Bank, UN-FAO, OECD-DAC, and UK-DFID. His book *Social Progress and Sustainable Development* (Rugby: ITDG Publications, 2002) was commissioned by the World Bank and UK-DFID.

Acknowledgements

This work has benefited greatly from a series of meetings and correspondence with fellow members of the *ProjectPlus* interdisciplinary happiness research group established and funded by Jean Timsit since 2009, to all of whom I am deeply grateful for their ongoing advice and warm friendship: Aaron Ahuvia, Robert Biswas-Diener, Ed Diener, Bruno Frey, Dan Haybron, Jennifer Michael Hecht, John Helliwell, Corey Keyes, Darrin McMahon, Matthieu Ricard, Jennifer Sweeton, and Stan Sweeton. I have also benefited from helpful advice from colleagues in various departments of the University of Edinburgh: Stewart Allen, Fabian Anicker, Francesca Bray, Gary Clapton, Jacob Copeman, Jennifer Curtis, Jan Eichhorn, Ian Harper, Toby Kelly, Christina McMellon, Sandy Robertson, Michael Rosie, Adrian Sinfield, Jonathan Spencer, Kay Tisdall, and Dimitri Tsintjilonis; and from colleagues elsewhere: Paul De'ath, Ivo Gormley, and Sarah White. Finally, many thanks to my wonderfully supportive and patient editor at The Policy Press, Emily Watt, and to three anonymous reviewers.

Preface: on happiness, rationality and empathy in scholarship and policy

> If you're poor, I hope you get rich. If you're rich, I hope you get happy. (Bob Dylan)

Everyday language can be refreshing in academic or policy discourse, improving their appeal and relevance. The sciences and policies of social transformation might engage more persuasively with a wider public if we sometimes made use of the experience-near concepts that people sing about, like love and happiness. We sing about these things because we care about them, and caring is the prerequisite of ethics and progress. If you care about the idea of personal or social progress, and think of any aspect of your life's work as 'progressive', you had better think carefully about whether you have enough understanding of happiness to pursue these ambitions. Even if, more modestly, you just want to 'matter' to other people, to behave 'ethically', and to be seen as a decent, caring person, do you honestly believe you can do these things without theories and knowledge about happiness?

Perhaps we all yearn for happiness and like to imagine ourselves as joy spreaders and purveyors of love, hope, empathy, and meaning. But by no means all of us find it acceptable or interesting to talk about happiness in public, or to make it an explicit personal aim or policy objective. To talk about values, or justice, or prosperity without reference to happiness, however, is perverse and potentially very damaging. Just having a happiness theory doesn't, of course, mean that your theory is a valid one, but no one can plausibly claim to be a force for the good in the world without some theory about how they contribute to happiness. Yet remarkably few scholars or change agents articulate such a theory. We have a long way to go before the study of happiness is routinely embedded in our instruction systems and policy discourse. Whether you're a social scientist or a someone who deliberately tinkers with society in any way, my aim is that by reading this book you will develop a clearer sense of what it means to apply a 'happiness lens' to your work, and of why this might improve your chances of making a benign difference to people's lives.

All happiness scholars need to be brave or foolhardy enough to confront big questions about the quality and meaning of life. Stephen

Jay Gould argued that there is 'no use writing a book on "the meaning of life"' and that 'you have to sneak up on generalities, not assault them head-on' (1983/1996, p 20). The argument for oblique approaches to happiness may well make sense as psychological advice or as a personal philosophy: it's not necessarily good for us to pursue happiness directly. But happiness scholars cheerfully disregard this kind of advice when it comes to the *study* of happiness, and an increasing number also advocate conscious *promotion* of happiness (though for a well-argued contrary view, see John Kay's excellent book *Obliquity*, 2010). By focusing on the positive aspects of life we reject also the view of Adam Phillips that 'the language of mental health – rather like the language of morality – comes to life, if at all, in descriptions of disability, incompetence, and failure' (2005, p 39). We don't believe that happiness can be effectively approached by stealth, or by detour of its opposites. This book is even broader than is customary in happiness books, insofar as it offers some degree of cross-temporal, cross-cultural, and interdisciplinary coverage, as well as exploring the social relationships and institutions that make personal subjective experiences possible.

The contemporary happiness-policy movement has been called a 'revolution', a 'new paradigm in development', and a 'new Enlightenment'. Radical or not, some significant shifts are occurring in both social science and social policy, from a concern with '*what's the matter?*' to an interest in '*what really matters?*'. The standard sociological motive is anger at social injustice, an anger that some believe the pursuit of happiness might displace, rendering us conservative and passive:

> This is not anger for which I need a therapist to help me 'come to terms with', displace, or sublimate [...] What really matters is tackling directly and virulently human suffering and social injustice globally [...] the reality of the human condition and global society is not happiness but misery. (Morrall, 2008, pp 5–6, 9)

These things matter, of course, and a bit of well-directed righteous anger makes life interesting and meaningful. But happiness matters too. And it is a social and public good, not just a private and individual concern. To understand and promote it, we must look between and around persons, not just within persons. Though the concept of happiness is vague enough to leave a lot of room for debate, the claim that happiness belongs in the centre of social science and policy discourse is a much stronger claim than the residualist rhetoric that 'the social' matters, that 'it's *not* just the economy, stupid'.

This book offers a positive response to rising doubts about whether our social sciences and policies are adequately engaged in questions of ultimate value, such as how people manage to enjoy life, find it meaningful, and sustain loving relationships. 'Life, liberty, and the never-ending struggle to minimise the worst forms of suffering' wouldn't sound great as a national or global ambition, but this has, in practice, been the guiding philosophy of most social research and social policy. Unlike cooking, gardening, or artistic creation, where your aim is to enrich people's experiences, in social policy the traditional approach has been to minimise harms rather than promote good lives. But several decades after Bhutan's king announced that 'Gross National Happiness' would henceforth be the guiding star for his country, many other countries are now following suit. Most western governments are measuring national happiness and their leaders are increasingly referring to happiness, if rather vaguely, as a key policy outcome. China's Prime Minister Wen Jiabao has told his vast army of bureaucrats that their performance is to be judged by how good they are at making people happy.

Bhutan and China, both with recent records of antidemocratic government action and weak respect for human rights, may not seem ideal sources of inspiration. Indeed, some very much worse regimes, and some far-from-saintly contemporary businesses, have traded on false promises of happiness. Yet this book asserts confidently that social research and policies must pay explicit attention to happiness. At the same time, it explains and illustrates how happiness, though typically conceived by psychologists and western publics as individual-level subjectivity, is itself essentially intersubjective and social. It is not just about private self-interest, it is about love, empathy, and engagement in the workplace and in communities, and about collective aspirations for a world that could be even better than it already is. Indeed, of the factors consistently found to correlate with happiness self-reports – marriage, relationships, employment, perceived health, religion, and quality of government (Bok, 2010, pp 17, 30) – nearly all are social, confirming that our happiness is socially constituted. Even if our primary ethical duty is to ourselves, we can't expect to fulfil this duty via narrowly selfish happiness pursuits. You may not entirely agree with educational philosopher John Macmurray's claim that 'All meaningful knowledge is for the sake of action, and all meaningful action for the sake of friendship' (1957, p 17), but it's a fair argument that, in general, we learn about the world in order to lead more fulfilling lives by engaging better with our fellow humans. That's what social happiness is.

The belief that drives the book is this: that by attending explicitly to the cultural and social construction of happiness, we can greatly strengthen the chances that our private and collective attitudes, our choices, and our actions will make benign contributions to personal and social progress. If we bring up children *for the sake of their happiness*, this is different from, and better than, bringing them up for the sake of their future roles as income providers, as soldiers, or as perfect examples of beauty or skill. If we see happiness as both an expected outcome of the realisation of human rights, and as a crucial contributor to their realisation, our promotion of rights will make better sense of the inevitable trade-offs involved. If we genuinely run businesses for the sake of the happiness of workforces, of customers, and of the wider public, this is a nobler and ultimately more sustainable calling than the short-term pursuit of profit. A happiness lens is not just lightweight truistic flannel: it implies a set of serious, difference-making concerns that deserve our full attention and investment.

As well as the private:social issue there is also a question mark over whether, if at all, happiness is best apprehended loosely through intuitions and personal experiences and stories, or whether it can usefully be studied in technical ways involving measurement, and/or in other scholarly ways such as philosophical and cultural analysis. I show here the valuable contributions of a wide variety of scholarly and unscholarly happiness theories, and from a range of diverse cultural contexts, although inevitably western-biased, since the bulk of writing on happiness comes from rich western countries.

My approach here is to make distinct contributions, complementing other texts so far on happiness policy by deploying the following qualities:

- **Interdisciplinarity:** I engage with scholarship from a wide range of disciplines, including not only those most commonly associated with happiness policy such as psychology, economics, and policy studies, but also anthropology, business studies, pedagogical studies, environmental studies, geography, development studies, moral philosophy, and religious studies.
- **Multidomain:** Unlike some thematic specialisms, happiness is something everyone has valid opinions on. So although this book is mainly based on academic scholarship, I also link this with happiness theories, policies, and opinions as expressed in various

walks of life, including media, business, government, and civil society organisations. I also make frequent reference to popular texts on self-help and life-coaching themes, which tend not to make substantial use of happiness scholarship but which are nonetheless important players in the development of happiness-aware culture at personal and collective levels.

- **Cross-cultural comparative approach:** Whereas most literature on happiness, and particularly on happiness policy, remains restricted to affluent western societies, this book considers evidence and prospects for application in a much wider range of contexts. As in many areas of social science, a huge percentage of the best literature is produced in the US. The book remains western biased but I have tried throughout to deparochialise by offering nonwestern examples where they seem helpful.
- **Meso-level:** Since there is already copious literature on happiness promotion at individual levels and at the macro-level of national policies, I try here to complement this by focusing on the middle ground in which 'social happiness' is culturally and socially produced through everyday interactions, in what the human ecologist Bronfenbrenner (1979) called the 'meso-system' of families, schools, neighbourhoods, and carers, and the 'exo-system' of wider social networks, media, and workplaces.
- **Morally balanced:** Though arguing strongly for more explicit attention to happiness in scholarship and policy-related discourse, I do also try to tread carefully between naïve promotion of happiness policy on the one hand, and exaggerated scepticism on the other. We do need to consider possible errors and harms of happiness policies, and the (still rather remote) possibility that happiness-focused research and policy could distract too much attention away from the more pressing needs of the world's more disadvantaged people.

It is odd that no other books have carried the title 'social happiness' and that happiness has yet to develop as a core theme in social policy disciplines. Perhaps everyone just assumes that policies are always social, and always directed towards happiness. I believe, however, that there are some surprisingly new currents of interest reasserting the need for policy and scholarship to be genuinely 'social' (on which subject please see my previous book, *Social Progress*, 2002) and truly focused on happiness. Some may see this as an unwarranted distraction from social repair and social protest, but I argue here that these latter aims can't be either efficient or virtuous without substantial attention to happiness.

In both parts of the book I address some unavoidably complex and controversial debates, but both in the more philosophical Part One and in the more directly practical and policy-engaged Part Two I have tried to offer a good range of empirical evidence and to simplify issues so as to make it clear and practical enough to be of interest to most readers outside of the relevant academic specialisms. It should therefore be useful to anyone who recognises that their academic discipline or their professional or voluntary work could be improved through better understanding of the social processes by which happiness is facilitated. I have not shied away from academic debates, but I have tried to make these accessible to those who don't yet have a full grounding in happiness scholarship or who have so far limited themselves to studying happiness from within one or two disciplines. Given the breadth of disciplines that I draw on, to avoid excessive weightiness I have simplified many debates and relied heavily on identifying key issues for debate and providing further reading recommendations on specific issues at the end of each chapter.

Part One provides an introduction to the (mainly European and North American) history of happiness themes in scholarship, policy, and moral discourse. It brings us up to date with recognition of the rapidly growing diversity of academic disciplines and policy domains in which happiness, along with empathy and respect for subjectivity more generally, is emerging as a much more explicit theme than was the case throughout most of the 20th century. I spell out what I see as the five core implications of applying a 'happiness' lens in these various domains of enquiry and practice, namely: *empathy* (showing an interest in people's feelings), *positivity* (attention to goodness), *holism*, a *lifespan perspective*, and *transparency*. I then explore the various ways in which, in principle, using a happiness lens can make particular kinds of difference to various aspects of the policy process – *causal analysis*, *goal-setting*, *ethical justification*, and choice of *indicators* for evaluation. A conceptual section explains why definitions of happiness matter but are not as difficult as is sometimes made out. This section also explores some of the sceptical objections to the ideas and values of happiness policy, before providing a basic introduction to happiness scholarship and its methods, analytical approaches, indicators, and tools.

Part Two explores more directly the actual and potential interplay between happiness scholarship and a wide variety of domains of social experience. This enters largely uncharted territory as far as explicit 'happiness' scholarship is concerned. Most happiness scholarship stops short of providing practical advice, and most texts that have begun translating findings into policy and practice have focused either at the individual self-help level or at the macro-level of national policies. Instead, I focus here on ways in which scholarship can help guide policy and practice in meso-level social environments – families, schools, businesses, and community organisations. In doing so, I draw on a great deal of scholarship that was not explicitly produced under a 'happiness' rubric but that is nonetheless relevant to the explicit promotion of happiness.

Neil Thin
Edinburgh, July 2011

Part One
Happiness in policy discourse and research

ONE

Introduction: prosperity debates and the happiness lens

'A quantum of happiness'

> Be happy while you're living, for you're a long time dead.
> (Scottish proverb)

Three core ideas underpin the current tide of enthusiasm for happiness policy worldwide: that *happiness is what counts*, that *happiness should be counted*, and that *happiness can be improved*. This book argues for stronger attention to a fourth, rather looser idea: that *happiness is social* – that it emerges from good social relations, from enculturation, and from fair institutions.

Lest any of these ideas seem so obvious as not to require research or explicit policy emphasis, it may help to start with a quick tour of the uneven development of these ideas since the Enlightenment. Different trajectories of similar ideas can be traced in many countries worldwide, but a convenient foothold in the modern history of happiness scholarship is offered by taking a quick glance at a handful of Scots who developed happiness theories in the 18th and 19th centuries, with extraordinary global effects. If this helps to dispel the popular image of a Scottish culture dominated by Calvinist dourness, so much the better.

The modern European version of the idea that happiness is what counts (and, just as importantly, that *everyone counts as one*) was first proposed by the Irish Scot Francis Hutcheson in the 1720s (1725). Against many potentially deadly religious fundamentalists and defenders of aristocratic privilege, he argued that the point of morality, and hence of governance, was to achieve the 'greatest happiness for the greatest numbers'. This 'utilitarian' principle was much later taken up by Jeremy Bentham, Thomas Paine, Thomas Jefferson and many other European and North American moral and political philosophers and reformers. Whether or not we agree entirely with utilitarianism, it is hard to dispute the moral and political significance of basing our morality on the appreciation of everyone's happiness. At the time, it constituted a radically new argument for rational, fair, and empathetic governance.

What it needed, but didn't get until late in the 20th century, was the support of systematic happiness scholarship.

Hutcheson's path-breaking work was followed by David Hume and Adam Smith, both of whom spread the idea that 'sympathy' – considering other people's (good or bad) feelings as if they were ours – is the 'natural' basis for our moral and political systems. Hume, arguably more influential than any other moral philosopher, and best known for his insistence that our rationality is rooted in our passions rather than being separable from them, developed the idea of scientifically studying the 'social virtues' – systematic links between the happiness of the individual and the goodness of society. At the core of his thinking lies the idea that 'benevolence' derives from individual passions and from our ability to recognise and appreciate other people's feelings. Social approval derives from our recognition of this quality of benevolence, of the contributions people make to social happiness.

Smith, founder of Economics and more spectacularly diverse in his interests and capabilities than Hume, similarly emphasised the importance of recognising that *happiness is social*: individual happiness matters, but pure individualism won't make us happy, because our happiness requires recognition of the happiness (and unhappiness) of others. Smith is best known as the original champion of capitalism: his most widely recognised contribution is the optimistic opinion that *commercial society performs better than any other at producing happiness*. But Smith was more complex than his reputation for optimism would imply. Sympathy may be natural, but so is greed both for material goods and for social esteem. Smith saw that *the greed that drives commerce is bad for individual happiness in its direct effects*. If commerce produces good happy societies by fostering excellent opportunities for fair governance and secure social order, it comes with a health warning. People are liable to make themselves miserable pursuing interim goods that can never provide them with the contentment they crave. In arguing that the poor in contemporary Europe were often happier than the rich, Smith the herald of capitalism was also an advocate of what is now known as 'downshifting' – drawing back from the self-destructive pursuit of wealth (Rasmussen, 2006). Smith wouldn't have been at all surprised by our current debates on the rethinking of prosperity.

Next up, John Sinclair published during the 1790s his 21-volume *Statistical Account of Scotland*. In coining the new term 'statistics', Sinclair laid the foundation-stone not just for modern national accounting, but more specifically for what has become the backbone of contemporary happiness scholarship and public policy discourse on happiness. He defined 'statistical accounting' as '*an inquiry into the state of a country, for the purpose of ascertaining the quantum of happiness enjoyed by its inhabitants, and the means of its future improvement*' (Sinclair, 1798, vol 20, p xiii). Hutcheson would have been proud to see this practical application of scientific study in support of national-level promotion of his utilitarian philosophy.

Then, in the mid-19th century, the aptly named Scottish politician Samuel Smiles published the world's first blockbuster self-help book, cunningly titled *Self-help* (Smiles, 1859). Though sharing Hutcheson's views that everyone's happiness is what matters, Smiles was a liberal who hitched the 'self-help' mantra to a political doctrine of *negative* utilitarianism. Governments, that is, should protect us from unhappiness rather than trying to make us happy. His core argument was that individuals must find and earn their own happiness and that 'the function of Government is negative and restrictive, rather than positive and active; being resolvable principally into protection – protection of life, liberty, and property'. The self-help and life coaching businesses that have followed in his wake are now said to have a turnover in excess of US$12 billion (http://answers.google.com/answers/threadview/id/786161.html). Self-help businesses have encouraged millions of individuals to seek their own private happiness paths, while until recently governments have tended to agree with Smiles that the direct promotion and assessment of citizens' happiness is not their business.

Whether the 18th- and 19th-century Scottish efflorescence owed more to the utilitarian spirit of Hutcheson, to Hume's antireligious emphasis on natural social conscience, to Smith's optimism about commerce, to Sinclair's magic of numbers, or to the self-help bootstrap spirit of Smiles (self-made business magnates such as Andrew Carnegie and William Lever read *Self-help* during their adolescence), we'll never know. But that era saw the export of an extraordinary number of the world's most important inventions from the tiny population of the Scottish intelligentsia: Watt's steam engine, McAdam's tarmac roads, Logie Baird's television, Fleming's anaesthesia, Patrick Geddes' idea of socially informed town planning, John Muir's wilderness heritage and national parks movement, and Walter Scott's revolution in popular fiction. Not to mention football and the kilt. None of these inventors, to my knowledge, offered their intellectual services explicitly in the name of happiness, but it's a fair bet that the colossal happiness benefits of all of their inventions have massively outweighed the costs, and that the cultural efflorescence that facilitated their work also illustrates the creative power of social happiness.

Another Scot, the utopian but also pragmatic socialist Robert Owen, did try to promote both social justice and social happiness in his model industrial villages. Owen came closer than any of the above to promoting social happiness policy through everyday social institutions, and though his experiments in Scotland and the US were not lasting successes, he did play an important part in spreading the idea that it might one day be possible to organise production in ways that were both efficient, fair, and enjoyable for everyone. This idea, that the value of work lies in the enjoyment of the *process* of working, rather than just in the deferred gratification of the end products, still sounds radical today, but is enjoying a renaissance.

The Enlightenment tide of scholarly and political attention to happiness did not, however, continue to rise steadily through the 20th century. Despite witnessing bloodshed and destruction on a bigger scale than ever before, the century also saw rapid democratisation of both politics and scholarship worldwide. These developments were driven more by concerns for removing harms and unfairnesses than by any explicit thought of maximising happiness. There was of course intermittent interest in happiness in many disciplines, but for much of the 20th century it remained a minority concern. As early as 1930, the psychologist Goodwin Watson noted that it was 'extraordinary almost beyond belief that so few attempts have been made to apply the techniques of psychological study to the understanding of happiness' (1930, p 79), but several years before his landmark study of students' happiness there had been several modern studies of marital happiness (Angner, 2004, chapter 2). Since the 1990s, happiness scholarship has again been flourishing and diversifying. Though still dominated by self-report surveys conducted either in rich countries or among comparatively affluent people (particularly university students) in poorer countries, it has been spreading to an ever greater variety of contexts and deploying a more interesting range of research methods. As it has begun to seem possible that more pressing concerns of food security, justice, and peace can be guaranteed for most of the world's population, so our interest has turned to post-scarcity, post-nastiness, post-injustice philosophical concerns which in the 19th century might more justifiably have been seen as luxury interests of the elite.

Even if democratic pragmatism explains the neglect of happiness in the 20th century, it is still weird that it should have so fallen out of favour that its contemporary renaissance makes people refer to public happiness as a 'hot topic', as if this were a temporary fad. A few years from now, I hope and expect that anyone engaging in social policy or practice, or in any discipline claiming to enhance the quality of life, or the quality of society, or the quality of specific domains such as the workplace, school, leisure facility, family, or community, will be expected to have at least a basic grounding in happiness scholarship or well-being studies. This is certainly not the same as saying that we will stop being concerned with harm and injustice, it's just that they will be increasingly complemented by attention to well-being. Also, the forms of ill-being will increasingly have more to do with philosophical challenges such as existential boredom, time poverty, relative deprivation, and unrealistic aspirations than with money and basic survival needs. And the questions about injustice will have less to do with deliberate nastiness and more to do with unintentional inequities that require positive imagination and cooperation for their resolution.

Filling the happiness-sized hole: towards more rational and sympathetic social science

Historians of 20th-century development will marvel at the happiness-sized hole in policy processes and academic discourse. They will be dismayed at how little attention was paid in policy analysis to the things that ultimately matter for us – our feelings, and our quest to find a good sense of purpose, meaning, and achievement in our lives. They will wonder how social scientists and development practitioners can have allowed this attention deficit to persist for so long. Although many policy-related texts on social development, health, gender, rights, and environment make frequent passing references to 'well-being' and 'welfare', remarkably few theorise or analyse these concepts and hardly any pay serious attention to people's happiness. Instead, they focus on harm, or on resources (money, property, technology), or on 'objective' indicators of progress (bodily health, longevity).

While some neglected happiness, others denied its relevance to governance. Karl Popper propounded a 'negative utilitarianism' philosophy, arguing that the business of politics is to ensure avoidance of unnecessary suffering, rather than (or as a higher priority than) to promote happiness (1962). Essentially, the proposal of negative utilitarianism is this: *if it isn't bothersome, don't bother with it*. Get rid of the weeds and pests, but otherwise let the garden take care of itself. It proved all too easy to show that the normally brilliant Popper let himself down badly with this obviously indefensible proposal. Popper grossly over-reacted to the possibility that utopian perfectionists might misuse utilitarian principles and try too hard to make people happy (Smart, 1958).

Like Enlightenment scholars, those of us advocating a happiness lens today propose that happiness matters, that it can be systematically studied, that its development requires empathic self-transcendence, and that we can increase it by applying scientific knowledge to personal and social transformation. The other claim we share with Enlightenment scholars is that, by attending to happiness, we can all potentially organise our thoughts and knowledge in more rational ways. Then and now, happiness promotion isn't just seen as morally desirable, it is also the most rational way of organising our plans and our evaluations. Conversely, failure to use a happiness lens is likely to result in worryingly irrational organisation of studies and policies. Both rationality and happiness have made immense progress since the Enlightenment, yet the organisation of our studies falls a long way short of rationality, and our policies are by no means clearly focused on the job of promoting happiness.

Indeed, this text is written in the belief that a happiness lens in scholarship and policy is a way of rekindling the Enlightenment project of organising scholarship rationally in order to improve the quality and the enjoyment of human life. If we are to make progress in linking academic studies with policies that offer better prospects for happiness, we could well start by recognising some general biases in the organisation of our academic disciplines. It would only be a slight exaggeration to say that none of the modern social sciences has a coherent sense of rational purpose with a suitable and clearly defined scope.

Each discipline has its own cultural histories that have produced remarkable quirkiness and embarrassing attention deficits, all of which would be substantially challenged by the introduction of a 'happiness' lens:

- **Psychology**, traditionally much more interested in mental pathologies than happiness even when applied to therapeutic work (but see Fava and Ruini, 2009), is rapidly being transformed by the Positive Psychology that has flourished since the late 1990s, though it has antecedents in the work of humanistic psychologists in the 1950s and 1960s. Still, Psychology's other bias, its ego focus and consequently inadequate attention to the social construction of identities and capabilities, had not been challenged enough (Parker, 2007; Biswas-Diener, 2011). This individualism explains why Psychology is often, counterintuitively, excluded from lists of the 'social' sciences.
- **Sociology**, **Social Policy** and **Social Work** have always been dominated by a deficit orientation obsessed with problems. Social Policy has miraculously transformed the concepts of 'welfare' and 'benefit' into stigma terms associated with undignified dependence

on state-funded pay-outs and protections. It has largely failed to theorise the concept of 'well-being' that so many of its proponents claim to be central to the discipline (Haworth and Hart, 2007; Greve, 2010). Positive qualities of relationships have received minimal attention in social analysis, as compared with social pathologies. Social Work has recently begun to develop an interest in positive strategies for constructive promotion of strengths (Wieck et al, 1989) and well-being (Jordan, 2007).

- **Anthropology** for much of its history showed minimal interest in how people actually experience the social and cultural institutions through which they organise their lives (Thin, 2005, 2008). The fairly recent trends towards analysis of emotion in Anthropology have mainly focused on adverse emotion, and prior to that the rare anthropologists who wrote about happiness tended to do so in appallingly undertheorised, romantic ways, celebrating the joys of non-western cultures with no attempt at developing a plausible evaluative or interpretive framework.

- **Economics** quickly departed from Adam Smith's idea of studying how private motives produce social happiness, and most economists have followed Jevons' (1871) assumption that interpersonal welfare comparisons must be done indirectly, since feelings are inaccessible. What they call 'the economy' has been grotesquely distorted and reduced from its 18th-century meaning. Reduced to monetised transactions, it excludes most of what we actually value and need. Echoing Schumacher's (1966/1973) plea for 'Economics as if People Mattered', or 'Buddhist Economics', there has recently been a chorus of declarations of the need for radical transformation of the discipline, from the Parisian students' manifesto of 'non-autistic Economics' (Fullbrooke, 2003), to Halpern's plea for recognition of the 'hidden wealth' in 'economy of regard' (2010), to a variety of 'Happiness Revolution' declarations (Layard, 2005; Anielski, 2007; Frey, 2008), and numerous revisionist manifestos steering economists in more humane directions: 'Caring Economics' (Folbre, 2001; Eisler, 2007); 'New Economics' (Boyle and Simms, 2009); and 'Compassionate Economics' (Norman, 2008).

- **Education Studies** have perhaps paid happiness slightly more heed than most other social sciences, and in a few rich western countries the potentially revolutionary concept of 'Social and Emotional Learning' is rapidly gaining mainstream attention (Durlak et al, 2011). But schooling worldwide remains the policy area that is most strikingly negligent in its systematic inattention to happiness. It is still astonishingly common to see educational studies, policies, and evaluations that fail to consider either the happiness of pupils (as a success factor or an outcome) or the contributions of education to lifelong happiness.

- **Development Studies** have largely focused on the poorer countries that have seen the least development, paying absurdly disportionate attention to aid-funded interventions and to those led by state or 'developmental' civil society organisations rather than the for-profit businesses that are responsible for most of development. More worryingly still, the sub-discipline of 'social development' within Development Studies has specialised mainly in the understanding of poverty and human rights abuses rather in the promotion of good lives and social goods, as if development were all about poverty and as if the only interesting stories to tell about poor people concerned their deprivations and sufferings, rather than their resilience and forms of thriving (Thin, 2002; Schimmel, 2009).

- **Gender Studies** and gender reform movements, although slowly and painfully struggling away from the 'women's studies' and 'women's liberation' traps, remain dominated by compensatory discourses by women, about women, and for women. Ironically, by largely ignoring the happiness of women and men, a great deal of feminist scholarship and gender reform policy remains fixated on the traditionally 'male' values of money, access to paid employment, status, and political power. The feminist ethic of care is exceptional in this regard, but has still a rather limited influence on mainstream feminism.

- **Childhood Studies** provide striking antidotes to the common vision of childhood as an exceptionally happy phase in life and the common belief that adults can become happier by recapturing the joyfulness and playful creativity of childhood and 'getting in touch with our inner child'. Most of the scholarly and therapeutic attention to childrearing and education addresses childhood pathologies and subsequent adverse outcomes or therapeutic treatments. Even reviews purportedly on 'good childhood' (Layard and Dunne, 2009) and 'child well-being' (Bradshaw, 2002) routinely focus almost entirely on suffering.

- **Human Rights Studies** have always been more about wrongs than rights. In our era of unprecedented progress towards universal enjoyment of rights, scholars and activists working under this rubric remain mesmerised by abuses and transgressions. Though professing the globalisation of respect and empathy, they have paradoxically proceeded in ways inimical to empathy, splitting humanity into rights-claiming victims on the one hand and duty-holding wrongdoers and neglecters on the other. Subjective experience, particularly if it is good experience, goes largely unrepresented in human rights reports.

- **Legal Studies** have treated legal processes as if they were mainly about achieving social order via abstract conceptions of justice. Empathy has deliberately been kept at bay among lawyers and legal students, for reasons of professional detachment (Bandes, 2000). Scholarly and professional interest in the relations between happiness, empathy, and legal processes is now rapidly gaining ground (Bagaric and McConvill, 2005; Sunstein and Posner, 2010). There is also growing recognition of epidemic levels of unhappiness and stress among lawyers and legal students, attributed both to the futile attempts to drive out empathy and to the distorted values of profit-seeking legal firms (Seligman, Verkuil and Kang, 2005; Peterson and Peterson, 2009).

- **Health and Mental Health Sciences** have focused mainly on illness and medicine. Worldwide, state-funded 'health' services remain medicine driven and patient focused, despite common understanding that it is much more humane and cost-effective to prevent illness by promoting health and well-being. Everyday production of normal health, largely due to non-medical factors, is taken for granted. It is considered 'progressive' to promote 'patient-centred' health services, as if the health of non-patients were not part of the remit of national health services. Even 'quality of life' research in medicine emphasises pathologies and disabilities rather than enjoyments and abilities (Bowling, 2003, pp 1–2). Inflationary prescription of anti-depressant drugs continues, despite clear empirical evidence that for most patients the benefits, if any, are largely due to placebo effects that could be achieved more cheaply, sustainably, and effectively by psychotherapy and/or social therapy (Breggin, 1998/2001; Bentall, 2009; Kirsch, 2009).

- **Leisure Studies**, which most of us would surely see as a form of happiness scholarship, are, unsurprisingly, more happiness-oriented than the rest of the social sciences. In fact, there have in the past been calls to relabel 'Leisure Studies' as 'Life Satisfaction Studies' (see critique by Rojek, 2005, pp 40–1). But even here it is not uncommon to find collections of essays on leisure that largely ignore the successful enjoyment of leisure, and instead focus mainly on the stresses and difficulties of coping with time pressure, and on new forms of leisure inequality.

- **Business, Organisation, and Management Studies** have attended to happiness since the development of worker satisfaction studies in the 1940s, broadening this later to the 'Total Quality Management' emphasis on stakeholder happiness (Ishikawa, 1985), 'socially responsible business', and 'conscious capitalism' (Aburdene, 2005). Since the 1990s there has been useful research on harmonies and conflicts between work and family, leisure, and prosocial commitments. If business guru Daniel Pink is right in claiming that we are in a new 'Conceptual Age' in which 'qualities of inventiveness, empathy, joyfulness, and meaning increasingly will determine who flourishes and who flounders' (2006, p 3), then we can expect that successful businesses will show increasingly explicit interest in happiness.

If these critiques of our collective academic irrationalities are fair, it should also be clear that these happiness-neglecting tendencies also entail some rather worrying *empathy barriers*. That is, they inhibit that extraordinary capability we have of allowing our own minds to reflect and experience the perspectives and feelings of other people. For example, the pathological bias puts up two kinds of empathy barrier. First, by focusing on people in trouble we screen out those whose lives are going fairly well, and so fail to learn about the miraculous psychological and social processes courtesy of which most of us – despite the horrors that dog our every step through life – manage to sustain moderate happiness. Second, regarding people in trouble, by attending to the harms they suffer we screen out those many other dimensions of their lives that are going well, and so we miss the many strengths and enjoyments of people living in poverty, of people living with disabilities, and so on. This road leads to compassion or pity, but not to empathy and respect.

Towards social happiness policy

In social policy and development ethics, the approach that comes closest so far to the happiness lens is the 'capabilities' approach that has been advocated by Amartya Sen since the 1970s and has been a key inspiration for 'human development' policies and assessments worldwide. Sen has long been seen as antagonistic to the idea of happiness as a policy goal for development. But in his recent work Sen has clarified that of course happiness is intrinsically valuable and important, that it is a good kind of capability, and that his objection is merely to the 'imperialist role' of happiness as the 'sole objective' of development (Sen, 2009, p 276).

To anyone who shares my view that governments, development agencies, and development scholars have been remarkably negligent of happiness, Sen's worries about excessive foregrounding of happiness come across as a bizarre fantasy, a straw target that seems to have been the basis of Sen's refusal until recently to make or encourage any substantial link between the 'capabilities' approach and happiness studies. The 'imperialists' Sen criticises are welfare economists, and his main contemporary example is his 'long-term friend' Richard Layard, who has worked so hard in recent years to bring happiness into policy discourse in the UK. Sen agrees with Layard that happiness matters, but objects to his claim that happiness is the only 'self-evident' good.

Sen's frequent critiques of welfare economics over several decades have been critiques of principle, warning us in general against being over-enthusiastic about the idea of happiness as the sole measure of goodness. But he hasn't provided evidence that such a worldview actually translates into bad policies, or practices that have bad outcomes. He argues, for example, that 'the utilitarian calculus based on happiness or desire-fulfilment can be deeply unfair to those who are persistently deprived' (2009, p 282). These moral warnings need to be substantiated by real-world examples of how 'unfairness', through bad policies, decisions, or practices, derives from the philosophical position of 'welfarism'. A philosophical theory that seems 'unfair' in the rarified, detached atmosphere of deliberately non-empirical reasoning may turn out, when translated into real-world applications, not to be unfair at all. Even after more than 60 years of happiness measurement, no one to my knowledge is yet out there using a 'felicific calculus' as the *sole* basis for personal or institutional decision making.

Our current era is experiencing a crescendo of interest in the possibilities for more happiness-focused policies. This builds on longer-running movements: environmentalism, communitarianism, social medicine, child-centred social and emotional education, and associated arguments in favour of looking at 'social indicators' and at 'quality of life'. But it adds a new, stronger emphasis not only on the intrinsic value of social processes but on the importance of understanding progress by looking at subjective experiences and listening to subjective evaluations rather than relying mainly on expert-driven 'objective' measures like money, physical resources, and bodily health. This tide of positivity and empathy is affecting a wide variety of policy domains and institutions:

- **Schools**, particularly in richer western countries, have begun introducing happiness classes and other activities intended primarily to promote enjoyment and to help children develop a positive approach to life.

- **Youth workers** are increasingly expected to focus on strengths, motivation, and resilience rather than assuming young people to be vulnerable, prone to crime, and in need of protection or saving.
- **Employers** are monitoring workplace happiness and taking active steps to enrich their employees' social lives, to facilitate meaningful and enjoyable work experiences, and to help people find positive synergies between work and other aspects of their lives.
- **Hospitals and geriatric homes** are paying attention to individual choice and sense of agency, flowers, pets, and views of nature as ways of facilitating the happiness that they now know speeds recovery and prolongs life.
- **Music and sports facilitators** are shifting emphasis from the excellence of a few elite players to the active and less-than-perfect but enthusiastic engagement of the masses.
- **Crime-fighters**, **therapists**, and others charged with reduction of pathologies are increasingly looking to positive activities that reduce harm by facilitating the collective enjoyment of meaningful activities.
- **Lawyers** are holding conferences with positive psychologists and rethinking the justification of law, legal processes, and legal decisions in the light of evidence about what makes people happy.
- **Environmental planners** are becoming less obsessed with pollution and are exploring the ways in which good environments facilitate good lives and good experiences.

Most public policy in most countries has hitherto normally proceeded as if happiness could be taken for granted, as if we didn't need to explore and explain how happiness emerges from harm fighting and from provision of interim goods like money and services. Happiness research has been slow to translate into policy and practice. Championed mainly for its rhetorical potential in macro-level political debate, empirical knowledge about happiness is rarely directed towards specific practical social policies. 'Social happiness policy' is doubly oxymoronic to many people: quite wrongly, people associate happiness with individualism, and 'social' with trouble. If scholars want to be taken seriously as promoters of social progress, they need to appreciate that what goes right with people's lives is at least as intriguing as the things that go wrong, and that social goods are every bit as worthy of study as social problems.

Efforts to apply happiness scholarship to real life have so far emphasised either individual-level therapy, life coaching, and self-help, or macro-level policies such as tax, employment, and wealth distribution. In this book, I address the vast middle ground of social transformations and more minor adjustments in families, teams, communities, workplaces, and networks that might derive from new happiness-related knowledge. The core proposal of the book is that we will engage with these middle-ground social realities more rationally, empathetically, and effectively if we apply a 'happiness lens' to all parts of the policy process.

This has two parts: *promoting happiness*; and *considering happiness*, which is often a good idea regardless of whether the policy in question is itself mainly aimed at promoting happiness. Many people have reasonable objections to naïve versions of the 19th-century utilitarian ideology of 'maximising happiness'. But those doubts are no excuse for neglecting happiness altogether. Use of a happiness lens in social policy analysis reminds us that happiness matters both intrinsically and instrumentally, and that promoting it and sustaining it requires collective actions, policies, and learning strategies, not just self-help and therapy.

Between the micro-personal and the macro-political there is a wide meso-world of 'society' – families, clubs, workplaces, community organisations, social movements, social networks, and thematic institutions – that is ripe for evidence-based guidance. It is in this sense, with reference to social relationships and institutions, that I advocate policies for 'social happiness' that help people to achieve personal happiness without losing sense of the importance of social and ecological embeddedness. As many scholars have argued (see for example Haworth, 2010; Biswas-Diener, 2011), social and cultural modification is essential for the promotion of well-being. Indeed, individual self-help and coping mechanisms are often best understood as responses to social and cultural pathologies (Zuzanek, 2004, p 139; Edgerton, 1992).

Until recently most happiness promoters in the giant and largely unregulated self-help business proceeded without reference to empirical research. Most empirical research on happiness has yet to be actively promoted as the basis for helping people to get happier. And of the research-based happiness advocacy that is available, most focuses on either individual self-help or (to a much lesser extent) on macro-level national policies. While some self-help advice is in some ways 'social' or 'environmental', much of it is micro-personal, addressing self-oriented bits of personhood rather than holistically seeking to improve lives as wholes embedded within wider societies and ecologies.

Translating from empirical happiness studies into policy

Since the late 1990s (Kahneman, 1999), scholars from a wide range of disciplines as well as media commentators and public figures have been celebrating the rapid rise of happiness studies and anticipating its maturation into a new phase in which the increasingly rich body of knowledge will be used in evidence-based policy. The boom in happiness research has potentially revolutionary implications for social and economic policy worldwide. As the evolutionary psychologist Geoffrey Miller puts it, 'if we take the happiness research seriously, most of the standard rationales for economic growth, technological progress, and improved social policy simply evaporate' (Miller, 2000). It isn't clear that we had 'standard rationales' for these policy objectives in the first place: happiness scholarship doesn't invite us to abandon them, but it does encourage us to rethink priorities and justifications to see if they can be organised better from a happiness perspective.

Happiness policies are all positive to the extent that they are meant to make people's lives go better than they otherwise would. But some emphasise attention to harm (its prevention, mitigation, or removal) while others are more positive and inclusive in that they emphasise attention to the good life, and so are meant to ensure that everyone benefits, not just sufferers. It is mainly these latter, 'good life' or 'eudaimonic' policies (Ryff and Singer, 2008) that this book will focus on, since there is no shortage of scholarly studies on remedial, harm-reducing approaches to well-being.

The idea of actively promoting uptake of happiness/well-being research findings in social policy has been rather slow to take off in happiness studies, and the few works that address this challenge substantially stick mainly to generalities plus some specific national-level interventions. There are now thousands of texts on international and intertemporal well-being comparison (see for example Diener et al, 2010), but only a tiny minority of these attempt to explore the policy relevance of their analysis and findings. The last few years have, however, seen a healthy efflorescence of texts arguing for plausible translations from happiness research into policies and applications. So far, most policy recommendations have been theories based on analysis of happiness survey responses rather than on analysis of real-world policy experiments. They have also been predominantly targeted at macro-level national policies rather than at middle-level changes in families, communities, and businesses that most of us might be able to influence fairly directly in our everyday lives.

In the UK, the Demos collection entitled *The good life* (Christie and Nash, 1998) presented an evidence-based challenge to governments and businesses to take happiness seriously as a policy objective. It seems to have achieved little, perhaps because its arguments were spoiled by a predominance of declinism and doom-mongery, making tokenistic use of happiness findings as an excuse for modernity-bashing. More persuasive arguments for evidence-based happiness policies were put forward in 2005 in the economist Richard Layard's mass-market book *Happiness: Lessons from a new science*. He argued for national-level economic policies such as higher taxation and reduced working hours, and health and education policy shifts towards 'preventive' mental health support. Since then, several collections have provided useful explorations of options for using happiness research to guide reforms in healthcare, environmental care, tax regimes, employment policies, promotion of family values, and social change policy arenas such as those relating to smoking and exercise, promoting socially responsible business and curbing advertising, but in general these have stopped short of trying to spell out how policy makers and implementers might use happiness scholarship systematically as a basis for changing their approaches (Dolan et al, 2006; Ng and Ho, 2006; Levett, 2007; Frey et al, 2008; Diener et al, 2009; Krishna Dutt and Radcliff, 2009; Greve, 2010; Graham, 2010).

Derek Bok's *The politics of happiness* (2010) is one of the most comprehensive attempts to draw constructive links between recent research on happiness and macro-level political and economic policies. His grand narrative of big policy questions is mainly of interest to political philosophers and politicians working at national and international levels, and pays little attention to the ways in which everyone, in business, in schools and universities, in clubs and community organisations, could improve their contributions to well-being by making use of research evidence. Worldwide, there are clear signs that governments are developing at least a theoretical interest in happiness. The *Report by the Commission on the Measurement of Economic Performance and Social Progress* is focused on macro-level statistics rather than social policy, but does argue for more attention to happiness and other well-being indicators, and makes clear its expectation that changes in 'the way in which our societies looks at themselves' will lead to changes in 'the way in which policies are designed, implemented and assessed' (Stiglitz et al, 2009, p 9).

The government-sponsored *Marmot Review* on health inequalities in England studiously avoids the term 'happiness', but is nonetheless replete with evidence on inequalities in a wide range of well-being and subjective experience, plus recommendations for more active promotion and monitoring of well-being (Marmot, 2010). Policy-related attention to happiness inequalities still lags a long way behind the attention to health inequalities, but the two themes are increasingly being linked and merged. The World Health Organization (WHO) Europe-wide review of mental health outcomes in relation to social inequalities and social capital argued for positive mental health policies complementing individual-level analyses and therapies with more understanding and interventions at collective levels (Friedli, 2009, pp v, 4). Based on the same twin principles of positivity and linkage between individual and social levels, in 2008 the UK government's *Foresight Project on Mental Capital and Wellbeing* reviewed and argued for evidence-based population-level mental health promotion (Jenkins et al, 2008).

Perhaps the most significant attempt to address the middle ground of social happiness policy is Thaler and Sunstein's book *Nudge: improving decisions about health, wealth, and happiness* (2008), which gives examples and analysis of how our social institutions and environmental arrangements could gently and subtly use 'choice architecture' to steer us gently towards better decisions for ourselves. They address the 'middle ground' in two linked but different senses. First, recognising the clear evidence that people everywhere are systematically likely to make bad decisions for themselves and for society, they reject extreme libertarianism but nonetheless avoid a lurch towards coercive and paternalistic 'nanny state' responses. Second, the 'nudges' they advocate would come at various levels between the interpersonal and national levels, and from a variety of kinds of social institution and social arrangement, many of which wouldn't normally be addressed under a 'social policy' rubric or even a 'policy' rubric at all. Finally, the middle-ground links between individual, 'community', and 'organisational' levels are addressed in Isaac and Ora Prilleltensky's book *Promoting well-being: Linking personal, organisational, and community change* (2006), signifying a new positive turn for the discipline of Community Psychology, which has traditionally between focused mainly on mental illness.

Trends and debates

The trend towards paying attention to 'ultimate' or 'good life' objectives in policy and planning is the most salient of various trends that support the case for social happiness policy. A related trend leads towards recognising the *intrinsic value of society*, due to the ultimate inseparability of our selves and our social lives. The explosion of interest in '*social capital*' since the 1990s has been arguably the most dramatic development in the modern history of social science (see for example Comim, 2008). This has drawn attention to the lower-level institutional, informal, and relational dimensions of progress that underpin or undermine, or are affected by, so many aspects of technical, economic, and macro-policy change. There have been numerous critiques of the positivity bias and economistic reductionism in 'social capital' discourse (Fine, 2010). It is equally important to contest the implicitly instrumentalist treatment of society in many economists' treatment of social capital (Thin, 2002). Fukuyama's book *Trust* (1995) is a clear example of this: it omits any recognition of the intrinsic value of social happiness, reducing conviviality and trust to the status of instrumental 'social virtues' that produce so-called 'economic' prosperity. But good social relationships are *intrinsically* valuable: love and empathy are the key social components of happiness. Social relationships actually *constitute* a major part of the quality of our lives. By contrast, since 'the economy' has only instrumental value, the commonly used concept of 'economic well-being' is inherently flawed.

Third, there is incipient recognition of the limitations and dangers of excessive liberal *individualism* in academic and policy movements focusing on well-being, such as the 'Positive Psychology', 'Self-esteem', and 'Capabilities' movements (Biswas-Diener, 2011; Thin, 2011a). Human well-being, including happiness, is so intrinsically social that it is wrong to try to conceive happiness or freedom or sense of self-worth or any other aspect of well-being in terms of pure, disconnected autonomy (Gore, 1997; Comim, 2008; Dean, 2009). Self-help books and individual-level therapies owe their enormous business successes not necessarily to their effectiveness: in large part they thrive on repeat business from people who, for a variety of personal and contextual reasons, don't get the social help they need. And to the extent that individual-level interventions are good for individuals, this doesn't necessarily amount to a social good in aggregate. For example, boosting self-esteem may help an individual but society can't be made up entirely of high-confidence people.

Finally, the tide of interest in *environmental responsibility* and *sustainable development* is strongly linked with the projects of rethinking prosperity, transcending short-termist and selfish 'materialism', and development of more socially responsible self-projects and business approaches. Although very often associated with fear-mongery, pessimism, and ascetic values, the sustainable development movement makes little sense without a concept of good lives and good societies that would be worth sustaining.

In addition to these philosophical and attitudinal trends, there are also several salient practical trends in empirical realities that will likely continue strengthening the case for policy attention to social happiness worldwide:

- **Democratisation:** As an ever greater percentage of the world's population come to live in societies that offer them (given the rapid expansion of access to education and information) ever more realistic opportunities to participate in decisions that affect their lives, it becomes more difficult for any government, business, or civil organisation to ignore the need to listen and respond to what citizens and members tell them about the quality of their lives and experiences (Inglehart, 2006).

- **Post–scarcity:** As basic material provisioning becomes more secure, capabilities for diverse happiness pursuits, and both private and public interest in happiness and life quality, increase. Unprecedented progress towards trusted reliability of *basic material provisioning* and *longevity* in most parts of the world means that an ever-increasing proportion of humanity is free to devote attention to discussing, pursuing, and even achieving happiness.

- **Post-inequality:** As life expectancy, and access to goods such as education, water, and positions of power become more equitable, substantial inequalities in happiness may persist, due to entrenched cultural and social factors. But even money, which many believe to be increasingly unequal in its distribution, is arguably more equally divided in some senses today than ever before. Instead of counting the billions that the new ultra-rich in theory call their own, if we ranked everyone's monetary wealth in terms of *effective spending power* on a scale from 0–10, it would doubtless be clear that monetary inequality has steeply diminished.

- **Choice, and new sources of both happiness and unhappiness:** Modernity and affluence have brought unprecedented health, longevity, and choice. Personal happiness theories therefore become more salient and more complex as people choose jobs, whether to work, what to do with leisure time, whether to marry, where to live, and so on. The risks of bad life choices have increased, and modernity has entailed new forms of alienation, new health risks, and downward hedonic adaptation.

- **Ageing populations:** Spectacular life extension worldwide has prompted endless debates and research on whether we can sustainably ensure that the extra years are good years, adding 'life to years', not just 'years to life'. This has been a key driver of research and policy discourse on life quality and subjective health.

- **Overconsumption and sustainability challenges:** As it becomes more difficult to imagine the planet sustaining high-consumption life-styles of increasing numbers, it becomes crucial to consider what kinds of livelihoods and life-styles can facilitate happiness without jeopardising the options of future generations.

So we seem set for long-term increase in public discussion of happiness and the social forces that influence it. There is a lot of catching up to do: most development ethics debate still proceeds without attention to psychosocial well-being (Clark, 2002, pp 838–9). The world will not simply live happily ever after once Happiness Studies has married Policy Studies and produced lots of chirpy little Happiness Policies. Such policies will always be fraught with complex problems of acceptability, political and personal implementability, and uncertain as well as diverse outcomes. As happiness scholarship matures, we will need an ever larger percentage of the movement's efforts to go not only towards devising evidence-based policies, but also towards exploring the challenges of translating good ideas into real-world progress for individuals and for society. Unlike the fairy-tale ending that denies a history to happiness, in real life, happiness means activity, debate, interest, and motivation.

The idea that policy as well as personal decision making should focus on personal happiness is, of course, not new. In some form it has no doubt been debated in every society. Jeremy Bentham, utilitarianism's most ardent and idealistic campaigner, no doubt over-egged his belief in the possibility of mathematical approaches to happiness, which he grossly distorted into the metaphor of a sum of pleasures minus pains. Still, there is no escaping the fact that the decisions we make in our everyday lives are guided by some kind of felicific calculus, some means – normally intuitive, no doubt – not only of distinguishing right from wrong but of betting on which action would bring the most happiness for ourselves or for others.

To conclude, the default assumptions of happiness policy, the ideologies that happiness promoters sometimes have to defend against sceptics and use to justify their approaches to policy, include the following:

- Happiness matters both intrinsically and because of its good effects.

- Though most people are moderately happy and 'complete' happiness is impossible, there is room for improvement (that is, most people in the world haven't reached optimal happiness).
- Because happiness derives from and is constituted by social relationships, we need social policies – guided by the empirical research, analytical tools, and philosophical insights of happiness scholarship – to help people make those improvements and to recognise them when they happen.

Five justifications for the happiness lens

By making happiness a more explicit focus in policy discourse, we can in principle make significant improvements in the following five aspects of social science and associated activism and policy: *empathy* (via respect for subjectivity), *positivity* (attention to goodness), *holism* (treating people as complex, rounded individuals), a *life-span perspective* (considering how current well-being emerges from the past and influences the future), and perhaps, above all the rest, *transparency* (making clear our usually implicit beliefs about the ultimate value of activities and policies for the goodness of life).

While all of these sound unobjectionable, after a century in which the seemingly obvious benefits of considering happiness have been brushed aside, we can't afford to neglect the likelihood that strenuous objections to happiness scholarship and happiness policy will continue for many years to come. In the following chapter we will explore the varieties of scepticism about happiness in more detail, but for now let me pre-empt three of the most likely objections to the use of a happiness lens in policy:

- First, I propose the happiness lens as *an enrichment to other approaches* to public policy such as those that focus on economic growth, poverty, rights, equality, or unhappiness, and not as a substitute for them.
- Second, it is therefore *not to be confused with a 'utilitarian' approach*, which in some form happiness-promoters might well favour, but which is much more ambitious and contentious in its insistence on treating happiness as the sole criterion of ultimate value and hence as the single overarching policy objective.
- Third, it is *not meant as a naïve celebration of the wisdom and virtue of subjective assessment*. People can be quite wrong about how healthy or well off they are, and they can seriously mispredict the effects that desired or feared events will have on their feelings. Though often misguided, people's feelings and perceptions matter, and

enquiries about happiness should be seen as an expected feature of any humane, empathetic relationship. Happiness or domain-satisfaction self-reports shouldn't be assumed to be a less reliable source of information on well-being than more 'objective' proxies such as biological or monetary indicators.

There is already a wealth of long-term experience in social happiness policies, not much of which has hitherto been explicitly aimed at producing happiness. Schools have always, to some extent, both promoted the immediate happiness of pupils and tried to increase children's prospects of lifelong happiness. For centuries, workplace managers and personnel officers have tried to improve working conditions, relationships, and the organisation of work so as to improve the work satisfaction and the broader happiness of workers. Mental health workers have experimented with community-based psychosocial approaches to mental health to complement or replace institutionalised, medicalised, and individually focused treatment of mental illness (Stein and Test, 1980; Burns and Furn, 2002).

Efforts to study happiness scientifically, and to translate new knowledge about it into new personal advice and policies, is one of the most intriguing and exciting developments of our era. Not all happiness writing is helpful: thousands of self-help books purvey lightweight and patronising truisms and encourage narcissistic attitudes through narcissistic anecdotes. Even scholarly findings often just confirm what most of us thought we already understood:

- that money is useful but becomes less so the richer you get
- that economic growth is good for happiness in poorer nations, but is much less relevant to happiness in richer nations
- that good relationships, relaxation, exercise, and engagement with the natural environment are good for happiness and health
- that happiness is good for our health and vice versa
- that the indignity and anxiety of enforced unemployment is devastating
- that happiness is socially contagious.

As research methods become more sophisticated and empirical findings are amassed, the ability of happiness scholars to provide strong, evidence-based steers to policy makers will improve. Meanwhile, though, it is worth considering in more detail the five a priori reasons I have given as justification for using a happiness lens to enrich research and policy discourse. It is important to recognise that these are all *desirable as a matter of principle*, and will remain valid as justifications regardless of whether happiness scholarship rewards policy makers with strong, unambiguous findings that require changes to the specific content of policies.

Empathy

To empathise requires considering people's feelings, respecting their humanity and agency by taking their perspective, listening to and trying to understand their feelings and viewpoints (Hodges et al, 2011). Scepticism about empathy was famously asserted by the economist William Jevons, who argued that 'every mind is ... inscrutable to every other mind, and no common denominator of feeling seems to be possible (1871, chapter 1). But empathy is at the heart of social happiness: to enquire about people's happiness is to welcome their views on the quality of their experiences – in specific domains such as health, relationships or work, or in life in general. Recognising all humans as people who want to be happy also makes us more well disposed towards them, rather than thinking of them as rivals in zero-sum competitions for status or goods. Even when emotional empathy isn't an option (for example, when other people seem bafflingly misguided or nasty), cognitive empathy can be facilitated by considering how their actions may be produced by implicit happiness quests or happiness deficits. When a man hits his wife and children, instead of closing off moral insight by labelling him as 'evil' and dehumanising him, we could pause to consider what unhappiness brought this action on, or what strange happiness theories might make him believe that either he or his family are well served by this practice.

By comparison, other key policy concepts such as well-being, welfare, health, rights, and wealth are often used to assess people's conditions or resources with no reference at all to how they feel or to how they evaluate or make sense of their situation. So the happiness lens insists on attention to subjectivity, albeit through objective analysis and objective indicators that can never be assumed to provide a definitive truthful version of how people feel. When poor people are asked about their satisfactions and their happiness, we quickly learn that their lives can't be characterised solely in terms of deficits and incapabilities (Camfield, 2006), but it also reveals that many of the most debilitating adversities faced by poor people are social and psychological, not just financial and physical.

Goodness (or 'positivity', and realism)

Happiness analysis may sensibly attend to adversity as well as enjoyment, but anyone using a 'happiness' rubric shows clear interest in people's enjoyment of good experiences. This not only steers us towards positive recognition of goodness, strengths, and enjoyment, it also adds a much-needed dose of *realism* to social science and social policy, since most people lead good, enjoyable lives and have lots of strengths and resilience. It is inexcusable for social research or policy to neglect people's strengths and well-being. Good moods, cheerful dispositions, enjoyment, and meaningful self-transcendence all matter both for their intrinsic value and for their desirable social outcomes. Policies and texts that fail to attend to them are inefficient, distorted, and lacking in empathy and vision.

The inherent positivity of the happiness lens therefore ensures that it transcends approaches that are *minimalist* (for example human rights), *abolitionist* (for example, many feminist approaches to gender reform, and many campaigns against child labour), *pathological* (poverty focus, most 'social work'), or *clinical and therapeutic* (most 'health' and 'mental health' practice).

Looking for goodness also steers our gaze towards *intrinsic value*. The happiness lens invites us to find the joy in a relationship, the fun of schooling, the happiness at work, the enjoyment of sport and music, rather than restricting our attention to the other ends that these are supposed to achieve.

Holism (and associated cross-disciplinarity)

Surveys of happiness or life satisfaction typically invite a holistic evaluation, for example, '*all things considered, how satisfied are you with your life as a whole?*' taking a 'holistic' (or, less academically, a 'caring' or 'humane') approach, recognising people as whole people whose whole lives matter to us. Unlike more specific domain satisfaction or customer satisfaction assessments or project assessment, happiness assessment necessarily draws attention to how the various bits of people's lives fit together − to the interactions, trade-offs, synergies among their resources, abilities, activities, relationships, and environments. That is to say, holism is not just about the comprehensive range of domains or aspects of life that are considered, it is also about the ways they interact.

Unlike gross domestic product (GDP) or 'human development' or 'health' indicators, a happiness lens draws attention to what the social psychologist and policy analyst David Halpern (2010) has called the 'hidden wealth of nations', the Australian economist Duncan Ironmonger (1996) calls the 'gross household product' and the 'economy of regard', and the economist and feminist Nancy Folbre (2001) has called the 'invisible heart' of the economy. These terms refer to those everyday activities and relationships that make life good, that too often go unnoticed in policy, unrecorded in economic valuations, or ignored in public evaluation. On average, at least in richer countries and almost certainly in the rest of the world too, we devote more time and effort to these than we do to the paid 'economy'. As far as market-focused economists are concerned, these products of love's labours can get lost. The happiness lens forces us to notice how those under-recognised aspects fit with those already well recognised in policy.

These latter demographic and environmental aspects of holism are particularly vital in fighting the tendency to make misleading associations between 'happiness' and individualistic selfishness: good happiness studies show how individual happiness is constituted through cultural, social, and environmental engagement, not just through atomistic personal agency. Just as development scholarship and practice requires interdisciplinarity, so too with happiness: you can't study or promote it well without drawing on a wide range of specialisms.

Any moral or pragmatic argument in favour of addressing people as culturally embedded wholes rather than addressing just part of a person (for example, medically attending to a body part, or bureaucratically attending to a social role or function) is advocating the happiness lens in this sense of holistic life improvement. In medical ethics, for example, Pellegrino and Thomasma (1993, chapter 6) argue that doctors must consider how they affect their patients' overall good and not just their specific physical ailments. In so doing, they are arguing that doctors should swap a reductionist biomedical perspective for a happiness or holistic well-being perspective (see also Friedman, 1997, especially chapter 7). Similar trends towards holism can be found in psychotherapeutic practice, in sport, and in the 'whole child' approach to parenting and education (Carey, 2003; Kline, 2007). As the moral philosopher Mike Martin has argued (2000), these 'caring' approaches that transcend minimal requirements are crucial components in the 'meaningful work' of 'engaged workers', and should be part of professional ethics rather than neglected and treated as idiosyncratic saintly behaviour that have nothing to do with normal work ethics.

Life span (or 'life course') perspective

Though less obvious than the other dimensions, it is also important that *'happiness' is a story about well-being and value that emerges over a lifetime* (McAdams, 2005; Potkay, 2010). The most telling happiness query is not 'how are you?' but rather the 'deathbed test' thought experiment: when you reflect back on your life, what aspects are you most likely to be pleased with? Would you wish you'd spent more time at the office, or that you'd bought more stuff? Would you wish your school had put more emphasis on academic achievement, or more emphasis on fun, sport, and the arts? Happiness scholars respect the minute-by-minute pleasures and challenges of everyday life, but they also insist that our evaluative processes make some use of the wisdom of cemeteries, inviting us to consider whether in some way our lives make sense or have value as wholes (Hatch et al, 2007).

Happiness is about life stories, not just momentary enjoyments. We have 'narrative identities' with plots, characters, and dramas through which we make some kind of sense of our lives as wholes (McAdams, 2009). Our relationships too, the core of our social happiness, develop as stories. Robert Sternberg's *Love is a story* (1999) distinguishes 26 varieties of common personal love narratives. People's own narratives of their life experiences are often side-lined by the dominant development-agency emphasis on quantified resources (Carr, 2010). Doctors and therapists who attend to how people's lives develop as stories, through 'narrative medicine' or 'narrative therapy', may be more effective (Charon, 2006). The interpretation of life narratives reminds us that happiness, though often useful for other ends (for example, making people nicer, more peaceful, more attentive, more productive) is also about 'ultimate value', not just about the 'interim' or 'instrumental' goods. It therefore makes us think about lives as wholes, about people's motivations, expectations, and sense of agency, and their memories, life stories, plans, trajectories, phasing, and so on.

The policy implication is that if it's people's whole lives that ultimately matter, then, agencies that address components or phases of people's lives must show an understanding of how that component or phase might be expected to relate to the whole life. In schooling, for example, specific academic attainments need to be linked with how schools have helped children to develop realistic aspirations: when linked with unrealistic aspirations or where career aspirations clash with other life goals, such as belonging in a community, schooling can lead to dangerous forms of unhappiness.

Transparency

In ethical debate and practical discourse, a 'happiness lens' ensures that our actions and our institutions are justified, as far as we can reasonably expect them to be, with reference to likely effects on how good people feel and how well they think their lives go. It invites us to render more explicit our motives, purposes, and theories of how benefits are brought about. Our everyday choices and our policies and attitudes are guided by happiness theories that for the most part remain implicit and therefore not easily subject to scrutiny and debate by others.

If a promoter of social change doesn't believe that this-worldly happiness is the core value, then anyone they interact with ought to know this. Parents and children have a right to know, for example, if head teachers value the elitist pursuit of academic excellence above the value of pupils' enjoyment of their school years. Women have a right to know if gender reformers who promote changes supposedly in their interest rate financial and political equality above the enjoyment of life. Members of faith communities have a right to know whether leaders of their faith want them to be happy in this world, or whether they require adherents to defer this-worldly happiness on the promise of happiness in some possible future life. Promoters of economic changes, especially those involving disruption of existing livelihoods, relationships, and communities, ought to make clear the assumptions by which they believe these changes will translate into better lives, not just into better income or productivity.

How a happiness lens transforms policy making

Many may agree that happiness matters, that in principle it sounds right that we should pay it some attention, but still doubt whether this would actually make any difference to how we manage our affairs or promote social change. So we need to consider the different ways in which happiness can be recognised in policy processes. The keys aspects of policy processes are: *analysing situations and causes*; *setting objectives*; *justifying* policy choices; and the *evaluating* processes and outcomes. Considering these will tell us whether social policies have implicit or explicit happiness theories:

- **Situational and causal analysis:** Does happiness feature, as empirical information or as a theory, in the analysis of the context in which the project or policy would take place? Does it feature in the causal analysis? Is consideration given both to the *intrinsic* value of happiness as an outcome and to its *instrumental* value as a cause of other valued outcomes (such as health, longevity, and peace)?

- **Objectives (goals, outcomes, and processes):** Is happiness (or enjoyment, fulfilment, and so on) listed as an objective? How do distinctive cultural values and visions of prosperity influence policy goals? Is the enjoyment of processes included as an objective, rather than assuming that enjoyment comes only from achieving goals?
- **Justifications:** Are the assumed links from immediate policy outcomes to sustainable happiness gains based on plausible evidence-based analysis?
- **Evaluation:** Are the indicators used in performance assessments and policy evaluation studies plausibly linked to happiness? Do the evaluative processes give adequate voice to people's subjective experiences of the goods and processes being examined?

Table 1.1 sketches some examples of the kinds of question that might be asked under these four categories in various policy sectors.

Table 1.1: Happiness in planning, policy discourse, and assessment

Policy themes	Form of happiness consideration			
	Situational and causal analysis	Objectives	Justifications	Evaluation
Promoting productivity	In what ways do people's happiness, and their beliefs about pathways to it, influence their productivity and economic choices?	Are productivity objectives sufficient in themselves as goals, or do they need ancillary objectives relating more directly to happiness?	Is the plan or policy based on an explicit, plausible, evidence-based theory of how productivity will translate into happiness?	Are 'objective' indicators of productivity or wealth complemented by 'subjective' indicators of satisfactions, happiness, or perceived wealth?
Education	How do factors such as motivation and self-esteem influence educational attendance and performance?	Is happiness recognised as an educational objective?	Are the intended direct outcomes of education (such as wisdom, skills, relationships and motivations) plausibly linked to happiness during and after childhood?	Is the enjoyment of educational processes to be monitored? Does educational research focus adequately on assessing correlations between happiness indicators and other educational indicators?
Health	Does socio-cultural context analysis focus adequately on the ways happiness influences health-related choices and outcomes? Are happiness makers recognised as key agents of health promotion? Is mental health recognised as a critical factor influencing overall health?	Do the goals describe how health outcomes form part of the good life?	Is the health intervention justified on the basis of evidence linking specific health outcomes to happiness?	Will subjective health indicators and/or happiness indicators be used? Will the enjoyment of health-promoting activities be assessed?

continued

Table 1.1: continued

Policy themes	Form of happiness consideration			
	Situational and causal analysis	Objectives	Justifications	Evaluation
Decent work	Are character traits such as cheerfulness and optimism recognised as key factors affecting productivity, teamwork, and access to decent work?	Are the happiness of the workforce, and/or work–life harmony, formally recognised as a desirable outcome?	Are plans for improving the quality of working life based on evidence of what workers enjoy, why, and with what outcomes?	Are workers' domain satisfactions and overall happiness going to be assessed? How will work–life harmony be assessed?
Environmental responsibility	Are positive attitudes such as love of the environment, and trust in long-term access to environmental goods, recognised as critical factors influencing environmental responsibility?	Do biophysical goals need to be intertwined with goals reflecting human enjoyment of those goods?	Is there a plausible theory of how environmental changes and happiness interact?	Will indicators of 'environmental' progress include enjoyment and/or subjective recognition of the value of those changes?
Governance and political rights	Are people's satisfactions or dissatisfactions with rights and political processes recognised as critical causal factors?	Are goals such as 'empowerment' or realisation of rights complemented by goals reflecting the enjoyment that these changes may deliver?	Are planned political changes based on evidence showing how those changes interact with happiness?	Will measures of good governance or rights include subjective appreciation of these?
Gender reform	Are happiness factors recognised among the causes of good or bad gender relations?	Is it clear how the goals of gender reform reflect better happiness prospects of men, women and children?	Is there good evidence that the proposed changes in gender relations, statuses, or aspirations have a realistic chance of promoting happiness?	Will evaluations pay attention to subjective views on gender progress and its outcomes? Will both male and female happiness be monitored?

Discussion points

- Modern social and policy sciences were originated by people strongly and explicitly interested in the promotion of happiness, but in much of the 20th century happiness was overshadowed by attention to harm and to interim goods such as market exchange, political processes, and technology.
- Reasserting the importance of a 'happiness lens' can greatly enrich and rationalise academic disciplines and policies by promoting *empathy*, *positivity*, *holism*, a *life course perspective*, and *transparency* (of purposes and causal theories).
- A happiness approach to social policy doesn't substitute existing approaches, but enriches them by complementing their attention to pathologies, interim goods, rights, and duties.

Key readings

Biswas–Diener, R. (ed) (2011) *Positive psychology as a mechanism for social change*, Dordrecht: Springer.

Haworth, J. and Hart, G. (eds) (2007) *Well-being: Individual, community, and societal perspective*, London: MacMillan,

Layard, R. (2005) *Happiness: Lessons from a new science*, Harmondsworth: Penguin.

TWO

What really matters: concepts, evaluations and objections

Who thus define it, say they more or less
Than this, that Happiness is Happiness?
(Alexander Pope, *Essay on Man*)

Positive definitions: happiness as a conversation about what matters and why

Happiness is best understood not as definable entity but as an evaluative kind of 'conversation' (broadly conceived to include internal dialogues) concerning how well our lives go. So construed, happiness, like all conversation, is dynamic and interactive, existing as a process rather than as an entity. These conversations tend to include good feelings (encompassing a wide range from calm contentment to wild excitement or extreme bliss), satisfactions, and more ambitious themes such as the fabrication of meaning or purpose or coherence. Despite all its complexities, happiness is an easy, experience-near concept to grasp and to translate: no other term gives us a more powerful invitation to discuss and assess how society facilitates or inhibits the enjoyment of good lives. We readily understand, without ponderous academic definitions, that a 'happiness' rubric requires us to consider enjoyment and to evaluate and interpret whole lives.

But beyond this clear 'shop window' function, there are lots of potential confusions. To agree on how to promote happiness, we need agreement on what we mean. Unsurprisingly for a concept of such importance and with such a deep and varied cultural history, happiness has diverse meanings that vary over time and between situations, individuals, and cultural traditions. We need to think about usage, and to develop analytical tools to help us parse its various referents.

Martin Seligman, author of best-selling book *Authentic happiness*, tells us in his latest book, *Flourish*, that he now 'detests' the word 'happiness' because it is 'so overused that it has become almost meaningless' (2011, p 9). This extreme view seems to miss the point of definitional discussions. Key terms like happiness, or self (which he also declares to be 'overused'), or love, or music, or society, are used frequently and with multiple meanings because they point to some of the more crucial aspects of our existence. The diversity and tendentiousness of common usage may often require academic users to tease out and analyse this semantic richness, but 'overuse' shouldn't drive us away from our most precious key concepts. To the contrary, it is the *underuse* of this concept in social science and policy that we should be more worried about.

'Well-being' is for many people a preferred alternative. This is more inclusive since it includes 'subjective well-being', which is often used as a synonym for happiness. Ironically, though, common usage of 'well-being' associates this term with much narrower concepts than happiness, typically focusing on the body, on basic provisioning, and even on ill-being (prompting the defensive term 'positive well-being'). 'Wellness', likewise, in western traditions has typically come to have a much more reductive reference to the body than is the case with well-being concepts in non-western traditions (Fahlberg and Fahlberg, 1997). Since 'feeling well' is never a synonym for 'feeling happy', it is risky to try to use 'well-being' as a synonym for 'happiness' (for a worrying example of trying this in research with children, see Gabhainn and Sixsmith, 2006). Happiness is in practice a much more expansive, complex, and motivating term, including numerous linked concepts that together combine to form much more holistic, narrative evaluations of lives. Without the 'subjective' prefix, 'well-being' is too easily understood in expert-led, paternalist ways that disregard people's own preferences and feelings. The street-level term 'happiness' seems more powerful and less clumsy than defensive concepts like 'positive subjective well-being' (Searle, 2008, p 36) and 'optimal human being' (Sheldon, 2004).

'Flourishing', 'thriving', 'self-actualisation', 'fulfilment', and 'the good life' are alternative terms used by philosophers for broader discussions about how well people's lives go, but these terms lack an emphasis on subjectivity and self-evaluation, which is the core point of 'happiness'. They are also tendentious: they imply approximation to some predefinable ideal model or to the individual's own earlier ambitions. 'Life satisfaction' is about subjective self-evaluation, but lacks clear reference to either feelings or meanings, so some people can claim to be satisfied with their lives without particularly enjoying their lives or finding them meaningful. Other concepts, like 'quality of life' and 'living standards', typically refer to external conditions rather than mental processing.

Box 2.1 provides a simple AEIOU model for mnemonic purposes, reminding us that happiness conversations can be about **Anticipation** of the future, **Experience** in the present moment, or reflection on **Outcomes**. They can also be about avoiding or coping with

Unpleasantness, and they sometimes emphasise **Interpretation** – cognitive evaluations, reflections on meaning or the development of life stories. Philosophers make a useful distinction between *hedonic* approaches, in which the core meaning of happiness is momentary pleasures, and *eudaimonic* approaches, in which the emphasis is on the evaluative interpretation through which we appreciate our whole lives. A eudaimonic approach incorporates attention to good feelings, but adds to these an interest in the complexities of how a sense of meaning or fulfilment is fabricated, plus a stronger emphasis on social approval and the different moral evaluation of different pleasures. To these two, we could usefully add a third variant: the *pathophobic* approach, which approaches the good life only indirectly, by looking at ways of minimising unpleasantness. As I've argued in the previous chapter, this third variant, which informs the 'negative utilitarian' approach to policy, was dominant in 20th-century social science and policy.

Box 2.1: An AEIOU model of happiness

Interpretation		
Anticipation	**E**xperience	**O**utcomes
Unpleasantness		

- **Anticipation:** Hope (for self, for others, for the world), ambition, expectations, coping with fears.
- **Experience:** Good feelings – current enjoyments including calm contentment, flow, excitement, and transcendent ecstasy.
- **Interpretation:** Appreciation and construction of the sense of one's life as a whole, through finding meaning, stories, and/or a sense of ultimate purpose.
- **Outcomes:** Retrospection on experiences in relation to hopes and expectations – pride in achievement, relief, surprises and unplanned successes, reliving nostalgic memories, coping with uncomfortable memories.
- **Unpleasantness:** Bad feelings, the ever-present possibility that any of the above may be undermined by fear, boredom, trauma, hate, anger, shame, alienation, disappointment, etc.

Too often, people use the breadth and variety of happiness concepts as an excuse for not even trying to talk about happiness. Coherent conversations about happiness do of course tend to require some degree of specification: are we considering feelings or life evaluation? Positive goodness or the avoidance of badness? Future, present, or past? Satisfaction with expected achievements or surprise joys? It may help in parsing happiness referents if we use some kind of table like Table 2.1, in which the rows represent orientations to future, present, and past, and the columns represent the various kinds of mental activity.

Table 2.1: A tool for analysing happiness

	Hedonic tone: good vs bad feelings	Evaluative interpretation: satisfactions vs disappointments	Existential interpretation: meaning making vs doubt and alienation
Future (anticipation)	Optimism vs fear	High vs low expectations	Life story imagined as coherent/ purposeful or not
Present (current experience)	Enjoyments vs sufferings	Belief that current life is good/bad	Sense of current fulfilment or purpose
Past (memory and synthesis)	Happy vs unhappy memories	Degree of satisfaction with achievements	Making sense of the past, or not

What happiness isn't

> Happiness is not a potato. (Charlotte Brontë)

Even if you agree that happiness is a kind of conversation rather than an entity, you could still believe it's an unhelpful kind of conversation. Happiness advocates must anticipate scepticism by noting some common misconceptions of what happiness conversations are about. Charlotte Brontë, like many sceptics, saw happiness as something so magical and elusive that it couldn't be cultivated – hence the potato analogy. Though this works well as a literary joke, it can't be taken seriously as a philosophical objection. Lots of other values, like beauty, love, and the transcendent joys of music and spiritual ecstasy, can be cultivated without running the risk of reductionism. To defend any deliberate societal or personal promotion of happiness, we must resist the fatalistic and romantic belief that happiness is not subject to manipulation.

Happiness is not just momentary or animalistic pleasures

Happiness overlaps with 'pleasure', but has broader emphasis on life appreciation and the fabrication of purposes, stories, and meaning. It isn't just a heap of pleasures but an ongoing constructive process of turning our various pleasures and sorrows into a meaningful and evaluative story about our lives as wholes. A purely 'hedonistic' evaluation of a person's life simply needs to check the proportion of someone's life that is spent enjoying pleasure, and as Daniel Kahneman (1999) and various neuroscientists have shown, we aren't very far away from being able to provide factual assessments of how much pleasure people enjoy. How much such an assessment would matter, in the grander scheme of 'happiness' or 'good life' analysis, would depend on how hedonistic one's personal philosophy was. A really committed hedonist could perhaps have a really good life by maximising pleasure, even primarily short-term pleasures. But nearly all happiness scholars and advocates of happiness policy are sensible enough to recognise that happiness is a great deal more sophisticated and interesting than just a heap of animalistic pleasures. We must assert this loudly in the face of sceptics like Daniel Ben-Ami, who has caricatured 'the happiness movement' as 'hostile to the notion of progress' and as advocating 'a dumbed down version of happiness' (2010, p 173).

Happiness is not just passive enjoyment

In one of Philosophy's most celebrated thought experiments, Nozick invited us to think about an 'experience machine' that would provide a perfect illusion of complete desire fulfilment. Most people agree that, even if offered a perfect machine of that kind, we wouldn't choose to hook up to it. This is often used, misleadingly, as an argument detracting from the value of happiness. It's better understood as an argument against overvaluing passive contentment, although even then it can't detract from the idea that contentment (even if derived passively from a machine, as increasingly becoming available through electronic media) has a valuable role to play in the happy life.

But recognition of the interpretative, meaning-making, story-telling dimensions of happiness makes us see the importance of *subjective agency*. Happiness isn't just a result or a gift or a character trait, nor can it be delivered to us ready made, nor does it just happen to us by luck (as the etymological origins of the term imply). It's an active process of engaging with the world, making sense of experiences, but also creating meanings and feelings by acting simultaneously on the self and on the environment. Proponents of the 'capabilities' approach to development ethics sometimes wrongly claim that it is better than a 'well-being' or 'happiness' approach because it recognises agency, but there is no good reason to suspect that a happiness lens in social policy would downplay the importance of agency.

Valuing happiness does not entail purely pathophobic objection to suffering

According to negative utilitarianism – the pathophobic, 'mental hygiene', and 'problem-oriented' approaches that dominate therapeutic practices and social policy discourse – happiness happens, if at all, as a by-product of harm reduction. Those who take this approach confuse the question of 'what matters' with the question of 'what bothers'. In real life, of course, any kind of bother that gets in the way of enjoyment is likely to be attended to. Still, most humans manage to enjoy themselves without trying, unrealistically, to have bother-free lives. Unpleasantness and struggles are woven into the story of a good life: we not only cope with them, we can turn them into positive sources of meaning and pattern.

The classification of emotions into two broad groups, 'positive' and 'negative' (or 'adverse') is normal in Psychology, despite the objections of Solomon and Stone (2002). Emotional experience worldwide is strongly dualised into 'positive' or desired emotions on the one hand and 'adverse' or shunned emotions on the other. But it would be implausible and quite possibly ethnocentric to portray the life struggle as one in which desired emotions are maximised and shunned emotions minimised. Even the happiest of people not only *must* feel sad, angry, and afraid some of the time, but actually *want* to experience those emotions to some extent – and probably every day.

A life without a rich mix of the full emotional repertoire would not be seen as a life well lived. The kinds of sad, angry, and fearful moments that all of us need and want reveal the positive potential in so-called 'adverse' emotions. The pursuit of happiness, then, is not just one of maximising those emotions that are normally seen as 'positive', but rather one of ongoing adjustment to the mixes and balances of emotions both 'positive' and 'adverse'. We need enough frustrations in our day (or our month, or our life altogether) in order to enjoy the satisfactions, enough fear in order to enjoy the comfort of safety, and enough challenges to stay engaged and avoid boredom.

Happiness isn't 'complete'

Sometimes, happiness is seen as a utopian ideal because it is a belief in 'complete' well-being that can never happen to us in real life and that would rob us of the will to do anything if it did. Happiness theorists who define it as a sense of 'complete' well-being – echoing the WHO's unrealistic definition of 'complete' health – may have let themselves be guided by the 'lived happily ever after' fictional concept of happiness, such as religious fantasies of heaven as a place where nothing ever happens. But they violate our normal understanding of the happy life as one full of motivation, action, and interest. For example, the proposition by the cross-cultural linguist Anna Wierzbicka that 'happiness' glosses as 'I can't want anything else now' (2004, p 36) simply doesn't ring true, except perhaps in a very momentary perspective. In similar perfectionist terms, Tatarkiewicz (1976) defines happiness as 'lasting, complete, and justified satisfaction with life'. This is wrong: optimal happiness is by definition incomplete, allowing for the continual invention of dissatisfactions and challenges. Recognising this is essential for the exercise of due caution in interpreting high-end scores in happiness or life satisfaction self-reports. Scores of 8 on a 0–10 scale could well mean that a person is already optimally happy, while scores of 10 could reflect unrealistic or fragile euphoria.

The celebrated positive psychologist Csikszentmihalyi, while recognising this sense of happiness as 'an illusion', still chooses to accept that perhaps happiness is 'simply the name we give to that unattainable state where nothing else remains to be desired' (2003, p 21). This doesn't make the happy person sound very appealing, or very interesting, or very human. If happiness is to refer to an enjoyable, meaningful, flourishing existence, it needs to be an active process, and activity requires dissatisfaction, motivation, and the ever-present possibility of making mistakes. He favours the term 'flow' (Csikszentmihalyi, 1997), a concept that is increasingly being deployed in many domains – health, work, exercise, and skill development. This state is achieved when we find a good balance between challenge and capability, between different categories of experience, between effort and relaxation, excitement and contentment.

Conceived as 'flow', active happiness thrives on ongoing challenges and abhors an excess of contentment. It is crucial for anyone trying to promote happiness policies to understand that what they are trying to promote is *not* a state of complete, passive contentment. A balance is required between intervention and leaving people to make their own mistakes and find their own goals. As Bertrand Russell put it: 'To be without some of the things you want is an indispensable part of happiness' (1930/1975, p 27).

Happiness is not about asocial individualism

Understanding happiness as an active, dynamic, and interpretive process also entails understanding it as a *social process* and not just a private judgement. Because we are social beings, 'subjective well-being' is also *intersubjective* well-being. This is also true of specific aspects of happiness, such as hope, which is as much a collective as an individual phenomenon (Snyder et al, 1997).

Following the discovery of mirror neurons, the new 'social neuroscience of empathy' can now give us visual proof of the intertwining of our thoughts and feelings with those of other people (Zlatev et al, 2008; Decety and Ickes, 2009; Franks, 2010). The self that pursues happiness can't just be conceived in egotistical terms, because it is interdependent with other people at least, if not also with the wider physical and cosmological environment (Markus and Kitayama, 1991; Charlton 2001; Markus and Hamedani, 2007; Leary et al, 2008; Dambrun and Ricard, 2011).

In general, happiness is associated with a range of life-enhancing and prosocial activities (Fredrickson, 1998). The goodness of happiness, therefore, goes beyond the ego-focused 'subjective' triad of wanting, liking, and evaluating, and includes the quality of our engagements with the world – with other people (empathy or 'intersubjectivity'), other species, with the natural environment, and (if we choose to believe in them) with deities and spirits. In this book, as the 'social happiness' term suggests, we will focus mainly on intersubjectivity, on happiness as an aspect of social engagement and as an everyday rubric in social discourse. Of course it has something to do with private emotional experience, but it is much broader than that and, unlike most emotions, it doesn't necessarily have *action tendencies* (other than trying to maintain the activity or situation that is understood to cause it) or *intentional objects* (you can be happy about something but you can also feel happy for no apparent reason, or you can conceive of happiness in detached evaluative, non-emotional terms).

No one has a valid claim to declare anyone else's happiness 'inauthentic'

Most people who look beyond the immediate appeal of happiness recognise that its value is to some extent qualified: we want good, or 'authentic' happiness that isn't based on something unworthy or illusory: 'People want to be happy, but for the right reasons, and they want certain valued things even in the absence of feelings of happiness' (Diener, 2003, pp 3–4). Furthermore, at the societal level, people judge social quality not just in terms of how happy people in general are, but also in terms of social justice (Diener, 2003, p 14). In other words *societal happiness, like individual happiness, is only valued if it meets with social approval*. All of us, throughout our lives, seek to authenticate our own happiness with reference to other people and by having conversations with them.

It is entirely right that we should recognise happiness as provisional, and subject to validation over time and to approval by others. But this doesn't legitimise judgemental declarations of other people's happiness as 'inauthentic'. We may find good reason to warn people that their happiness is based on illusions, or that it is undignified or selfish or unsustainable, but we must also remember that the happiness lens requires us to respect each person's own subjectivity. Blanket judgement on the 'authenticity' of some sources of happiness is intellectually and ethically unsatisfactory, even if it is expressed with benign intentions. The attempt to authenticate happiness is explicit in the title of Martin Seligman's book *Authentic happiness*; in Matthieu Ricard's view that transient pleasures 'have nothing to do with happiness' (2007, p 41); in Seamas Carey's advice that parents must insist that children aim for the 'highest goals in life' and instruct them that 'pleasures' are not 'true happiness' (2003, pp 8, 30); and in Aristotle's embarrassingly smug efforts in *Nicomachean ethics* to persuade us that the only really good life is that of the philosopher. Throughout these views runs a common thread, a disapproval of 'pleasure', a refusal to admit that happiness is ultimately composed entirely out of pleasures, and an insistence that there must be some elusive criterion that allows experts to rank some aspects of happiness as 'better' or 'higher' than others.

The most common resort is to the metaphor of the great chain of being, with humans at the top of the heap, so that within humans our 'animal' pleasures are 'lower' than our distinctively human 'spiritual' or 'intellectual' pursuits. Its modern pedigree goes back to J.S. Mill's insistence that 'It is better to be a human being dissatisfied than a pig satisfied: better to be Socrates dissatisfied than a fool satisfied.' Mill purports to help us distinguish good from bad satisfaction, but all he really does is tell us what most of us probably think we already know: that it's better to be a human than a pig, and better to be a bit like Socrates than to be foolish. Most commonly, the attempt to authenticate happiness is linked with the opposition between sustainability and evanescence: what is uniquely good and uniquely human is the ability to generate a lasting, abstract sense of happiness that is to some extent detached from fleeting pleasures.

But the idea that brief pleasures are intrinsically 'false', sub-human, undignified and therefore not part of 'true happiness' is philosophically untenable. We may well understand goodness and virtue better by distinguishing sincere from insincere expressions of emotions, fleeting or simple animalistic or selfish pleasures from more complex, lasting, meaningful, and self-transcendent pleasures. It is even possible that after the fact we may reflect on the 'affective ignorance' of our own previous belief that we were happy, thereby calling into question our faith in our own subjectivity and forcing us to question whether we really 'know how happy we are' (Haybron, 2007). But it is not at all helpful to imagine a clear distinction between 'true' and 'false' happiness. Whether we are judging the happiness of others or telling ourselves a story about our own happiness, we must always accept that it ain't necessarily so.

Sceptics and objectors

> To be stupid, selfish, and have good health are three requirements for happiness, though if stupidity is lacking, all is lost. (Gustave Flaubert)

> A lifetime of happiness! No man alive could bear it: it would be hell on earth. [...] courage consists in the readiness to sacrifice happiness for an intenser quality of life. (George Bernard Shaw)

Show me anything that's fun and I'll show you a horde of sceptics and worriers who have conspired to discredit and forbid it. Like money, freedom, ecstasy, food, and sexual thrills, happiness is so good that people get suspicious: they worry about its reality, about the ethics of its sources, about its sustainability, and about the social responsibility of displaying it. Sceptical psychiatrist Richard Bentall suggested in 1992, in light of the diagnostic proliferation in psychiatric disciplines, that happiness could be classified as a psychiatric disorder 'of the pleasant type', on the grounds that it has a cluster of symptoms, is statistically abnormal, and is associated with cognitive abnormalities.

Philosophers have always questioned whether it's good for our happiness to think about it and pursue it. Although there is a great deal of research on the happiness benefits of 'altruistic' or 'prosocial' activities, recent empirical evidence from deliberate happiness–promotion experiments, shows that the motivation to make ourselves happier has a significant and lasting positive effect on the happiness benefits of interventions (Lyubomirsky and Dickerhoof, 2010, pp 234–5). Still, most good things can turn toxic in excess: too much talk of happiness could give rise to a new Happiness Anxiety Disorder to add to the myriad of existing Self-Actualisation Disorders and worries about our bodies and our clothing that have been the subject of formal enquiries and interventions.

The disapproval and neglect of happiness in both scholarship and policy is strongly patterned and institutionalised, sometimes amounting to learned incompetence rather than random negligence. Happiness scepticism has a rich, varied, and long-standing cultural heritage and we would be foolish to expect an easy ride in arguing for happiness-oriented policies. If we want stronger emphasis on happiness in scholarship or policy we must try to understand and respectfully engage with the sceptical objectors and worriers, but not pander to them. I hope the above section has shown that there is enough common ground at least to argue in favour of having policy-related conversations about happiness. Many self-declared sceptics turn out to use 'happiness' and 'pleasure' interchangeably, and/or to confuse pleasure with a small set of short-termist, selfish, and undignified, socially denigrated, and animalistic gratifications. Others assume, equally naïvely, that happiness and its pursuit are inextricably intertwined with narcissism and selfishness.

The most common position is not to engage at all, and simply to proceed as if there were no need to mention happiness. When people entertain doubts about the value of happiness or of some variety of happiness promotion, they often aren't very clear (perhaps not even in their own minds) what exactly they are objecting to. The above typology can help us to analyse objections by asking what the objectors are querying: it is the value, the personal pursuit, the promotion, or the display of happiness that they doubt? Or is it assumptions about causality, or the methods used to study happiness that are causing the disagreements?

Box 2.2 combines various objection themes and kinds of objectors to produce a list of the varieties of objection to happiness policy. Not all of these are necessarily meant as arguments against taking happiness seriously in scholarship and policy. Indeed, some arguments purportedly against 'happiness' or against 'happiness policy' really aren't anti-happiness but are in favour of better kinds of happiness pursuit or happiness policy.

Box 2.2: Varieties of objection to happiness policy

Against life itself: Human life is so inevitably prone to suffering that there's no point trying to make it worth living (Benatar, 2006; www.vhemt.org; www.churchofeuthanasia.org).

Against happiness: Happiness either isn't intrinsically good, or isn't as good as other contenders for the status of ultimate human value, such as wisdom, virtue, freedom, or knowledge; happiness is associated with inauthentic, short-sighted, short-lived, animalistic, unsophisticated pleasures (Belliotti, 2003; Farrelly, 2008; Wilson, 2008; van Deurzen, 2009).

Against the pursuit of happiness: Pursuing happiness is futile, either because increasing happiness is impossible or because it's only achieved indirectly, by other means (Freud, 1930).

Against narcissism and selfishness: The pursuit of happiness is selfish and individualistic, antisocial (Lasch, 1980; Hewitt, 1998; Ben-Ami, 2010, chapter 8).

Against happiness studies and subjectivism: Happiness is too trivial, funny, boring, personal or elusive for scientific study; people are often poor judges of their own mental health and poor predicters of what is good for them (Ormerod and Johns, 2007).

Against compulsory/compulsive jollity: Too much happiness display is socially irresponsible; making people feel they ought to be happy and cheerful all the time can be psychologically damaging (Huxley, 1932; Held, 2004; Horwitz and Wakefield, 2007; Ehrenreich, 2009; Ahmed, 2010).

Against utilitarianism: Our policy guide should be *negative* utilitarianism, that is, we should focus on harms that can be avoided, minimised, or mitigated, and let goods take care of themselves (Popper, 1962; Ryan, 2010).

Against greedy, status-obsessed, and self-defeating consumerist happiness pursuits: Capitalism promotes false consumerist happiness promises and win–lose status competitions (Frank, 1999; Kasser, 2002; James, 2007; Jackson, 2009).

Against romantic anti-wealth and anti-consumerism: Happiness surveys should not be used naïvely and selectively to bolster utopian agendas for improving the world by putting an end to economism and consumerism (Johns and Ormerod, 2007; Ben-Ami, 2010, chapter 8)

Against paternalism, interventionist happiness policy, and the 'nanny state' or 'therapeutic state': Even if people make bad choices by mispredicting their own happiness, individuals should be free from state interference (Polsky, 1991; Furedi, 2006b; Harsanyi, 2007).

Against ethnocentrism: Happiness is an obsession of western and post-scarcity culture, and may not be such a high priority for most of the world's population (Marar, 2003; Wirtz et al, 2009).

Against cynical and tokenistic use of happiness-related promises: Governments and businesses may just be using the promise of happiness as a euphemistic smokescreen for bad services and products (McMahon, 2006; Vitale, 2008).

Against smugness and conservatism: Postindustrial societies aren't very happy, so are il equipped to promote happiness; and happiness policies tend to be promoted by the rich with inadequate consideration of the priorities of less affluent people (Russell, 1930; Lane, 2000; Easterbrook, 2003).

Against empirically unverified claims: There is pitifully inadequate evidence to support a lot of the advice promoted in self-help and life-coaching literature (Mary, 2003; Salerno, 2005).

Against this-worldly happiness: 'True' happiness, or bliss, is to be expected only in some different kind of post-human existence (Bible; Koran; most Buddhist texts; Walls, 2002).

Against wrecking it by talking about it: Happiness, like sexual thrills and aesthetic or spiritual ecstasy, is far too precious, magical, and personal to risk spoiling through academic analysis and bureaucratic discourse. I haven't yet come across this argument in print, but it seems to me the most persuasive of all possible objections. Nel Noddings, advocate of schooling for happiness, comes close when she says: 'I dread the day when I will enter a classroom and find Happiness posted as an instructional objective' (Noddings, 2003, p 10).

Discussion of literature and debates on these various kinds of objection and scepticism would fill many more books, but it is worth at least considering them briefly with a view to minimising confusions and unnecessary arguments. Arguably, the most common source of confusion arising from happiness scepticism is the refusal on the part of sceptics to concede that 'happiness' can be a more versatile concept than pleasure, and that pleasure itself can't in any case reasonably be reduced to the scorned category of simple, animalist, short-lived gratifications. As Carol Ryff has argued (Ryff, 1989; Ryff and Singer, 2008), empirical research into 'positive human functioning', or eudaimonic flourishing as moral philosophers call it, needs to explore a broader range of indicators than just the good feelings or life satisfactions reported in surveys, and must include the Aristotelian concept of 'striving toward excellence' within the concept of flourishing, not just as a contributing factor.

This opposition between 'hedonic' (pleasure-focused) and 'eudaimonic' (fulfilment-focused) conceptions of the good life, though wheeled in to answer the hedonophobic critiques, is itself a source of confusion. As Laura King as persuasively argued, the distinction is overdrawn, since research clearly shows that fulfilling, virtuous, eudaimonic activities tend to bring more pleasure, more sustainably, than disapproved short-termist gratifications. This is partly why the latter are disapproved of, although they are also frowned on because they tend to be selfish and antisocial. Happiness isn't just about pleasure seeking, but we must also resist 'anti-pleasure' critiques. There are many forms of pleasure, and many of them are derived from virtuous, prosocial, beautiful, admirable activities. Any objections to pleasures are morally suspect if they aren't supported by evidence that the pleasures in question are worrisomely fragile or harmful.

Since there is no obviously correct balance between freedom and restriction, or between individual-level and social-level benefits, or between gratification and a hard graft, many cultures and many people through the ages have exaggerated the need for anti-fun, often with grotesque outcomes such as the female genital mutilation that is still inflicted on so many girls in so many countries. Unsurprisingly, therefore, few aspects of cultural tradition display the range of human ingenuity better than the restriction of fun and the pursuit or promotion of painful activities.

Some of these counter-hedonic institutions and pursuits are done in the name of happiness and may well actually contribute in some ways to happiness, while detracting from it in other ways. Largely through the work of Freud, psychologists have long been aware that no individual and no society can get by without a great deal of psychological and behavioural repression – the conscious or unconscious denial of desires and impulses. Repression tends to get a bad press, but it is not all bad. Many individuals seem to enjoy their lives without pleasures (for example sex, alcohol, exercise) that others see as crucial. The repression of one impulse leaves space to enjoy another, perhaps more enjoyable, more prosocial, or longer-lasting alternative pursuit. The repression of painful knowledge such as horrible memories is often essential for peace of mind. And social life would be troublesome without a great deal of restriction of people's freedom to express their desires.

But the collective, traditional, and personal pursuit of pain or avoidance of pleasure is sometimes hard to understand. For any happiness theorist, indeed for any interpreter of human meaning and motives, *masochism* (the deliberate pursuit of pain), *asceticism* (the avoidance of pleasure), and *puritanism* (the forbidding, repression, or strict social control of pleasure) present major interpretive challenges. It is not just that we explain the motives of many of our actions in altruistic rather than selfish, hedonistic terms (Harsanyi, 1996), but that happiness and pleasure are deliberately avoided by all of us for some of the time and by some of us for most of the time. Some people therefore question the status of pleasure or happiness as a core human value. While there is enormous individual and cultural variety in the extent to which pleasure and happiness are explicitly valued and pursued, it is doubtful whether any cultures or even individuals can persist without some degree of public and private masochism, asceticism, and puritanism.

Discussion points

- Happiness is a more inclusive and culturally powerful rubric than other 'good life' concepts. It is not a single definable entity, but it is commonly understood that conversations about happiness are likely to address five ways in which we think about and evaluate the enjoyment and meaning of life: Anticipation; Experience; Interpretation; Outcomes; and coping with or avoiding Unpleasantness.
- Happiness promotion tends to be wrongly confused with the selfish pursuit of short-term pleasures, with naïve attempts to avoid all suffering, and with antisocial individualism.
- Many sceptical objections to happiness promotion seem reasonable but can often be resolved through conceptual clarification.

Key readings

Bowling, A. (1995) 'What things are important in people's lives? A survey of the public's judgements to inform scales of health-related quality of life', *Social Science and Medicine*, vol 41, no 10, pp 1447–62.

Rath, T. (2010) *Wellbeing: The five essential elements*, New York: Gallup Press.

Seligman, M. (2003) *Authentic happiness*, Boston: Nicholas Brealey.

Sheldon, K.M (2004) *Optimal human being: An integrated multi-level perspective*, New Jersey: Erlbaum.

THREE

Effects of happiness (and unhappiness)

The good life, as I conceive it, is a happy life. I do not mean that if you are good you will be happy; I mean that if you are happy you will be good. (Bertrand Russell)

Success is not the key to happiness. Happiness is the key to success. (Albert Schweitzer)

Happiness ... *is never a means*: on the contrary, it is the only goal which is impossible to instrumentalise. (Bruni, 2006, p 19)

The 'pursuit of happiness' implies goal orientation, but is it not rather the 'happiness of pursuit' that really matters? A common and wise cliché has it that happiness is the journey, not the destination. This points to the potentially liberating recognition that the good life is there to be enjoyed *in the process* of living and striving. But by default, our happiness theories tend to be end weighted: we want, strive, achieve, and finally thrive. Understood as a goal, outcome, or reward for effort or achievement, happiness is anticipated as pleasurable pride or sighs of relief and contentment. Although much of the justification for happiness policy is provided on the basis of its status as an 'ultimate' value, happiness also matters because it is *generative*. As a source of inspiration for sustained action, and a disposition to believe in and seek out the good in other people, happiness has key roles to play in social progress. A lot of happiness science has emphasised the outcome version of happiness, but in recent years considerable evidence has been amassed of the *instrumental* value of happiness as a driver of good actions that not only spread happiness but also enhance other goods such as health, artistic creativity, and social solidarity.

Russell and Schweitzer may have underestimated the role of virtue and success in bringing happiness, but they're certainly right about the effects of happiness. Bruni is wrong to claim that happiness can't be instrumental as a means to other ends. Like Aristotle, whose beliefs he is approvingly reproducing, Bruni entertains the implausible notion that the intrinsic value of happiness somehow disqualifies it from having instrumental value. Bruni is simply agreeing to the commonly held conceptualisation of happiness as the end of the causal chain. A moment's common-sense thought confirms that happiness has extremely important effects on behaviour, which in turn affect valued life outcomes. Yet treating happiness as (in part) an interim good, examining the outcomes of happiness rather than happiness as an outcome of other factors, seems to be understood by Aristotle, Bruni, and many others as flouting what we might call the *standard grammar* of happiness analysis. The Russell and Schweitzer quotations would pack no rhetorical punch if we didn't feel a little jolt of surprise at hearing happiness in a causal position, prior to the outcome at the end of the sentence.

In happiness studies, the default 'outcome' status of happiness is so dominant that the term 'reverse causality' is used to refer to the effects of happiness, meaning that this inverts our expectations. Perhaps these expectations derive from a previous context in which happiness was determined to a much larger extent by conditions external to individuals. If you live in abject poverty, constantly under the threat of other people's physical or verbal abuse, frequently falling ill and seeing loved ones die, and with no control over your critical life decisions such as marriage and employment, the chances are that your happiness is determined by your conditions more than vice versa. Today, however, it seems likely that *for most of humanity, the mind has more influence over the conditions and processes of life than ever before.* A happy disposition becomes more helpful in an environment of abundance and security.

Even if it is so, then either due to cultural inertia or genetic hardwiring, we seem reluctant to change our grammar: happiness is still seen primarily as an outcome. In a fascinating large-scale diary study of creativity in various kinds of workplace, researchers found that although emotional tracking showed that positive emotion was often closely followed by improved creativity, respondents were much more likely to report good emotion as an outcome rather than as a cause of creative events (Amabile et al, 2005, pp 395–6). The other, puzzling aspect of this bias is that whereas happiness has relatively rarely been studied as a likely cause of health benefits, unhappiness has for a long time been a standard part of explanations of illness (Cohen et al, 2003; Cohen and Pressman, 2006) and, of course, of suicide (Koivumaa-Honkanen, 2001).

Grammatically, happiness typically comes at the end of causal sentences, just as it comes at the end of children's stories. It tends to be conceived as deferred gratification, as an 'ultimate' value. 'The more you *x*, the happier you are likely to be' is common, but 'the happier you are, the more you are likely to *x*' is much rarer. There is an *implicit default assumption, often unstated and unconscious but revealed in sentence structures, that the causal arrow points towards happiness (or unhappiness) rather than the other way around.* More generally, feelings are rarely seen as causes, and are normally seen as outcomes of events, institutions, relationships, and attitudes.

This same bias pervades happiness scholarship and everyday happiness discourse alike. The inadequate treatment of happiness as a cause rather than an effect, and the default assumption of one-way causation of happiness by factors such as income, relationships, health, and success, have been critical areas of weakness in happiness studies that few scholars have tried to address. Even when scholars do explore the benefits of happiness, they sometimes seem reluctant to admit that they are doing so. For example, the authors of an excellent paper justifying public mental health promotion by exploring the many public and private benefits of mental health gave their paper the title 'The intrinsic value of mental health', even though it was mainly about the *instrumental* value of mental health, recognising it as a 'resource' as well as a good thing in itself (Lehtinen et al, 2005).

Tired of seeing too many scholars making lazy assumptions about one-directional causality of economic growth, the economist Charles Kenny examined 40 years' worth of happiness surveys in rich countries and boldly asserted that 'if there is a link between growth and happiness, it does indeed appear to run from happiness to growth, not vice-versa' (1999, p 14). Kenny overstates his case: it is implausible to suggest that in poorer countries economic growth doesn't contribute to happiness. In richer countries its contributions to happiness may be more debatable, but it still adds to life-years and hence to the average happy life-years a person enjoys. Kenny is right, though, to insist that *happiness matters as a cause, not just as a desired outcome.*

We will see in the forthcoming section on causality that in most examples of mistaken causal inference the direction of causality is assumed to run from some factor to happiness rather than vice versa. Happiness-as-outcome by default crowds out recognition of happiness-as-cause. Yet intuitively, all of us appreciate that feeling happy or being a happy kind of person affects our behaviour and the way our lives go.

Back in 1989, Veenhoven and Hagenaars compiled a collection of essays under the title *How harmful is happiness? Consequences of enjoying life or not*, which addressed a significant gap in happiness texts so far. Nearly all, they argued, had looked at the factors that cause happiness or correlate with it, rather than at outcomes of happiness. This is a critically important issue for the valuation of happiness, for debates about whether interest in it is primarily associated with self-concern or with altruism and public goods, and for questions concerning the policy relevance of happiness studies. For everyone but those who see happiness as the only ultimate good, happiness matters not just because it is intrinsically good for the individual who feels it, but because in general it is assumed to bring good outcomes. We prefer to stick around happy people, provided that we see their happiness as authentic and socially responsible; and this isn't just because we empathise, it's also because we seek the benefits of positive emotional contagion: we expect better things from happy people, and we anticipate that they will be nice, productive, fun to be with, and so on.

The essays in that collection found that happiness science did not support the common beliefs that happiness buffers stress, prolongs the life of cancer patients, makes patients and citizens more docile, or has a detrimental effect on work motivation and commitment. They did find some evidence that happiness predicts longevity, but perhaps only for women, that unhappy people are less likely to get married, and that job satisfaction is good for productivity and reducing staff turnover. Overall, the contributors were most confident in their findings that happiness has good effects on other valued outcomes, and in their rejection of specific beliefs that happiness causes laziness and political disengagement. For example, challenging popular myths about the miserable creative genius, they showed research evidence that in general, happiness fosters creativity rather than killing it.

Since the warning from Veenhoven and Hagenaars in 1989, happiness research has largely failed to get rid of the default assumption of happiness as an outcome. There have been some important efforts to counter this, such as Barbara Frederickson's 'broaden-and-build' theory of the evolutionary benefits of positive affect, which argued that good feelings broaden the options for action that we consider, making us more creative and adaptive (Fredrickson, 1998, 2011; Fredrickson and Losada, 2005). The biased interpretation of correlations derives from the dominant Aristotelian philosophical assumption of happiness as the *ultimate* good, as an end rather than a means. As the philosopher Roger Crisp puts it, 'well-being is most commonly used in philosophy to describe what is non-instrumentally or ultimately good for a person' (2001). But the term 'non-instrumentally good' can be misleading, since it is ethically legitimate and practical common sense to see well-being or happiness also as a means or a cause. Experimental and survey-based information supports this view:

When pleasant emotions are experimentally induced in the laboratory, a number of characteristics seem to follow: sociability, activity, altruism, self-confidence, positive perceptions of others, and flexible thinking. Thus, it appears that happiness causes these characteristics, not just results from them. (Diener, 2003, pp 13–14).

In cross-national comparison, it has been argued that happiness is necessary for democracy, and that widespread unhappiness makes it easier for dictators to gain popular support: 'societies with happy publics are far more likely to survive as democracies, than those with unhappy publics' (Inglehart, 2006, p 2). In Belgium and the Soviet Union, declines in happiness *preceded* major constitutional changes, rather than following them, and in general 'democratic institutions do not necessarily make a people happy' (Inglehart and Klingemann, 2000, pp 177, 179). The common fear that mass happiness may lead to political apathy appears to be unfounded.

After a long period in which happiness studies flourished while largely neglecting Veenhoven and Hagenaars's arguments about the causality of happiness, Lyubomirsky, King, and Diener (2005) have at last begun to challenge the 'happiness as effect' paradigm in happiness studies by proposing that although success may bring happiness, happiness may also bring success. They base their argument on experimental and longitudinal studies that have suggested that good feelings lead to good outcomes such as prosocial behaviour, self-esteem, likeability, creativity, and longevity, and hence to successful marriage, work, and health. Veenhoven himself regularly publishes reviews based on the best evidence of the causality of happiness, based on his World Database of Happiness. For example, he reviewed numerous studies on happiness and health, and found the consensus view to be that happiness helps people avoid ill-health, conveying major longevity gains (perhaps 7 or 8 years, as compared with unhappy people), but that 'studies of the sick and old show mixed results', with no general pattern supporting the idea that happiness helps recovery from sickness (Veenhoven, 2008a).

We don't yet know whether the often dramatically good effects of cheerful disposition that have been identified in rich western countries might be found in all cultural contexts. Would the cheerful Milwaukee nuns (Box 3.1) have lived longer than their gloomier sisters if they had lived in Cambodia or France, for example, or would their unrealistic optimism have led them into life-threatening trouble or made them social outcasts in a less cheer-rewarding culture? Could their initial cheerfulness have been due to some mainly innate bodily capability (better sleep, stronger immune system) that benefited them throughout their lives? With suitable caution, Xu and Roberts (2010) acknowledged that these differences may be 'partially or completely mediated by social networks', and that in any case the life-winners in their Alameda County study may have been people who were simply born happier, or with clusters of gifts including happiness, rather than people who made good life choices. Although evidence of the health benefits of happiness is now mounting, most of this comes from western countries where happiness is highly valued as an objective and as a character trait (Cohen et al, 2003; Pressman and Cohen, 2005; Chida and Steptoe, 2008; Guven and Saloumidis, 2009).

Box 3.1: Inspiring studies indicating possible effects of happiness

Most texts inferring causes from correlations between happiness and life conditions assume happiness to be the outcome. Some, however, have argued that the evidence from correlations over long periods makes it look very likely that happiness causes desirable outcomes.

- In the famous **Milwaukee nuns' diaries study**, the life courses of 178 nuns were compared with their self-appraisals in diaries written in the early 1930s. Of the quartile who wrote the most cheerful diaries, 90% were still alive at age 85, and 54% at 94, whereas only 34% of the least cheerful were alive at 85, and 11% at 94 (Danner et al, 2001).
- The **Mills College photo study** ranked 141 women students' faces in 1960 photos for cheerfulness and beauty. Nearly all were smiling, but some had more genuinely cheerful 'Duchenne' smiles with crinkly eyes. At ages 27, 43, and 52, the ones who in 1960 had the crinkly eyes were more likely to be married, to stay married, and to report high levels of life satisfaction at all ages. Beauty ratings were irrelevant to these outcomes (Harker and Keltner, 2001).
- In the **Harvard ageing study,** 45 years' worth of information on the same individuals through their life course showed that happiness is the strongest predictor of physical and mental health in late life (Vaillant, 1990).
- In the 1950s, Italian immigrants in the Pennsylvanian town of **Roseto** had less than half the national heart-attack mortality rate, despite a fat-rich diet and heavy smoking. The 'Roseto effect' was explained by social happiness theory – that social cohesion, homogeneity, cultural dispositions to have fun, and the absence of status anxiety, enabled them to keep stress levels remarkably low (Albright et al, 2011).

- In a **US longitudinal 1976/1995 college outcome study**, the self-rated cheerfulness of both female and male students was a good predictor of higher income, higher job satisfaction, and continuous employment history 19 years later (Diener et al, 2002; and for a similar finding on young Australians' happiness and subsequent pay rises, see Marks and Fleming, 1999).
- The **'Whitehall study'** has monitored over 10,000 civil servants' health in the UK since 1967. Though most texts on this avoid causal speculations and report their findings using the language of 'correlation' and 'association' (Steptoe et al, 2005), some have claimed that the study has shown the likelihood that happiness reduces the risk of heart disease and diabetes (Bhattacharya, 2005).
- In the **Arnhem Elderly Study** in the Netherlands, 1,012 elderly subjects were tracked and their initial happiness levels correlated strongly with survival over 15 years. But when adjusted for levels of physical activity and morbidity, the correlation disappeared, showing that the apparent long-term 'effects' of happiness on morbidity are mediated through synergetic links between happiness, exercise, and health (Koopmans et al, 2010).
- Other compelling findings on long-term correlations between happiness and health outcomes include the **Framingham Heart Study** in Massachusetts (Christakis and Fowler, 2010); the **Alameda County Study** (Xu and Roberts, 2010); and the **British 1946 Birth Cohort Study** (Richards and Huppert, 2011).

Still, as the Arnhem case study in Box 3.1 exemplifies, the case for evidence-based health and happiness promotion requires cautiously optimistic rather than overstated claims about the causal benefits of happiness. A synthesis study of 160 reliable studies on correlations between happiness and health outcomes over long periods found very strong evidence in nearly all of the studies showing that happiness is associated with better health and longevity, even after controlling for the initial health of subjects (Diener and Chan, 2011). The authors remain less confident about the associations between happiness and health in longitudinal studies of people who were already ill at the start of the study, although many such studies do show better outcomes for happier people. In places, the authors are suitably cautious in reminding us that causality remains uncertain, and that what the longitudinal studies primarily show is correlations. This caution seems essential for two reasons: first, it could be that people who were more cheerful at the start of longitudinal studies weren't yet manifesting significantly better health but already had some innate or early nutritional difference that gave them better underlying health that throughout their lives caused both their cheerfulness and – increasingly as they got older –

their manifestly better health. Second, even if innate cheerfulness is the main cause of the health benefits, it remains to be seen whether *acquired* cheerfulness (for example through the pursuit of happiness-promoting exercises as advocated in self-help books) is associated with long-term health benefits.

Nonetheless, the authors were sufficiently confident of the causality of happiness to say in their title that it 'contributes to health and longevity' and in the main text that 'the case that subjective well-being influences health and longevity is compelling'. This is because animal experiments, and quasi-experimental studies of humans, complement the longitudinal studies by showing that positive and negative emotions induced by environmental changes lead to changes in health. Still, reminders of the uncertainty of causality really do matter because they require us to continue investigating the many possible causal pathways to both health and happiness.

A similarly cautious approach leading to confident statements about causality is Cahit Guven's work on longitudinal studies comparing happiness, social capital, and good citizenship behaviour (voting, volunteering, public participation) in the German Socio-Economic Panel from 1984 to 2005. Recognising that cross-temporal correlations don't in themselves show causality, he developed sophisticated statistical analytical tools to eliminate the 'endogeneity problem' (that is, factors such as personality characteristics that vary with happiness) to measure variations in 'residual happiness' (in people whose characteristics are otherwise similar). Thus able to show how this variation correlates with variation in good citizenship in later life, he was able to make a much stronger case for causality (Guven, 2009).

Probably the most well-established genre of research on the effects of happiness is work exploring how workers' happiness affects workplace goals such as productivity, creativity, workforce stability, and harmonious teamwork. Reviewing scores of studies since the 1930s, Zelenski et al (2008) confirm that although the studies and findings are very diverse and often contradictory, the overwhelming evidence is that both happy character ('trait' measures) and happy mood ('state' measures) help people to work well. Policies promoting job satisfactions and good feelings (even temporary ones) in the workplace are likely to bring dividends not just in the intrinsic value of worker happiness but in the instrumental outcomes of better productivity and better workforce relationships.

Thanks to a large amount of fairly recent research on the consequences of happiness, we can now assert with reasonable confidence that people who feel good are more likely to work well, be nice, stay healthy, and live longer than those who feel bad. We also need to distinguish the 'happiness brings benefits' argument from the linked but separate 'unhappiness causes harm' arguments. It has been argued that 'the major finding of modern Psychology is simply that unhappiness is the basis of all social evils. Unhappy people commit unhappy acts; either on themselves or others' (Fordyce, 1987/2000). Reviewing evidence from cross-sectional, longitudinal, and experimental studies on happiness and work-related outcomes, Boehm and Lyubomirsky (2008) have recently shown convincingly that happiness genuinely precedes good outcomes, and that experimental generation of happiness produces predicted benefits. A major recent WHO review of mental health outcomes has found that there are many demonstrable benefits from 'positive mental health', such as better health, recovery, relationships, and academic performance, that are not just the result of avoiding mental illness (Friedli, 2009).

Discussion points

- Happiness and unhappiness have important effects on other valued goals such as health, longevity, and productivity.
- Not enough is yet known about how much of these effects is attributable to 'trait' happiness (mainly genetically determined), or to 'state' happiness (which varies by circumstances and effort).
- It is not therefore clear whether, by making ourselves and others happy, we can bring about other good effects. But this seems more likely than not, and in any case because happiness is intrinsically good we should want to promote it anyway.

Key readings

Diener, E. and Chan, M. (2011) 'Happy people live longer: subjective wellbeing contributes to health and longevity', *Applied Psychology: Health and Well-Being*, vol 3, no 1, pp 1–43.
Fredrickson, B.L. (2011) *Positivity*, Oxford: Oneworld.
Huppert, F.A. (2009) 'Psychological wellbeing: evidence regarding its causes and its consequences', *Applied Psychology: Health and Well-Being*, vol 1, no 2, pp 137–64.

FOUR

Thinking ourselves happy: on the policy relevance of both subjectivity and objectivity

Happiness depends upon ourselves. (Aristotle)

Objectivity requires taking subjectivity into account.
(Lorraine Code, 1991, p 31)

It isn't what you have or who you are or where you are or what you are doing that makes you happy or unhappy. It is what you think about it. (Dale Carnegie)

What is inside is also outside. (Goethe)

Traditionally, public policies tended to focus on changing people's 'objective' (external) life conditions, whereas the effort to transform 'subjective' feelings and interpretations tended to be left to individuals unless things got so bad that they needed the help of counsellors or psychiatrists. Happiness policies, and the rise of positive life coaching, are changing this. But this new emphasis on subjectivity mustn't be seen as a proposal to put 'mind over matter', expecting citizens to find their own 'inside-out' pathways to happiness.

An argument commonly used against public happiness policy is that, to the extent that our happiness is modifiable, it is we ourselves who can do this, through the power of deliberate control of our own thoughts and feelings. A strong version of this is to be found, for example, in Ricard's popular book *Happiness: A guide to developing life's most important skill* (2007), which presents the pursuit of happiness as largely a mental exercise, although without denying that external circumstances are at least to some extent relevant. Politicians and confidence gurus advocating self-help will tend to quote sayings like Abraham Lincoln's line that 'most folks are about as happy as they make up their minds to be'. In a tirade against the shallow, materialistic hedonism of contemporary US 'popular culture', parenting guru Jim Taylor writes that in contrast to pleasure, 'Happiness ... comes from within. It does not come from what we do, but rather from who we are and what we value. Happiness can never be provided to us, but we can only find it ourselves' (Taylor, 2005, p 178).

Happiness, in more extreme versions of this argument, is all or nearly all controlled by the mind. We get happy by deliberately changing the way we understand and appreciate the conditions and events that seem to affect us. For example, in his chapter on happiness in his book on parenting, Carey makes the all-too-common claim that 'happiness … is only minimally affected by external circumstances' (Carey, 2003, p 33). Authors of the hundreds of self-help publications with titles like *Choose happiness* and *Happiness is a choice* have a vested interest in marketing similarly optimistic beliefs in the power of mental self-help. In her otherwise excellent evidence-based self-help book *The how of happiness*, Lyubomirsky overstates the comparative influence on our happiness of personal intention versus circumstances – which she claims account for '40%' versus just '10%' of our happiness, respectively (2008, p 20). This obviously untenable claim is explicitly provided for the sake of optimism: 'If we can accept as true that life circumstances are not the keys to happiness, we'll be greatly empowered to pursue happiness for ourselves' (2008, p 22). Good ethics, perhaps, but bad science. Few readers will be persuaded that we can make a measurable, sharp distinction between individuals' intentions and their 'circumstances' (under which Lyubomirsky would presumably have to include physical environment, physical health, personal psycho-histories, employment, and all relationships with other people). The inside-outside distinction can be useful for structuring conversations about the mind and its environment, but has no validity in measurement of influences on happiness.

We mustn't let this tendency to exaggerate the power of self-help goad us into knee-jerk rejections of the whole idea of emotional self-help. The substantial psychological and philosophical literature on emotional regulation and self-regulation does demonstrate the extraordinary diversity in people's capabilities to influence their own emotional experiences and evaluations, as well as those of other people (Solomon 2004; Nyklícek et al, 2010). There is also, in happiness science, a well-established school of those who study the structure of motivation and explore possibilities for deliberate modification of our own motives, or those of other people, in favour of motives that stand a better chance of being both prosocial and happiness inducing. For example, in a study of students' motivations in 15 different cultural contexts around the world there was found to be a high degree of cross-cultural consistency in the organisation of motivations along two axes: *intrinsic* versus *extrinsic* (activities that are rewarding in themselves versus those aimed at some expected exterior reward) and *spiritual* versus *physical self ('hedonistic')* (Grouzet et al, 2005). As noted above in the section on happiness experiments, experimental manipulation of activities towards extrinsic or intrinsic motivation has had very striking results (Sheldon et al, 2010).

One warning about these 'inside-out' approaches to happiness is that even if the power to affect personal happiness lies largely within our own minds, social and physical environments do still influence personal happiness. There is also Goethe's more sophisticated argument that the mind is in any case shaped by the external world. There are no resources for personal happiness that exist only 'in your head': changing happiness must obviously be a lifelong process of recursive engagement between the mind and its environment. 'Inside-out' versus 'outside-in' debates, like 'mind–body', 'self–society', and 'nature–nurture' debates, are useful conversation starters, but are misleading when people forget that the dichotomy isn't real. Another, slightly different, approach is to adopt the 'construal' approach, which recognises that 'objective' circumstances do have significant influences on our happiness, provided that we see those circumstances as important: 'how people construe and think about (using top-down processes) objective events and situations in their lives plays an important role in determining how happy they are' (Lyubomirsky and Dickerhoof, 2010, p 231).

In any case, if policy goals include bringing about changes in people's subjective experiences rather than just changes in their living conditions, policy evaluation requires subjective assessment. It may of course make sense to include subjective assessment anyway, regardless of whether experience is included in the policy goals. For example, the goal may be to improve academic scores or to improve objective health outcomes, but it can still be useful for process monitoring and/ or for evaluation to ask people how they feel about the changes.

Another argument sometimes deployed against the use of happiness assessments as a policy guide is that happiness is too 'subjective' a matter for 'empirical' investigation. But we should never let anyone get away with peddling false oppositions between 'subjectivity' and 'empiricism'. In fact, the meanings of 'subjectivity' and 'objectivity' in the past were pretty much the inverse of today's common usage, with subjectivity being about real, substantial facts, and objectivity being about people's perceptions (Williams, 1976, pp 308–12; see also Torras, 2008). Similarly, two different meanings of 'empirical' tend to take us in opposite directions:

- **Empirical as factual, external information:** In this sense, happiness self-reports seem less empirical than the 'revealed preference' that economists have traditionally used as a proxy for happiness, which is implicitly 'concealed preference'.
- **Empirical as experience:** In this sense, verifying the happiness of birthdays and Christmases, and the truth of subjective health, is an empirical matter.

If we measure human progress using monetary indicators, as economists have traditionally done, we are basing our assumptions about well-being on theory. To test this theory empirically, we must ask people about their experience – how they feel. Anyone trying to improve people's lives through income gains, schooling, medical services, or some other kind of benefit has an implicit theory about translation from these benefits to a better life, and when we ask people about their happiness or their feelings we are complementing theory with experience. The empirical investigation of happiness therefore has two experiential components: the felt experiences of the people whose happiness is being investigated, and the experiences of the investigators.

The happiness lens insists on the practical and moral significance of subjectivity. Generations of philosophers have debated subjectivist versus objectivist apprehensions of reality and of values and morality, but polarised views are pointless because we all know that reality and goodness consist of *both* subjective and objective components. The world we experience consists of both mind and matter, both of which (despite our objectivist language) matter. The good life consists of good feelings and thoughts, not just of good things. Well-being isn't just some external reality, it is to a significant extent constituted by the experiencer's recognition of it, just as beauty is, partly, in the eye of the beholder. Bodies and external conditions matter, but everyone also fabricates their own happiness or misery in their own minds. We learn how to do this largely through parental enculturation and through social engagement with other people, which is why the concept of 'social happiness' matters as a complement to individualistic self-help.

As a prudential guide (that is, attending to our own good), the happiness lens is a reminder of the possible benefits of introspection: unless external conditions are truly awful, we can build our own paradise in our own minds. And conversely, no matter how wonderful the external conditions might be, we can also fabricate our own mental miseries. As a moral and policy guide, the happiness lens amounts to an insistence that empathetic engagement with people entails considering their minds, not just their bodies, their productivity, their incomes, and their physical environments.

In modern bureaucratised and professionally specialised society, the subjectivity reminder becomes particularly necessary because specialised and formalised attention to objective goods often entails empathy barriers. These make us treat people as objects rather than subjects, and encourage us to focus narrowly on selected aspects of factual reality rather than on the full range of human experience and meaning. Medical specialists treat patients as bodies with particular diseases. Managers, often against their better nature, end up treating workers as factors in production rather than as fully rounded human beings. Lawyers, as the blind justice statue reminds us, are often constitutionally required to treat litigants non-empathetically as victims or wrongdoers, without regard to their feelings. Hurried or bureaucratically pressured schoolteachers treat pupils as vehicles for scores in academic tests. The specific objective goods that these specialists promote – health, wealth, objectively fair legal decisions, and knowledge, respectively, all play important parts in the good life; but pursuit of these goods without regard to subjective feelings and evaluations can be counterproductive and dangerous.

No one can talk about happiness for long without bumping into debates about the synergies and trade-offs between 'subjective' and 'objective' routes to happiness, that is, between efforts to improve our interpretations of the world, or efforts to improve the world itself. Nor can anyone can engage in policy discourse for long without encountering debates about the respective merits and complementarities of 'subjective' and 'objective' indicators of reality, and associated 'subjectivist' and 'objectivist' approaches to learning – that is, between an emphasis on perceptions and opinions on the one hand, and solid 'facts' on the other (referred to by Veenhoven, 2002, p 36, as distinctions of 'assessment' and of 'substance' respectively). Put these two distinctions together, and you have a useful matrix for facilitating discussions about these different aspects of the good life and about different ways of learning about these different aspects, as shown in Table 4.1.

Subjective assessments may be criticised as simply *incorrect* (for example, Marxist accusations of 'false consciousness', or behavioural economists' findings on systematic misremembering of experience), *invalid* (for example, where survey questions are inconsistently understood), *unreliable* (for example, different understandings of the meaning of scores on a 0–5 scale), or *systematically distorted* (for example, by cultural norms such as the 'social desirability' of self-reporting happiness) (Veenhoven, 2002, p 37). These potential weaknesses must be remembered when weighing up the value of different information sources. But responsible policy making requires knowledge about people's subjective and objective well-being, obtained through a combination of methods and indicators using varying degrees of subjectivity and objectivity.

Table 4.1: Subjectivity–objectivity matrix

	Subjective indicators and learning methods	Objective indicators and learning methods
Subjective life quality components	Asking people about their feelings and satisfactions (for example emotion diaries, life-satisfaction surveys, focus-group discussions of happiness)	Externally observing indicators of subjectivity (for example, scoring facial expression, neuroimaging)
Objective life quality components	Asking people about their life conditions (for example, subjective wealth, subjective health indicators)	Recording factual data about life conditions (for example, actual income, bodily health measures)

Source: Adapted from Veenhoven, 2002, p 36.

The distinction between subjective and objective conditions matters, because if we excessively prioritise the one or the other we are apt to misconstrue the quality of someone's life: very happy people can be living in awful conditions that are morally unacceptable, while others may seem to have excellent objective conditions, but if they are really miserable their lives aren't going well. A government that focuses solely on the objective well-being of its citizens could end up in charge of a desperately bored, anxious, unhappy population. The same is true of any social institution: hospitals that focus only on objective health won't perform very well on that aim, because health and recovery prospects are strongly influenced by happiness and subjective factors like hope, feelings of agency, trust in doctors, and so on. Schools that focus only on academic excellence won't do very well at that because academic performance is strongly influenced by subjectivity.

It is harder to think of examples of major institutions that privilege subjective over objective conditions, although dystopian fiction such as Huxley's *Brave new world* (1932) and James Gunn's *The joymakers* have tried to depict what they might be like. But there are plenty of examples of more minor social institutions that could be accused of overemphasising subjectivity at the expense of objective well-being: psychotherapists who treat mental illness as if it were all in the mind, ignoring socio-economic factors; businesses that sell only alcohol, psychotropic drugs or cheap thrills; or religious institutions and doctrines that purvey faith, hope, and nonchalance but do nothing to question or fight poverty and illness. Indeed, anyone who specialises in subjectivity, however well-intentioned, runs the risk of being accused of purveying false consciousness, unrealistic optimism, and conservatism. Marxists are very explicit in insisting that our morality should be guided by observation of material realities: under capitalist relations of production, the proletariat are alienated, whether or not they believe this to be the case.

Yet those who emphasise 'objectivist' approaches to the good life, by focusing on material wealth and health for example, are perhaps unwittingly influencing people's subjective experiences in ways that they might not intend. A sports instructor who overemphasises physical capability without attending to psychological aspects of sport can lead pupils to obsessive body fixation and exercise dependence, and to forgetfulness about the hedonic value and existential meaning of sport and fitness. Feminists who attend only to the objective injustices of gender-based inequalities in wealth and power can end up making women pathologically interested in these objective goods, instead of persuading women and men to consider the ways in which gender reform might make everyone happier, or how an attention shift to psychological goods like love and intimacy might itself lead to gender reform. Parents who overemphasise the achievement of academic scores, or who encourage their daughters to entrap rich, high-status husbands, can set their children up for a lifetime of anxiety, guilt, and disappointment.

The objective/subjective distinction is itself to a large extent fluid and subjective, because it is a cultural construct, and hence to some extent arbitrary. For example money, the obsession of so-called 'materialists' and the supposedly objective representation of wealth and value that economists are so interested in, exists only as a cultural belief system backed up by social institutions and transactions. It is simply an objectification of ultimately subjective realities, the value concepts that we hold in our minds and transact with other people, just as numbers based on surveys of life satisfaction are objectifications of momentary self-evaluation. As Adam Phillips puts it, 'what the desire for money has been a desire *for* has never been clear' (2005, p 188). 'The economy' may seem real, and it certainly has real effects, but it is produced by collective make-believe, as Black Mondays and currency collapses periodically remind us.

Rising interest in the assessment of happiness is driven by the feeling that we have been let down by false promises of economic growth. Our ability to organise our environment – or at least the non-human parts of it – does seem over recent generations to have made much more dramatic gains than our ability to organise our minds. Many people doubt that humanity is in general any happier today that 100 years ago, despite astonishing gains in longevity, technical capability, freedom, choice, and health. Throughout world history, when considering how to get happy, people have always pondered and debated the trade-offs and relative prioritisation between efforts to manipulate our inner selves and efforts to change our external circumstances.

Like any organism, we need to combine assimilation (adapting our surroundings to suit us) with accommodation (adapting ourselves to fit our environments). As humans, we must accept that our main environmental consideration is other people. So, ongoing happiness projects must operate at both individual and social levels. As individuals, we are constantly trying to adjust others' behaviour and attitudes towards us, but also adjusting ours to them. Collectively, we adjust our non-social environments to fit our social preferences, and adjust our societies in the hope that we will interact better with our non-human environments. But, unlike other species, we have the unique ability to modify the way in which both our social and non-human environments affect our happiness. The self is perhaps not infinitely manipulable, but sometimes it seems that way.

A final point is that listening to and respecting 'subjective' accounts of well-being is not at all the same as being 'subjective' about well-being. Being 'objective' means considering phenomena as objects in a detached, scientific way. Hence, it isn't incoherent to talk of 'objective happiness' (Kahneman, 1999), and 'the task for positive social science is to provide the most *objective* facts possible about the phenomena it studies' (Peterson and Seligman, 2003).

Discussion points

- Life quality is composed of both objectively real conditions and people's own feelings and evaluations: responsible policy making addresses people's objective and subjective well-being.
- Knowledge about each of these two aspects of life quality needs to be obtained through a combination of methods and indicators using varying degrees of subjectivity and objectivity.

- In scholarship and in policy and planning a simple mnemonic device such as a subjectivity–objectivity matrix can serve as a helpful check, facilitating discussions about the optimum balance of emphasis on subjectivity and objectivity in methods and in intended outcomes.

Key readings

Nyklícek, I., Vingerhoets, A. and Zeelenberg, M. (eds) (2010) *Emotion regulation and wellbeing*, Dordrecht: Springer.

Veenhoven, R. (2002) 'Why social policy needs subjective indicators', *Social Indicators Research*, vol 58, nos 1–3, pp 33–46.

FIVE

Who makes happiness happen? On emotion work and psychosocial contagion

> Nothing is so interesting as happiness. (Florence Nightingale, cited in McDonald, 2001, p 94)

Anyone interested in the deliberate promotion of social happiness needs to think about the key players, the positive deviants who are exceptionally good at spreading joy. Yet, if asked to justify our patterns of social and professional recognition and remuneration, how articulate would we be in spelling out the different contributions people make to social happiness? From a happiness perspective we can re-evaluate individual capabilities such as leadership, effectiveness, responsibility, charisma, and success – rethinking what it means to 'bring out the best' in people and the social processes and contexts that make that happen (for a more cross-cultural version of these arguments, see Thin, 2011a). Since, throughout our lives, we learn how to be happy (or unhappy) from other people, it makes sense to try to enrich our analytical understanding of how some people – mood elevators, morale boosters, and meaning providers – use their characters and positions to bring out the best in other people.

For example, Florence Nightingale was famously good at promoting well-being through her determined attention to hygiene, statistics, and morale-boosting. Her life-long ailments often made her miserable, but her diaries show that she understood clearly that social contagion transmits feelings as well as germs. So she performed mental hygiene, keeping moderately cheerful by keeping busy helping others. And she taught others the importance of mental hygiene too, complementing her battles against soldiers' insanitary practices and alcoholism with more upbeat work keeping their spirits up by helping them run cafes and write letters to loved ones. Biographies all too rarely dwell on these illuminating aspects of the lives of positive deviants.

Happiness scholarship has so far focused much more on individuals' own happiness than on the roles of happiness facilitators. Yet we all know that happiness is socially contagious, and that it has to be culturally learned along with all other aspects of emotional regulation, self-evaluation, and meaning-making. It isn't just consumer habits, activities, afflictions, and suicide that are 'socially contagious': our (self-reported) happiness itself is strongly influenced by the (self-reported) happiness of the people in our social networks (Christakis and Fowler, 2010).

When toddlers fall, they check their minders' faces for advice on whether to laugh or cry. From birth, we learn about our emotions, and about the feeling rules that will steer us towards emotionally responsible interaction with others, from interactional experience. Emotion guides such as teachers, counsellors, leaders and carers therefore do a lot more than the immediate nudging of temporary emotions in specific situations: they teach us all how we should feel and how we should communicate our feelings. Life coaches and philosophical or spiritual guides go further still: they encourage and show us how to find meaning and purpose in life, and how to harmonise and balance our diverse desires and pleasures.

If we want to understand the positive social, emotional, and philosophical contagion that facilitates happiness, we must try to develop a sense of the variety and capabilities of the people who make these processes happen. To study or promote happiness while neglecting the happiness makers is weird, a bit like studying music without looking at musicians, composers, conductors, or musicianship. But do we really recognise and understand the full array of charismatic enthusiasts and quiet moral exemplars whose mysterious energising and feel-good forces bring out the best in people around them? There are some striking features of contemporary happiness and social science discourses worth bearing in mind:

- **Ego focus:** Happiness scholarship and guidance on self-help and character strengths have generally been ego focused and experiential rather than ethnographic and socially analytical. They have mainly explored how happiness correlates with personality traits, generic conditions, attitudes, and life events. People are recognised as agents and communicators of their own happiness but not of other people's happiness. Training in life coaching and therapy does, of course, pay some attention to the joys and skills of making other people happy, but even here the ego focus is dominant, with only rare attention to positive social contagion (see Biswas-Diener and Dean, 2007, especially chapter 7, 'Coaching social strengths').
- **Adverse social contagion:** Social sciences and organisation and human resource studies have specialised more in toxicity than in positive contagion. Their copious work on toxic socio-cultural

environments, on trouble makers, and on adverse social contagion hasn't been substantially complemented with research on the capabilities and effects of life enhancers.

In Business Studies, in workplace coaching, and in scholarship on management, leadership, and human resources, there has been substantial work on positivity, strengths, charisma, and emotional intelligence, focused largely on interim goods, harm avoidance, and efficiency rather than on the intrinsic goodness of relationships. The standard organisational management approach remains a 'deficit' orientation, emphasising coping with problems, but some researchers are trying to supplement this (but not replacing it) with an 'abundance' approach focused on strengths and promoting self-reinforcing positive 'heliotropic effects' (Cameron and Lavine, 2006). Copious research has been conducted on the characteristics of successful entrepreneurs and team leaders, much of it relevant to understanding life enhancement, but little of it teasing out the factors that contribute to happiness rather than productivity and profit. There are signs of a movement towards using a happiness lens in 'Positive Organisational Scholarship', 'Psychological Capital', and 'Servant Leadership' (Cameron and Lavine, 2006; Luthans et al, 2007; Trompenaars and Voerman, 2009).

'Emotional labour', 'empathy', and 'social/emotional intelligence' research areas are the most promising from the perspective of prosocial happiness promotion. These areas of scholarship go beyond ego focus, beyond pathologies, and beyond productivity and profitability to explore the goodness of social relationships at home, in the community, and in the workplace. Even in these fields, happiness has yet to emerge as a prominent theme. Neither 'emotional labour' nor 'social/emotional intelligence' theories tend to predict that these actions and capabilities will actually spread happiness, nor do they generally enquire into whether this happens.

If it's interesting to read books on how people get happy, it ought to matter at least as much to learn the secrets of people who are exceptionally good at persuading and showing others how to be happy – good parents, teachers, carers, entertainers, leaders, and team-mates. These life enhancers, whether they be professional mood elevators or inconspicuous meaning providers, are the opposite of toxic. We all owe a great deal of our happiness to them, and it is likely that we could ourselves become more virtuous and happier by trying to copy at least some of their skills. Their moods and attitudes are known to be contagious, yet for all the hundreds of publications on social 'toxicity' (particularly in the workplace but also in schools, homes, and public places), it is hard to find any on positive social contagion.

We already tend to be quite sophisticated at identifying and analysing trouble makers – the toxic co-workers, disruptive pupils, bullies, and dangerous spouses who wreck other people's lives. Indeed, there's a colossal literature on adverse social contagion (on toxicity in the workplace, see for example Kusy and Holloway, 2009 and Durre, 2010; on toxic personalities and bad relationships in general, see Grant, 2003; on toxic cultural and social environments you can choose from countless thousands of contemporary social science texts, but for popular generalisers see for example James, 2007 or Palmer, 2007). Most of us, thankfully, aren't like that, but nor are we like those exceptional individuals who actively generate contagious good cheer and help others to strengthen their sense of dignity and meaning.

Indeed, a recent spate of books, much of it in the 'assertiveness training' tradition, has been advising us against the 'nice guy syndrome' (Glover, 2003) or 'nice girl syndrome' (Engel, 2008). We are advised not to try too hard to be one of those adorable people, because we can damage both ourselves and others by trying to be nice, especially if in doing so we are being inauthentic (Rapson and English, 2006; Grzyb and Chandler, 2008). We can also damage other people if our efforts to promote positivity are experienced as a kind of emotional bullying (Ehrenreich, 2009). And at the level of teamwork, 'niceness' can detract from performance objectives and competitiveness (Miller, 2010). Given all this pessimism about niceness, and in light of the fact that evolutionists have tended in the past to advise us that nice guys get beaten and eaten, it's a relief to explore some more upbeat literature both on the rich evolutionary heritage of altruism and empathy, and on the apparent civilisational expansion of these traits (Wright, 2000; Pinker, 2007; De Waal, 2009). It's also comforting to notice a rapidly expanding body of research evidence demonstrating the happiness and health benefits of 'prosocial' activities and attitudes (Aknin et al, 2010).

There is also, comfortingly, a rash of academic and popular publications in the fairly recent 'Positive Organisational Scholarship' and 'Servant–Leadership' traditions advising us that even in the cut-and-thrust world of business it is possible to flourish as a leader, co-worker, or salesperson by being nice (Thaler and Koval, 2006; Quinn and Quinn, 2009). In studies of business ethics, it has been noted that job satisfaction is reduced when the belief spreads that unethical practice leads to success (Viswesvaran and Deshpande, 1996; Elci and Alpkan, 2009) or, conversely, that happiness makes workers more interested in business ethics (Heinze, 2005).

Life enhancers are not necessarily the most noticed people, nor the most popular, nor are they necessarily also best at being 'productive' or 'efficient' when judged by non-eudaimonic criteria. In fact, there are sound socio-evolutionary reasons why prosocial acts such as generous sharing and peace making should go uncelebrated and unadvertised, especially by the do-gooder, since recognition of such acts can cause friction by highlighting inequalities, tensions, and suspicions of people's motives. Also, although prosocial joy making is no doubt generally a rather uplifting way of behaving, joy makers aren't necessarily the most cheerful or inwardly happy people. And though we think of cheermongers as kind and considerate, altruistic people, there are also some rather stern and perhaps even selfish characters who make vital contributions to happiness.

In practice, we can usually recognise people who are sources of positive emotional contagion. Positive emotion work is an astonishingly rich and complex human capability that we are all born capable of developing. In some people, the role of providing emotional and philosophical support to other people becomes their signature strength. In others this potential atrophies through disuse. Like musical and artistic skills in many cultures, cheermongery tends to be left largely to a few experts and to be seen as a mysterious gift that the rest of us can't understand or emulate. Despite or perhaps in some ways because of its importance, the powerful capability of joy spreading is often invisible and is sometimes actively downplayed or denigrated – again, much as is the case with musical and artistic capabilities. As with happiness itself, a major part of the ability to spread happiness may well be genetically fixed for us, but that still leaves a lot of room for deliberate improvement. We may not all be able to copy the natural warmth, kindliness and cheerfulness of born cheermongers, but we can surely learn a lot from observing how they behave – how they speak, how they listen, what they do with their time. And we can learn about the culture of happiness more broadly by considering how people are trained in happiness-facilitating skills, how they are placed socially and institutionally, and whether and how they are rewarded and celebrated. Box 5.1 provides a suggested start-up typology for anyone interested in analytically considering the variety of social roles through which people facilitate happiness.

We need to distinguish the short-term *mood elevators* (cheermongers, entertainers, distractors) and medium-term *therapists* who specialise in episodic happiness, from the *life enhancers* who promote chronic happiness. And we should recognise that happiness can be enhanced in the short or longer term by helping people to get what they need, helping them to get what they want, and helping them to want what they get. Further, we should distinguish private facilitators who promote the happiness of a few individuals from those who promote social happiness as a public good. Some people no doubt enhance other people's lives in multiple ways, performing all of these roles in different contexts.

Box 5.1: Generic categories and examples of happiness-facilitating roles

- **Home makers:** Those who design and maintain the physical and social infrastructure, the flows of goods, and the stocks of goodwill and security that provide us with a secure, meaningful, and pleasant home base.
- **Carers:** Parents, home carers, nurses, social workers, and other pastoral care specialists.
- **Therapists:** Psychotherapists (but not Freudian psychoanalysts, who see happiness as an unrealistic aim), bereavement counsellors, marriage guidance counsellors.
- **Meaning facilitators:** Good managers, story tellers, life coaches, teachers, religious leaders.
- **Empathy pioneers and solidarity facilitators:** People brave and/or creative enough to break through the empathic barriers and thereby promote sociality, understanding, love, and prosocial behaviour.
- **Ethos brokers and eudaimonic exemplars:** People who wittingly or unwittingly generate collective moods and longer-term cultural norms of goodwill and realistic optimism within any social unit – families, schools, clubs, businesses, venues. (For example, some people seem to energise and optimise people around them simply by seeming to run their own lives well, perhaps by being exceptionally cheerful or pleasantly calm, perhaps by combining excellence and commitment in multiple domains without ever seeming to be in a hurry.)
- **Entertainers and short-term cheermongers:** Specialists in light-hearted everyday banter, musicians, comedians, artists, fiction writers, producers and presenters of media entertainment; leisure and travel experience managers – cabin crews, waiters, and some hotel staff.
- **Cultural pioneers:** Courageous breakers of social taboos (homosexuals who come out; interracial couples), solvers of collective-action dilemmas (men and women who insist on flexible and family-friendly work practices; dowry refusers in India; casual dressers in stuffy organisations).

Facilitating the happiness of others is more complex than mere joy making, and if we are to develop our policy sciences of life enhancement we must analyse the skills and dispositions involved, and the ways in which these are advanced or inhibited by social processes. The invisibility of happiness as a theme in our assessment of what people do for society not only weakens our understanding of society, it also distorts our reward systems. We notice, celebrate, and pay for people's impact on the world without adequately evaluating their contributions to happiness. Happiness science is already well advanced in its assessment of the factors that are likely to affect or be affected by personal happiness. But the systematic study of who helps others achieve happiness, and how, has barely begun. I have searched in vain for examples of analytical tools that would assist anyone wanting to start analysing the people who, in their organisation, might be the experts in facilitating happiness. Box 5.2 is a first tentative and simple step in this direction.

Box 5.2: Checklist for positive emotional labour in organisations

- **Mission:** Is the happiness of the workforce, and/or of other stakeholders formally recognised as a valued principle and goal of the organisation?
- **Recruitment:** When hiring staff, is their capability for spreading happiness explicitly assessed?
- **Understanding strengths:** Is it clear who is best at facilitating happiness (of staff, customers, and other relevant stakeholders), and in what ways?
- **Deployment:** Are exceptionally gifted cheermongers placed in roles that play to this strength?
- **Performance and incentives:** In reviewing staff performance, is their contribution to the happiness of others (fellow staff, clients, other stakeholders) considered? What is done to reward, thank, or celebrate those who spread happiness?
- **Social events:** Are there ample occasions – festive events, social lunches, coffee breaks, and so on – for informal social interaction?
- **Infrastructure:** Is infrastructural layout conducive to a suitable amount and variety of informal social interaction?
- **Protection:** What is done to limit the contagion of toxic emotion in the organisation?

Sources: Cherniss and Goleman (2001); Berger and Berger (2003); Fineman (2003); Biswas-Diener and Dean (2007); Hughes and Terrell (2007); Manz (2008).

The neglect of happiness in biographical and theological literature also speaks of a gender bias: the crucial roles that women play in facilitating happiness go un-narrated. Arlie Hochschild's *The managed heart* (1983) was a ground-breaking theoretical work promoting analysis of emotional labour in the workplace, based on a fascinating ethnography of the training and work experience of flight attendants. Though inspirational in directing our attention to the under-acknowledged and often both skilful and stressful management of the self that is required for some forms of emotional labour, Hochschild's approach is in the end a worryingly distortive approach to her subject. Her Marxist and feminist adversarial persuasions require her to see paid 'labour' (and hence all 'commodified' emotion work) as intrinsically exploitative, alienating, and unpleasant.

The possibilities that we might celebrate and marvel at the life-enhancing skills of professional peace keepers and joy makers, or that these people might find their work deeply rewarding, are hidden in Hochschild's attack on the exploitation of these mainly feminine virtues by male managers and businessmen. So critics have pointed out, for example, that supermarket check-out staff might take great pride in their role in facilitating enjoyable shopping experiences (Tolich, 1993, p 372), and that 'emotion work' might be a better term to describe, for example, the 'gift' of care that nurses love bestowing on their patients (Bolton 2000, p 584). Table 5.1 illustrates some of the variety of emotional labour through which people facilitate happiness.

Most people who do socially responsible work make important contributions to happiness, whether their work is paid or unpaid, and regardless of whether they think of it as work or as prosocial. A happiness lens invites more specific exploration of positive social epidemiology, looking at ways in which viral happiness spreads through the processes and outcomes of good work. The most obvious categories of joy makers are those who are professionally required to cheer people up or help us make sense of events and avoid alienation and bewilderment. These tasks can be temporary expedients, to help people through difficult circumstances like bereavement or illness, or longer-term challenges. Or they can be directed at longer-term goals, helping people to rethink and make positive sense of their lives and develop realistic, motivating aspirations.

Table 5.1: Varieties of happiness facilitation

Domain, activity, or disposition correlated with overall happiness	Key facilitators	Supportive cultural and social context
Good marriage/intimacy	Parents, marriage brokers	Family-friendly work policies, secure local employment
Health	Nutrition/healthcare advisers, doctors, nurses	Food production and distribution systems, food safety organisations, sanitation and cleanliness systems, medical and therapeutic services
Strong relationships	'[C]onnectors, mavens, and salesmen' (Gladwell, 2000, chapter 2)	Socially inclusive infrastructure, education, and leisure facilities
Realistic aspirations (and benign social comparisons)	Parents, teachers, coaches, close friends	Public media, advertisers, organisers of competitions and other talent-celebrating processes
Being intrinsically motivated	Non-interfering, autonomy-supportive guides and appraisers (parents, teachers, managers)	Societies and cultural traditions that offer opportunities for autonomous choice in key life roles – marriage, paid work, social functions; secure environments allowing experimentation with life options
Good work	Careers advisers, managers, fellow team workers	Strong economies and businesses, vibrant voluntary sectors, sociable workplace infrastructure and supportive organisational culture
Financial security	Financial advisers, employers	Stock markets, insurance
Coping well with adversity	Counsellors, therapists, fellow sufferers	Social support networks, cathartic and resilience-enhancing rituals
Social justice	Anti-poverty and human rights campaigners	Legal justice systems and enforcement agencies
Education	Teachers, educational media producers/authors	Schools, further education, lifelong education institutions, libraries, internet/media
Benign biophysical environment	Urban planners, conservationists	Environmental, heritage and conservation organisations;
Arts and leisure	Musicians, artists, organisers of arts and leisure clubs	Good leisure infrastructure; vibrant culture
Regular exercise	Sports club organisers, architects and town planners who design exercise-promoting environments	Educational and workplace institutions and clubs that encourage sport and exercise
Religion/spirituality	Religious leaders, charismatic providers of existential meaning, facilitators of bliss and self-transcendence	Religious organisations; belief and value systems that make people receptive to charisma and bliss, and a sense of self-transcendent meaning

Finally, one particularly interesting and under–celebrated category of joy maker is people who see the potential for fun and beauty in unexpected places and forms, and who then share this with other people. Guerilla gardening (Box 5.3) is one example, but there is something of this capability in a great deal of artistic and literary creativity, and in less conspicuous creativity in most organisations, and increasingly via idiosyncratic websites and online networks.

Box 5.3: Guerilla gardening

'Guerilla gardening' was first developed by a young freelance advertising planner called Richard Reynolds in London in the late 1990s (www.guerrillagardening. org), as a way of relaxing after work and meeting other people both face-to-face and through internet links. He began simply planting flowers in neglected patches of land such as disused flower beds, traffic islands, and tree pits in his neighbourhood of Elephant & Castle in south London. In doing so, he enriched the already well-known happiness benefits of gardening by adding a frisson of illicitness, a pinch of cheerful public engagement, and the possibility of making subtle political statements about urban environmental neglect. Reynolds launched a 'Pimp Your Pavement' campaign in March 2010, which has won support from the London Festival of Architecture, the Conservation Foundation, and the London Sustainable Development Commission, who have formally appointed Reynolds as a 'London Leader'.

A more specifically artistic version of this was developed in 2006 by a class at the California College of the Arts in San Francisco (www.potholegardens.org) as a way of simultaneously embellishing drab urban spaces and promoting awareness of global environmental sustainability issues.

This idea was transformed into a delightfully beautiful and entertaining public art form by Steve Wheen in the UK (www.thepotholegardener.com), and by several 'guerilla knitting' organisations (www.flickr.com/groups/guerilla-knitting/).

Sources: Tracey (2007); Reynolds, (2009)

Discussion points

- Happiness develops through a set of culturally learned and socially constituted capabilities.
- It is therefore important to understand how people facilitate the happiness of other people, paying particular attention to their

dispositions, actions, roles, and the social contexts that optimise their work in this regard.

• While a great deal of happiness-related scholarship has been excessively ego focused, and a great deal of social and biographical research on factors influencing happiness has been toxicity focused, there are good signs of new emphasis on the social facilitation of happiness in business and community development.

Key readings

Biswas–Diener, R. and Dean, B. (2007) *Positive psychology coaching*, Hoboken, NJ: John Wiley.

Cherniss, C. and Goleman, D. (eds) (2001) *The emotionally intelligent workplace*, San Francisco, CA: Jossey-Bass.

Fineman, S. (2003) *Understanding emotion at work*, London: Sage.

Goleman, D. (2007) *Social intelligence: The new science of human relationships*, London: Arrow Books.

Nelson, D.L. and Cooper, C.L.E. (eds) (2007) *Positive organisational behavior*, London: Sage.

Quinn, R.W. and Quinn, R.E. (eds) (2009) *Lift: Becoming a positive force in any situation*, San Francisco: Berrett-Koehler.

Values-In-Action, VIA Classification of Strengths, www.viastrengths.org.

SIX

Governance and responsibility: towards the eudaimonic state?

Worldwide, governments of rich and poor countries alike have been showing dramatically increased interest in monitoring national levels of self-reported happiness. This is a major shift from previous positions whereby governments and parastatals in richer countries saw their roles primarily in terms of ensuring law and order, facilitating economic growth, and remedying the pathological sources of psychological suffering, particularly among the poor and marginalised. This latter role has been known by sceptics as that of the 'nanny state' (Harsanyi, 2007) or 'therapeutic state' (Polsky, 1991). Note that these terms, which on the face of it refer to the not unreasonable idea that states might want to look after the well-being of their less fortunate citizens, are almost invariably used as terms of abuse. Now it seems that many governments want to move beyond therapeutic into eudaimonic roles, facilitating happiness rather than just minimalising suffering. Is this a clear sign that they want to use this information as a guide for policy and practice, and that they recognise their responsibility to do so? In the UK, a BBC survey in 2006 found that 81% of people thought the government should see happiness, not GDP, as its main objective (Easton, 2006).

Bhutan remains the only country in the world to have chosen 'Gross National Happinesss' (GNH) as the overarching policy objective (see www.bhutanstudies.org.bt). Although lots of political leaders, government bureaucracies, and business leaders worldwide have insisted on the importance of measuring happiness in order to balance so-called 'economic' indicators with attention to people's reported experiences, few have even dabbled with the idea of spelling out the kind of difference that this might make to policies. Even in Bhutan, the GNH idea has until recently had mainly rhetorical status, with little systematic attempt to back it up with distinctively happiness–promoting strategies. Bhutan's government has in practice put much more emphasis on economic growth than on happiness, achieving (albeit from a low base) some of the world's highest growth rates in recent years. It seems almost certain that recent major improvements in Bhutanese happiness, health, and longevity are largely due to the economic growth induced by liberalisation policies. Bhutanese citizens are well aware of this:

when they responded to the open-ended question on 'what makes you happy?' in the national happiness survey, the most common response by far was 'financial security' (52%), followed by 'access to roads' (32%), with 'family relationships' mentioned by only 26%, and 'community' by just 9%, perhaps because they take the quality of these social goods for granted (Centre for Bhutan Studies, 2008).

In any case, the 'Gross National' part of the rhetoric may work well as a joke, but has an uncanny ring to it as a new version of the old counting-house metaphor for happiness. Jeremy Bentham, the godfather of utilitarian politics, argued for maximising happiness, which he thought of as a 'sum of pleasures minus the pains'. He was right that governments should give happiness proper attention, but completely wrong to reduce happiness to just a sum of pleasures. This is a bit like saying that the objective of gardening is to produce a big heap of flowers minus the weeds, or that music is a heap of nice sounds minus the discords. Happiness needs to be understood not only in the 'bottom-up' sense of cumulative pleasure, but also in the 'top-down' sense of how we interpret our experience (Diener, 1984, p 565).

Although it is desirable that governments and statisticians should address happiness, we mustn't forget that in democratic societies governments need to show accountability and short-term performance by making heaps of things and counting them. So they will much more readily tell us how much they have spent on their citizens' welfare than try to develop more complex stories about how those expenditures may eventually translate into sustainable well-being. All democratic governments have to some extent succumbed to the obviously ridiculous idea that 'the economy' is reducible to a sum of measured monetised transactions called 'Gross Domestic Product', as if the uncounted and unmarketed activities on which we rely at least as much were of no value. In terms of 'economic' management, government policies have tended to be a version of utilitarian philosophy: they have imagined that ever bigger heaps of economic activity would provide ever bigger heaps of wealth that people would be able to turn into ever bigger heaps of pleasures of their own choosing.

Regarding so-called 'social' policies, governments have, as argued above, been excessively led by *negative* utilitarianism, focusing on the removal of harms. They fight crime when they could be doing a better job of facilitating the happiness that would make crime unnecessary. The so-called 'health' and 'mental health' services are mainly about the extremely inefficient investments in medicine and therapy, downplaying the potentially much more efficient promotion of good physical and mental health. Education fares slightly better, but even here too much of the emphasis is on schooling as a battle against ignorance and as the production of a heap of measurable knowledge, rather than holistically exploring how schools and other educational processes facilitate good lives from childhood onwards.

In the spirit of new millennial optimism, in 2002 the UK government Cabinet Office produced a think-piece paper on the implications of life-satisfaction research for government policy. The paper came to the common-sense conclusion that life satisfaction must be a central concern for government policy making. But what is most interesting is that this idea is presented so cautiously and defensively, as if it were novel and controversial:

> If we accept that life satisfaction is an important objective and can be influenced, then the literature throws down a fundamental challenge to policymakers. If decades of legislation, economic growth and increased life expectancy have barely affected the life satisfaction of the British people, then what should government be doing? (Donovan and Halpern, 2002, p 33)

Higher officials seem to have been worried about the radical implications of this paper, forcing the authors to head every single page with the strikingly defensive caveat: 'This is not a statement of government policy').Yet, in Organization for Economic Co-operation and Development (OECD) member countries, high-level rhetorical interest in happiness has suddenly become so prominent that the recent United Nations Economic and Social Commission for Asia and the Pacific (UNESCAP) report on the OECD's Global Project on Measuring the Progress of Societies felt the need to clarify that this project is 'not purely about measuring happiness' (UNESCAP, 2009a, p 9) – as if (against overwhelming evidence to the contrary) it were now normal worldwide for progress assessments to dwell mainly on subjectivity. At the other extreme, Kesebir and Diener have unrealistically claimed that government policies and performance assessments worldwide have until recently put an 'almost total emphasis' on 'economic outcomes' and 'indicators such as GDP' (2008, p 60). Faith in such indicators has been excessive, but most governments have for decades been using lots of 'social' indicators (health, life expectancy, crime and divorce rates, and so on) that reflect quality of life more directly than do monetary indicators.

One of the most outspoken and politically experienced promoters of evidence-based happiness policies is the British economist and politician

Richard Layard. His chapter on happiness policies (2005) makes several bold recommendations for national-level policies: promoting work–life balance through higher taxation; discouraging zero-sum status rivalry; promoting intrinsic motivation at work; tightening controls on advertising; wealth redistribution through higher taxation; employment protection; promoting social capital by reducing geographical mobility; promoting mental health through higher investment in psychotherapy. Another commonly cited collection of happiness advice at a generic policy level is the 'Wellbeing Manifesto' promoted by the New Economics Foundation (NEF) (Shah and Marks, 2004). It argues that governments should promote well-being mainly by 'encouraging and incentivising good citizenship', by facilitating better work–life balance, better environmental care, and stronger communities, that is, by making us happy indirectly rather than by trying to achieve direct happiness impacts. It recommends eight key areas for consideration: national well-being accounts; ensuring access to meaningful work; a maximum 35-hour week, more flexibility in working hours, and more bank holidays; all schools promoting emotional, social, and physical well-being, with more emphasis on thriving and less on performance; a health service that promotes health; more support for early childhood and parenting; discouraging materialism and promoting authentic advertising; and strengthening active citizenship.

I would expect most readers to sympathise with many of both Layard's and the NEF's policy objectives, but it is harder to agree on government roles in promoting these changes. Particularly in Layard's more overtly government-focused and expensive prescriptions, the risks of becoming excessively interventionist are all too evident. Also, while many of these policy recommendations look like good common sense strengthened with scientific evidence, they are also open to some fundamental questioning. Status competition may be damaging in some ways, but is also part of human nature and in many ways fun, so any interference in competition would have to be approached cautiously. But it is certainly valid to question the tendency, for example, in western schools and businesses, to promote competitiveness on the assumption that it is good for us. The rationale for redistribution of income sounds immediately plausible, but leaves a lot of questions about how it could be done without impinging on the motivation and dignity of the poor. Perhaps we could benefit from more psychotherapy in the UK, but are there not more sensible no-nonsense alternative ways of promoting happiness that don't involve narcissistic soul-baring to professional strangers? Sharing work more equitably and reducing overwork sounds good, but are there not lots of people who have good reason to want to work more than 35 hours per week, and lots of jobs that are hard to do well without long hours? And is 'materialism' anything other than a vague slogan, and if it can be defined is it really so bad that we should, in principle, discourage it? In both the Layard and the NEF examples, it quickly begins to look as if happiness research is being used in a very tokenistic way to justify long-held idiosyncratic policy preferences.

In any case, happiness science could just as well be used to question some of these policy themes. Like many others with concerns about environmental sustainability, the NEF clearly hopes that happiness research will lend support to arguments against capitalist overconsumption. Some research does indeed show that some kinds of consumptive greed and shopping addiction are associated with unhappiness (though they may often be more the outcome rather than the root cause of unhappiness). But just about all serious studies show strong correlations between income, or economic growth, and happiness (especially in poor countries, but also in rich countries), so if 'discouraging materialism' means losing income and growth, only wishful thinking points to this as a would-be happiness policy.

If the NEF's Wellbeing Manifesto looks slightly weak in terms of its evidence base and policy analysis, its 'Happy Planet Index' (HPI) (www. happyplanetindex.org) is frighteningly naïve in its pretensions to link happiness with environmental wisdom. For many countries ranked in this system, it has no reliable information on happiness at all. Worse still, its scores on what it calls 'environmental impact' are arrived at via pure anti-capitalist prejudice, based on the questionable concept of 'carbon efficiency', with no recognition of the massive environmental improvements achieved thanks to capitalism, nor any recognition of the horrific environmental harms faced by people in poorer countries due to poor technology and lack of environmental care. In the HPI, therefore, a country whose citizens say they are happy and that has a low carbon footprint can come near the top of the world league even if its citizens live in such atrocious environments that they have a life expectancy of 40 and suffer multiple illnesses throughout their lives. The HPI, though developed sincerely with the best of intentions, is an insult to the intelligence of those of us who would like to develop synergies between happiness scholarship and policies for sustainable development.

Layard, in contrast to the NEF, assumes that financial wealth is good for happiness provided that most of it is controlled by governments. His wealth redistribution and high taxation recommendations both imply that heavy government 'welfare' expenditures are good for happiness. Unfortunately there is as yet no substantial evidence that this is so. Given the enormous importance of state welfare expenditures and of political debates about their effects and effectiveness, remarkably little systematic research has been done on the effects of these on happiness. The first substantial attempt was Veenhoven's analysis of comparative data on 40 nations from 1980 to 1990 (Veenhoven, 2000). To his surprise, he found no correlations between social security expenditures and the degree to which citizens led healthy or happy lives, nor between these and well-being equality, and neither did increases or decreases in welfare expenditures over time correlate with changes in health or happiness.

These are astonishing and disturbing findings that merit further study. However, policy analysts in all domains are well aware that expenditure is only one indicator of what governments and development agencies are doing, and that for policies to have effects other factors such as quality, commitment, and institutionalisation are crucial to the translation of funds into effects on people's lives. It is quite possible that if these other factors could be systematically compared we would find them correlating with well-being outcomes. This is what Pacek and Radcliffe have tried to do in their 2008 paper, which concludes that life satisfaction *does* correlate positively with three welfare regime indicators: the 'decommodification of labour' as measured by citizens' ability to opt out of paid employment without risking their livelihoods; the 'social wage', that is, the share of national income allocated to social need rather than by the market; and the degree to which regimes follow in general 'left-wing socialist' principles.

Intriguingly, whereas Veenhoven expressed surprise at his finding that state welfare generosity had no effect on happiness, Rothstein, conversely, says that he finds it 'counterintuitive' that state welfare generosity should correlate with happiness, since welfarism is commonly believed to have various perverse effects such as dependency and stigmatising the poor, paternalistic bureaucratic intrusions into private life, reducing economic growth, and interference with civil society and voluntarism (2010, p 444). Rothstein supports Pacek and Radcliffe's positive finding and cites other studies that likewise lend it support, strangely ignoring Veenhoven and many others who have made similarly negative findings on welfare policy outcomes. Both Veenhoven and Rothstein, therefore, are using surprise as a rhetorical tool to persuade us that they are simply responding to what the numbers tell them. In reality, these authors who draw opposite conclusions from similar data sets are just doing what has always been done with national statistics: steering the evidence in tendentious ways, perhaps quite unwittingly so. It seems most unlikely that happiness scholarship will in the foreseeable future give us clear consensus messages on whether and, if so, how state welfare generosity is good for citizens' happiness.

Looking at studies of correlations between happiness or life satisfaction and government expenditures as a percentage of GDP, the findings are similarly recent, few, and mixed. Bjørnskov et al (2007a) explored cross-sectional data from the World Values Survey for 74 countries and found no significant correlations between national governments' 'social spending' and life satisfaction, confirming the common suspicion of 'public choice theory' that high government-consumption spending correlates with lower life satisfaction – that is, that 'life satisfaction depends negatively on the size of the state sector', as they put it (p 269). Particularly interesting was their finding that this adverse correlation is stronger for men in lower- and middle-income brackets, especially if the government is left wing. Though fleetingly mentioned and unanalysed, this is a rare example of researchers taking seriously the very different relations between policy and well-being that may pertain for women and men, and for people of different class. Sadly, like so many authors of cross-sectional studies, these authors wreck their argument by repeatedly making unwarranted causal claims (for example that their data tell us about the 'harm' and 'impact' of spending). The correlation may simply reflect a tendency of unhappier populations to vote for high-spending left-wing governments. But the correlational information remains an interesting challenge, nonetheless.

In another paper specifically on decentralisation (Bjørnskov, 2007b), the commonly cited correlation between political decentralisation and life satisfaction, when assessed over 60,000 individuals in 66 countries, turned out to be entirely mediated by the correlation with fiscal decentralisation. Local fiscal autonomy may well be good for happiness, but political decentralisation has no independent effect. Kacapyr (2008) found no correlation, in a study of information from 63 countries, between life satisfaction and the ratio of government spending to GDP. Ram (2009), looking at a wider range of countries and a wider range of indicators of happiness and life satisfaction, found mixed results, but no evidence that high government expenditures systematically reduce life satisfaction.

Unsurprisingly, given his findings, Bjørnskov's (2005) policy prescriptions for governments that want to promote happiness contrast with those of Layard's. Essentially, Bjørnskov whittles these down to just four positive recommendations (in addition to potentially limitless negative recommendations for harm avoidance). Believing that the statistical evidence from cross-country comparisons doesn't show correlations between happiness and democracy, inequality, or state welfare spending, Bjørnskov argues more or less that governments should focus on economic growth: growth-conducive policies in poor countries; trade policy that furthers participation in globalisation; policies that affect the business climate; and policies that limit government's share of total income (2005, p 6). Though these arguments are consistent with evidence of steep rises of happiness in some poorer and middle-income countries that have liberalised, such as Bhutan and post-soviet countries, they seem nonetheless to miss a lot of potential for less 'economistic' government actions in favour of happiness.

A more cautiously nuanced approach to government responsibility for happiness is taken by Derek Bok in *The politics of happiness* (2010, chapter 11). Arguing against a variety of overhasty conclusions commonly drawn by dabblers in happiness science (for example, anti-growth, over-generous welfarism, income redistribution, happiness lessons), he argues that we do, by contrast, have good evidence from happiness studies that could help to promote happiness. He favours programmes to develop better childcare and education, recognising broader educational objectives; to strengthen marriage and family; to encourage active leisure; to protect against unemployment; for universal healthcare; for secure retirement income; to prevent and treat mental illness and sleep disorders; and to improve urban planning so as to reduce commuting.

David Halpern's similarly cautious but well-informed and persuasive *Hidden wealth of nations* (2010, chapter 6) offers rather more general categories for governmental happiness policies, including: strengthening the 'economy of regard' (promoting parenting and care skills, supporting complementary currencies); improving supply of information to and from citizen-consumers; braver practical responses to local and global environmental threats; fighting drug and sex pathologies; and devolution and democratic innovation to promote citizen participation. The Young Foundation, while emphasising that governments must stop short of believing they can 'make people happy', provided empirical evidence in favour of a similar list of various policies and practices that seem to give people a better chance of achieving happiness: promoting children's resilience in schools; providing social support for health as a holistic experience rather than just focusing on specific maladies; planning, transport, and school policies that encourage more exercise; and provision of systematic support to isolated older people to help them create and maintain social networks (Bacon et al, 2010).

The sensible and promising categories for progressive social policies identified by Bok, Halpern, and the Young Foundation require some degree of government intervention and investment. They therefore seem unambiguously to imply a moral duty on the part of governments, even if much of the most useful action has to take place at individual, family, and community levels. It is philosophically and morally untenable for governments to aim to 'maximise' happiness, since this could encourage policies that increased self-reported life satisfaction without increasing well-being, and even if well-intentioned could likely lead to perverse outcomes, such as downplaying citizens' interests in the process of participation (Frey and Stutzer, 2007; Duncan, 2010). But between ignoring happiness, and seizing it as the sole objective, there is a wide range of government options and responsibilities.

Discussion points

- Despite strong public and expert support, in principle, for some degree of government responsibility for civic happiness, fear of the accusation of 'paternalism' and the need to show accountability for measurable progress have tended to dissuade democratic governments from overt happiness promotion. But most governments are now measuring national happiness, which indicates a willingness, in principle, to consider actions to promote and protect it.
- The doctrine of 'negative utilitarianism' remains pervasive worldwide, at least in its soft version – that governments should concentrate mainly on the removal of harms and unnecessary constraints on freedom. This, in effect, acts as a strong bias against active promotion of social happiness.
- In very recent years several important texts have started to provide substantial evidence-based policy guidance for government action to promote happiness. Though sometimes used opportunistically to support existing prejudices, happiness science can effectively increase the moral pressure on governments to become more explicit and active promoters of happiness.

Key readings

Bok, D. (2010) *The politics of happiness: What government can learn from the new research on well-being*, Princeton, NJ: Princeton University Press.

Haworth, J. and Hart, G. (eds) (2007) *Well-being: Individual, community, and societal perspectives*, London: Palgrave Macmillan.

Krishna Dutt, A. and Radcliff, B. (eds) (2009) *Happiness, economics and politics: Towards a multi-disciplinary approach*, Cheltenham: Edward Elgar.

SEVEN

Assessing happiness: measurement and beyond

Happiness makes up in height what it lacks in length.
(Robert Frost)

Prosperity debates: the power of happiness indicators

In policy discourse, the assessment of public happiness is at the heart of the happiness movement's insistence that policy evaluators must look 'beyond GDP'. But is this radical enough? Why substitute or complement one measurement exercise with another when the key weakness may have been the overemphasis on measurement itself, rather than the choice of measure? People often overrate numbers as the core tool in the process of political persuasion. They trot out claims like 'if it isn't counted, it doesn't count'. But in reality, policies at all levels are much more influenced by stories, pictures, personal charisma, and arguments than they are by numbers.

Towards the end of 2010, there was feverish debate in the UK media on the wisdom and sincerity of Prime Minister David Cameron's decision, at a time of recession and massive cutbacks in public spending, to require the Office of National Statistics to conduct regular happiness surveys as part of national well-being assessment. What's odd is that, after so many decades of happiness surveys, this should be seen as a controversially novel idea. But the Canadian economist John Helliwell, who has for many years tirelessly tried to persuade his government to give happiness assessment a higher profile in policy making, argues that 'What is or could be dramatically different in the UK is for the government not just to undertake more widespread and thorough collection of subjective well-being data, but also to give them a central place in the choice and evaluation of public policies. That would be a global first' (Stratton, 2010).

There is, however, a puzzle at the heart of happiness scholarship. It has come to prominence in policy discourse, and is known to the public, via the number-crunching of surveys. We have finally come to believe that something so elusive as happiness can, after all, be represented numerically, and (still somewhat less confidently) that those numbers will be useful guides for policy. Yet surveys are the least empathetic of all social science tools. And numerical representation is, as the historian Theodore Porter persuasively argued in *Trust in numbers*, a 'struggle against subjectivity', a universalising discourse that, like western law, deliberately seeks to bypass empathy in order to avoid parochial personalism (1995, p xi). It is therefore profoundly ironic, and unsettling for both numerophiles and subjectivists alike, that public awareness of trends in subjective experience should come to us mainly in numerical form. As authors of one of the earlier happiness studies noted, translating subjective experience into numerical form presents us with 'excruciating problems of definition and measurement' (Campbell et al, 1976, p 4).

There is no simple way of escaping this dilemma. Social scientists' interface with public policy and media will continue to be dominated by measurement and by indicators that reduce complex realities to fact-like objects. People often fall victims to the false dogma that numbers are essential for all management decisions. As Porter argued, it is the demands of culture and politics, not the demands of science, that persuade us into irrational over-reliance on the 'mechanical objectivity' of numbers (1995, pp 4–5). And so a major and not necessarily rational feature of modern bureaucracies large and small is participation in periodic indicator-fests at which unwieldy lists of indicators are chosen that are then theoretically meant to be monitored and – even more theoretically – expected to be used to generate an evidence base for evaluation and future policy direction. Businesses have been partly inoculated, due to the dominance of the 'bottom line' as the main indicator, but the new 'triple bottom line' ideology is now requiring two extra teams, in addition to the accountancy team, to specialise in devising and reporting on indicators of social and environmental responsibility.

Most progress indicators are 'proxies', things that are relatively easy to observe and count, that are plausibly linked with the changes we are hoping for. Money is a proxy for choice, which is a proxy for the well-being we get from choosing freely and well. Obstacles and harms removed serve as negative proxies for a sense of progress. Test scores are proxies for knowledge or wisdom. But the most powerful and the most democratic indicator of them all is the happiness indicator, the one that in the past few agencies have dared to employ, even though they knew it was what they hoped to point towards. This is now rapidly changing: more and more agencies and governments are daring to use happiness indicators as indicators of progress. It is just possible that this could work an economic miracle for bureaucracies: if the happiness-measurement trend continues, some of those shopping lists of scores or hundreds of proxy indicators could shrink as the colonising power of the happiness indicator becomes evident. Who needs to check up on everyone's wish lists if everyone can just tell us how happy they are in general? As the economists of the Stiglitz report argue, the single-question happiness self-report provides 'a natural way to aggregate various experiences in a way that reflects people's own preferences' (Stiglitz et al, 2009, p 145). They go on to claim, bafflingly, that 'this approach makes it possible to reflect the diversity of people's views about what is important in their lives' (p.145). This is the opposite of what a single-item question does: it *disguises* the diversity of values that people cherish.

The philosopher Jeremy Bentham would have been proud to witness how his rhetorical concept of a 'felicific calculus' became the backbone of robustly scientific modern happiness scholarship in the late 20th century. Though the numbers reported from happiness surveys don't normally reduce happiness to Bentham's sum ranking of 'pleasures minus pains', in practice it is the numbers rather than the complex evaluative processes behind them that seem to attract attention. However, assessment is a lot more sophisticated than measurement, which is just one tool in the assessor's toolbox. Quality of life (and happiness within that) is an arena for evaluative conversations, not an entity reducible to 'barometric' readings, as rhetorical labels like 'Eurobarometer' and 'Social Weather Reporting' would have us believe. And happiness is much less obviously an issue for national assessment than a relatively private matter for conversations between friends. But the magic of numbers and the concept of national prosperity ensure that public discourse on happiness often, paradoxically, takes its cue from debates about national-level numerical representation. How is Sweden doing, happiness-wise, compared with Portugal? Or how is Chinese happiness doing, compared with its GDP or compared with trends in 'welfare' expenditures? These are the kinds of question that have so far tended to engage the public in discussions of happiness assessment.

Public attention to happiness studies has so far put more emphasis on indicators than on the kinds of actual change in policy and behaviour that happiness studies might persuade us to undertake. It is easy to confuse debates about policies and priorities for debates about indicators. The so-called 'social indicators movement' and the 'human development' movement, both objecting to the overuse of 'economistic' indicators, were both important precursors to the late 20th-century efflorescence of happiness studies, so it is not surprising that the emphasis on indicators remains. 'Social' and 'human' indicators are often loose labels for harms or goods that so-called 'economic' indicators don't indicate adequately, and drawing attention to these (schooling, health and healthcare, crime, and so on) has often been strongly associated with shifts in policies and in deployment of resources. 'Happiness' indicators that tell us about generic or domain-specific feelings and satisfactions may not be so easy to link to real-world changes.

For some people, what primarily matters is not so much that governments and other institutions specifically redesign policies and interventions to maximise happiness, or that they base these on specific kinds of happiness-related information, but rather that they simply *give happiness the public recognition it deserves*. They want governments to stop giving such high priority to indicators of 'economic growth', and to complement economistic assessments by funding research on happiness. And they want that information used in public discourse, though not necessarily as a decision-making tool. They want to see politicians and political analysts making reference to happiness and life-satisfaction indicators when they discuss the state of the nation. A key problem is, however, that the demand for use of happiness indicators is strongest in those countries with strongly 'post-materialist' values, where economic growth has already done most of the good it's going to do, and where self-reported happiness levels may already have just about reached the highest level they can reasonably be expected to reach.

Bogus comparisons: minding the 'gap' between affluence and well-being

Happiness scholarship's most well-known and powerful message so far has been confirmation of the surprisingly weak connection between wealth (whether individual income or national 'economic growth') and happiness. This begs three questions: who is really surprised by this? Is it possible to compare trends in wealth and happiness? And what possible implications might it have for policy or practice?

If information based on happiness surveys is to be useful for policy, it is worth taking a careful look at how messages are conveyed. Unfortunately, a huge amount of scholarly and popular writing has been deeply flawed in its representation of happiness–wealth and other happiness–progress correlations. It is very common, for example, to read false claims that happiness has declined or failed to rise in rich countries, despite economic growth, or even that there is no correlation between wealth and happiness. Worldwide, when surveys are reliable there are clear correlations (over time and between nations) between national wealth and national happiness. In rich countries, there is more room for debate. In Gregg Easterbrook's book *The progress paradox* he claims that people in rich countries today have 'more of everything except happiness', as compared with the past. To be sure, some surveys have shown national happiness self-reports flatlining since the 1950s, and others have shown declines in those who say they are 'very happy'. In their review of Gallup survey information from 140 countries, economists have recently found compelling evidence of robust correlations between income and life satisfaction at individual and national levels, over time, in all countries, rich and poor alike (Sacks et al, 2010). In any case, even if happiness has flatlined in rich countries, the 2010 population of a rich country is very different from its 1950 population: there are more people, they live longer (so that's a lot more happiness if average happiness has flatlined), many of them come from different countries, and all have very different aspirations than people had in the immediate post-war years.

Even the more cautious writers tend to refer, bafflingly, to some vague notion of a 'growing gap', due to happiness having failed to 'keep pace' with economic growth (Layard, 2005; Anielski, 2007, p 43; Jordan, 2008, pp 13, 25; Jackson, 2009; Searle, 2008). Even the archdeacon of Positive Psychology, Martin Seligman, makes the same basic representational mistake when claiming in a recent article that 'happiness ... has not remotely *kept up* with improvement in the world' (Seligman et al, 2009, p 294, emphasis added); his latest book, *Flourish*, includes a whole section titled 'The divergence between GDP and well-being' (2011, p 222). It doesn't require specialist training to understand what's wrong with 'gap' and 'pace' metaphors. You can only talk meaningfully of trends as a 'growing gap' if the trends are commensurate – for example, if money and happiness were both subjective self-reports on a 0–10 scale.

Everyone accepts that the benefits of money are subject to the law of diminishing returns, so the 'gap' shouldn't surprise us. Perhaps money may also be subject to what we might call the *law of toxic reversal*: like flavour, sound, exercise, and heat, it can be beneficial up to a point, but too much of it may be toxic rather than just wasteful. If so, the weak relationship between income and happiness in rich countries is no more surprising than the weak relationship between additional hot water and bath comfort once the bath is already quite full and pleasantly warm. What is perplexing – though still not all that surprising – is that people who have become rich find it hard to undo a lifetime's habit of pursuing wealth even after they have reached the optimum wealth–comfort zone.

So there is obviously no real 'gap' between 'economic' activity and happiness, and anyone who claims there is one is not making a valid contribution to knowledge. What's going on here is that a highly complex set of social transactions is being reified as 'the economy', or 'welfare', or 'purchasing powers' so that it can be represented numerically as a growing heap, while another complex set of self-evaluations is reified as a 'happiness scale' or 'well-being' – a different kind of heap that, unlike the 'economy' heap, is inside a container, like mercury in a thermometer. The 'heap' metaphor is implicit in any attempt to make quantified comparisons between trends in happiness and anything else. There are no heaps of either happiness or wealth. Economic relationships and values are not objectively real stocks and flows: they are highly complex webs, only some aspects of which are reflected in numbers. Happiness and well-being, more obviously still, refer not to measurable things but to highly complicated evaluative processes.

Inappropriate comparisons between very different kinds of scale are also apparent in statements about how the influence of wealth compares with other factors influencing happiness. For example, Greve's introduction to *Happiness and social policy in Europe* confidently informs us that 'factors such as health, age and marital status are strongly related to the level of happiness, whereas income is to a lesser degree' (2010, p 2). But *none of these is a meaningful comparison of 'degree'*: income is an open-ended scale, health status can be scaled any way you choose, age is a limited scale, and marital status isn't a scale at all. Policy makers can't afford to pay heed to such misleading non-comparisons. All we need to know is whether each of these factors correlates significantly with happiness because, if they do, we should then start investigating causal pathways in the hope that we might learn something useful about how the unequal distribution of happiness comes about in our society.

My point here is not simply to poke fun gratuitously at clumsy use of metaphors and unrealistic faith in numbers. If some of the above sounds unduly pedantic, bear in mind that *our investments in the numerical assessment and analysis of happiness can only be useful if we are able to make rational sense of the information*. If we can't do that, we might as well just talk about happiness and not bother with the numbers. The really interesting challenges in rethinking prosperity lie in trying to understand how people juggle with and make sense of synergies and trade-offs between the various kinds of goods that we pursue and enjoy, many of which we aren't used to apprehending numerically. Numbers may help here and there, but their importance mustn't be overestimated and we mustn't indulge in numerical analysis to the extent that we mistake statistics and analytical tools for reality. Scholars and journalists alike make a host of basic analytical and representational errors when they use happiness-survey data. This doesn't render survey-based studies futile, but it does require us to be much more cautious than many authors have been in using the data to tell policy-relevant stories.

Surveys

When we consider our own happiness or that of others we are likely to think about its qualities, its sources, its effects, its narrativity (how its story unfolds), its existential significance, and so on. But in empirical happiness research so far, quantification has been the main starting-point. Ruut Veenhoven, the energetic founder of the World Database of Happiness and of the *Journal of Happiness Studies*, observes that 'happiness is commonly understood as *how much one likes the life one lives*, or more formally, the degree to which one evaluates one's life-as-a-whole positively' (2009, p 45). With the current explosion of interest in happiness-survey findings, it is possible that even outside of academic circles, conversations about happiness may come to be dominated by this kind of 'how much' approach. But there is clearly a lot more to happiness than questions of degree. And there is a lot more to the assessment of happiness (whether self-evaluation or institutionalised assessment) than survey measures. Nonetheless, it is startling how easy respondents seem to find it to put a number on their happiness, and this fact has facilitated a flourishing and influential enterprise of survey-based happiness research worldwide.

For most of the past 50 years, the scientific study of happiness has consisted largely of collecting and analysing survey responses to questions about overall happiness and life satisfaction, and about domain and sub-domain satisfactions such as health, relationships, work, aspects of work, and so on. Survey responses allow us to identify correlations between happiness and various other surveyed factors, and to make comparisons of self-reported happiness over time or in different places.

Perhaps the most emphatic finding from all of this is that, contrary to what many people expect, most people do provide answers to seemingly blunt questions about how happy they are, and their answers are not just random noise but have been shown to have strong validity and reliability. *People everywhere in the world give reasonably consistent and reliable answers that correlate very strongly with other measures, such as ratings made by observers or friends.* This doesn't mean, of course, that we can simply accept survey self-reports as the only indicator we need. There are various contextual and cultural influences on responses, so they need cautious interpretation. We should try to triangulate with other information, such as ethnographic reports, autobiographies, focus-group discussions, and people's own explanations of why they chose to give particular answers to survey questions. But neither can survey responses be dismissed as pseudoscientific non-information: each individual may feel somewhat unsure of their responses, but in aggregate their answers give us a great deal of very important information about cultural differences and trends in happiness, and about which factors (personality, relationships, life conditions, national trends) correlate strongly with happiness and which don't.

The would-be interdisciplinary happiness scholar is caught between a rock and a soft place. On the one hand, the rapid rise of happiness scholarship into policy discourse has been facilitated by thousands of surveys of many millions of people in all the countries of the world, supported by several decades during which the scientific rigour of happiness measures and statistical analysis have been strengthened. On the other hand, of all social and psychological research methods, the survey is the least suitable for facilitating the kinds of conversations and narratives that allow us to develop empathy and to strengthen our understanding of cause and effect. Diary studies, oral histories, focus-group discussions, ethnographic accounts, and visual methods can all provide much more humane and relevant understanding of happiness than the cold numbers of survey responses, but they lack the scientific precision that gives policy makers the confidence to make use of their insights.

There are now literally hundreds of formal happiness-measurement survey tools and other happiness-assessment methods in circulation. Erasmus University's World Database of Happiness now covers 4,704 surveys among general population samples in 225 nations, with time-series for more than 20 years for 15 nations (worlddatabaseofhappiness. eur.nl). Readers requiring a basic introduction can easily refer to some of the many excellent introductions to those methods, starting perhaps with Veenhoven's web-based 'measures of happiness' introduction at http://worlddatabaseofhappiness.eur.nl/hap_quer/hqi_fp.htm. There are a number of significant distinctions worth bearing in mind when we consider the various sources of happiness information available to scholars, policy makers, and evaluators:

- **Single-item** questions (such as 'how happy are you?' and so on) versus **multi-item** questions (for example, covering satisfaction with life conditions, enjoyment, contentment with achievements, optimism about the future).
- Questions emphasising **cognitive** appraisal (for example, life satisfaction) versus questions emphasising **feelings.**
- Whole-of-life versus domain-specific evaluation.

- **Happiness** surveys versus broader **quality of life** surveys, which may include happiness questions.
- **Subjective** (such as income satisfaction, self-rated health) versus **objective** indicators (for example, brain scan, income).
- **Self**-evaluation versus **other**-evaluation (for example, generic peer evaluation, observation of faces and postures, analysis of language in diaries).
- Satisfaction with personal well-being versus satisfaction with one's society, conditions, or context.
- Momentary versus memory-based or predictive assessments.
- Presentist versus intertemporal assessments.
- **Representative** (for example, whole population randomly sampled) versus **non-representative** samples (for example, when students on a particular course are used as evidence of national culture).
- **Comparative** evaluation (for example, happier/less happy than expected, than before, than peers, than people in other regions or eras) versus **non-comparative**.

If you're not already familiar with happiness surveys, you may find it counterintuitive that happiness-survey response rates are so high and so reliable. Perhaps you are thinking that something so elusive, personal, subjective, and ill-defined as happiness can't be measured. Perhaps you worry that measurements are somehow reductionist, that they only parody the ultra-complex processes by which we evaluate our experiences and our lives as wholes. Yet we measure other complex goods both ordinally (for example, expressing musical and other artistic or aesthetic preference rankings) and cardinally (for example, using machines to measure time). That people can put a number on their happiness, and that systematic analysis of those numbers might be useful, isn't as strange as it might at first appear.

There is a reasonably strong consensus among the academics who review the validity and consistency of those findings that they are very strong indeed by the standards of social psychology surveys, indicating that they do give us real and potentially very useful information for international and intertemporal comparisons, if only we can interpret that information wisely. To do so, we need to apply a great deal of lateral thinking, triangulated evidence from other kinds of assessment, and ethnographic evidence on the cultural contexts from which the survey findings emerge. The problem is that the surveys themselves have progressed a long way ahead of our analytical powers and ethnographic information.

Recorded statements about subjective feelings are filtered in so many ways that some researchers and policy makers choose to reject them as too distorted, and their interpretation and evaluation too morally fraught, to be worthy of policy consideration. We know that people are surprisingly confident in their responses, but much less is known about what goes on in people's minds in the brief moments in which they think up a response. We also know that it is very easy to manipulate those responses by inducing short-term mood changes (Schwarz and Strack, 1999). What I tell a researcher about my satisfactions will in the first place reflect not simply my actual feelings and views (which in any case may be highly volatile and uncertain, varying from moment to moment and from one encounter to another) but also my preferences for what I want the researcher to record about me. This may be distorted in major ways by my expectations of what the study ought to report, my desire for approval or recognition or pity, and so on. Even if I were given a truth drug that forced me to give the most accurate rendition of my true feelings, those feelings would in any case be strongly influenced by many factors other than objective circumstances. For example, my current life satisfaction reflects my previous experiences, my views on what a good life should be like and on what I deserve, my expectations for the future, my perceptions of what selected individuals or categories of relevant other people have and what I think they enjoy.

Multiple-item and domain-specific questions can introduce an element of external influence over people's self-assessment, but this can be offset by asking respondents to specify and rank the issues that matter most to them. Happiness or satisfaction (whether single-item or multiple-item) is typically embedded within broader surveys, but is sometimes studied in stand-alone surveys, in which case it would normally be studied via multiple-item questionnaires.

Experience sampling and diary methods

If all of this makes the meaning of survey responses on global happiness look too unclear, an alternative approach is to try to get as close as possible to assessing momentary happiness through the day, and then aggregating up to assess how much of our time is spent enjoying ourselves or not, and comparing the kinds of activity and location associated with enjoyment (Kahnemann et al, 2004). This approach, which places greater trust in people's momentary assessments of the 'currency of life' than in people's longer-term memories and global self-assessments, is advocated and exemplified in the recent collection of essays on 'National Time Accounting' (Krueger, 2009), which will without doubt stand as a landmark text in the history of well-being indicators. Krueger et al demonstrate and propose the use of the 'U–Index', based on Experience Sampling and/or Day Reconstruction Methods, measuring the percentage of time that people spend in an unpleasant state. A very promising recent innovation in this regard is the development of an iPhone application that already involves many thousands of volunteers in tracking momentary enjoyment in the UK (www.mappiness.org.uk).

Despite the apparent pathologism of the U–Index 'misery' calculus, it relies on a core assumption that the study of well-being is to a very significant extent the study of enjoyment: those who subscribe to the approach must agree to a largely *hedonic* concept of well-being and declare the sum of good feelings to give us a better guide to the goodness of people's lives than their own declarations about how good their lives are as a whole. The approach has an openly ambiguous relationship with people's declared subjectivity: on the one hand, it is strongly participatory and respectful of momentary hedonic self-assessment, but on the other hand, it is disparaging of people's more holistic and eudaimonic self-assessment.

Eudaimonists who doubt the intrinsic moral value of pleasure may be slightly reassured by the authors' insistence that enjoyment is not just about easy gratificatory pleasures, but about how much people value the activities they spend their time on. The affective valence of time, then, becomes the measure of well-being, as defined by people themselves taking into account their views of what a good life should be. Furthermore, advocates of the method aren't claiming that this should be the only criterion for assessing citizens' well-being.

Other approaches to understanding well-being (including the standard economistic National Time Accounts) and fulfilment are needed, too. In case anyone should feel that the assessment of subjective self-evaluation is becoming too prominent, it is worth remembering that, until recently, most major work on the assessment of life quality worldwide has proceeded without attention to subjective experience. Box 7.1 gives some examples of major life quality assessments that could be significantly enriched with the addition of some subjective information.

> **Box 7.1: Major surveys in dire need of giving attention to happiness and subjectivity**
>
> The following are all examples of important, high-investment surveys purporting to convey major reviews of progress towards better quality of life. They are all useful so far as they go, but none pays attention to how people feel about or evaluate their experiences and life conditions. This conveys the implicit message that the funders and authors are uninterested in how people feel about their lives. The Canadian and Australian examples also display the rampant pathologism that is so common in social surveys, focusing on poverty, crime, unemployment, and so on, conveying the impression that the concept of social progress can be reduced to the reduction of harm.
>
> * World Bank: World Development Indicators (formerly 'Social Indicators of Development'), http://data.worldbank.org/
> * UNDP National/Global Human Development Reports, hdr.undp.org/en
> * UN: Millennium Development Goals, www.un.org/millenniumgoals (and see indicator lists at http://mdgs.un.org/unsd/mdg)
> * Vital Signs (Canada), www.vitalsignscanada.ca
> * Australian Bureau of Statistics: Measures of Australia's progress, www.abs. gov.au/AUSSTATS/abs@.nsf/mf/1370.0?opendocument

Responding to the 'data graveyard' problem

We all know that in the modern era we collect and file away far more information than we could ever conceivably use. And even though information technology and ease of travel allow us to keep expanding this information base at extraordinary rates, we still seem to find policy makers and analysts complaining of inadequate evidence on which to base their decisions. In principle it seems sensible to add lots of new information on happiness into this data heap, but we must realistically accept that most of the information we collect won't be used, whether it's collected in informal local studies or in highly systematic, national-level surveys. There are two main ways of responding constructively to this problem:

* **Reduce wastage:** Cut back on survey fatigue and information pollution; think more carefully about who might be able to use or be influenced by what kinds of information, when, and for what purposes; use simpler, quicker, cheaper methods when rough information will do; quantify and number-crunch only when

necessary; focus on areas of doubt and stop confirming the obvious; and pay more attention to promotion of uptake.

- **Emphasise *learning processes* rather than findings:** Promote intrinsically valuable, enjoyable, participatory information gathering; choose information gathering and broader learning methods not just for their hypothetical instrumental value, but as tools for encouraging people to pay attention to things that really matter.

In organisational scholarship, the 'Appreciative Inquiry' approach was originally developed as a way of scientifically studying things that go right in organisations, as an antidote to the standard deficit orientation. But in an exploratory study of the development of egalitarian relationships within a large hospital, the researchers found that the process itself led to the desired outcomes they sought to study:

> [I]nquiry itself can be an intervention. Inquiry is agenda setting, language shaping, affect creating, and knowledge generating. Inquiry *is* embedded in everything we do as managers, leaders, and agents of change. Because of the omnipresence of inquiry, we are often unaware of its presence. Nevertheless, we live in the worlds our inquiries create. These experiences suggested that the best intervention might be to simply be an inquirer, seeking to understand organizational life and to create a spirit of inquiry that invites others to collaboratively do the same. Inquiry itself *intervenes*. (Cooperrider and Sekerka, 2003, p 232)

Recognising this process is crucial to appreciating the likely effects of happiness studies. While we may hope for some instances where studies lead in a linear and rational fashion to useful new knowledge that is then applied, it is quite likely that many of the benefits of happiness studies seep in gradually, iteratively, and unseen, via subtle changes in attention. By making good things like enjoyment, meaning, empathy, and personal strengths salient to our assessments, it seems quite likely that this will result in appreciation, in elevating feelings that help us to evaluate our situations, organisations, and relationships more positively.

Let's consider the hypothetical example of a school. Suppose the school already evaluates progress using a wide range of performance indicators – academic test scores, attendance and completion rates, sporting achievements, and so on. And suppose I argue that the school ought to assess pupils' happiness and domain satisfactions. If I simply advocate another costly information-gathering exercise, the head teacher is likely to be sceptical about affordability and usefulness. I might then discuss with all stakeholders how happiness assessments could enrich existing assessments and substitute for some of the less useful ones. Still, even sympathisers might be sceptical about the practical usefulness of such information as a guide for decisions. Perhaps a more persuasive argument would be that it is *intrinsically* important for staff, pupils, and parents to be invited to reflect on happiness during and after schooling (or, conversely, that it is simply rude not to invite such reflection). Such exercises might produce new, useful information, but even if they didn't, the process would be intrinsically interesting and a good form of social engagement rather than just a costly information-gathering exercise. If, in the process, people have become more conscious of what they want, and of what makes them and others happy or unhappy, *the exercise could be worthwhile regardless of whether anyone reads the reports or analyses the data*. But if this is to work, we'll need some methods that are a bit more exciting than the traditional clip-board survey.

Writing about the politically fraught process of 'Social Weather Reporting' in the Philippines, Mangahas and Guerrero argued that participatory monitoring of social change and well-being had three purposes: 'firstly, to stimulate the eye; secondly, to influence the heart; and finally to guide the mind' (2008, p 32). In more prosaic terms, I have similarly been arguing here that evaluative monitoring of well-being is useful not just for the rational planning function ('the mind'), but also for drawing attention to issues and to subjective views on the issues, and perhaps above all for motivating people to work towards ultimate goals rather than just interim goods.

Simple, low-cost, and participatory happiness assessment methods

So we have a problem and an opportunity. The problem is that happiness scholarship, which promises to facilitate more empathetic and humane social policies, has hitherto been overwhelmingly focused on surveys and analytical methods that are not only expert led and costly but are also, ironically, much more reductionist and less empathetic than other research methods we might use. The other part of the problem is that the wide range of more humane, holistic, interesting, participatory, cheap, and simple social learning methods, such as story-telling, focus groups, role-play, and appreciative enquiry have tended to pay little or no attention to happiness.

The opportunity, of course, is to put these two together, enriching happiness scholarship and participatory social research by complementing happiness survey work with happiness-focused participatory learning.

In a series of collections on *Community Quality-of-life Indicators* (Sirgy et al, 2011, etc), case studies have been published on local, mainly urban, and mainly US and European civic participation in quality-of-life monitoring. All cases show the tremendous energy and enthusiasm people are prepared to put into discussing and monitoring environmental and social progress in their neighbourhoods. Many of these grew out of concerns about unsustainable development during the 1970s to 1990s, which in 1992 at the UN Conference on the Environment in Rio led to a 'Local Agenda 21' agreement that governments would encourage decentralised monitoring of sustainability. Increasingly, emphasis has tended to shift from environmental and social pathologies to well-being indicators.

Discussion points

- Happiness-measurement techniques, particularly surveys, have been in use since the 1940s and have been regularly used for many years in most parts of the world.
- There is broad agreement that well-prepared happiness-survey findings can be reliable and useful for intertemporal and international comparisons. But cultural and situational influences make their meaning uncertain, so they can only complement rather than replace other well-being and progress indicators.
- Though the public face of happiness scholarship remains dominated by surveys, this form of knowledge is inadequate for the promotion of empathetic, holistic, narrative, and contextualised exploration of happiness. These are better served by ethnographic, participatory, and analytical happiness research.
- Investments in happiness measures and numerical analysis of findings have not yet been adequately complemented by investments in consultations as to what uses might be cost-efficiently derived from what kinds of study.

Key readings

Diener, E. (2006) 'Guidelines for national indicators of subjective well-being and ill-being', *Journal of Happiness Studies*, vol 7, no 4, pp 397–404.

Møller, V., Huschka, D. and Michalos, A. (eds) (2008) *Barometers of quality of life around the globe: How are we doing?* Dordrecht: Springer

Stiglitz, J.E. et al (2009) *Report by the Commission on the Measurement of Economic Performance and Social Progress*, Paris: OECD, www.stiglitz-sen-fitoussi.fr/documents/rapport_anglais.pdf.

Veenhoven, R. (nd) 'Examples of measures of happiness', http://worlddatabaseofhappiness.eur.nl/hap_quer/hqi_fp.htm.

Journals: *Journal of Happiness Research*; *Social Indicators*; *International Journal of Wellbeing*.

EIGHT

Correlations and causal theories

Interpreting happiness self-report surveys

Surveys are difficult to do well, and many ill-conceived surveys provide little or no useful information for comparative purposes. The main trouble with survey information, however, lies not in the design and implementation of the surveys, nor in the numerical analysis of findings, but in the interpretation of what the findings tell us. The quality of analysis of happiness surveys is often embarrassingly plagued by basic interpretive errors deriving from deliberate or neglectful extrapolation from correlations to assertions about causality. Even when written by the finest of happiness scholars, survey interpretations ought to come with a health warning: look carefully, and you'll usually find lots of tendentious and unwarranted use of causal language about factors that 'determine' or 'predict' or 'affect' or 'lead to' happiness.

Causality can also be subtly implied in the way sentences are ordered when reporting correlations. Saying 'the wealthier people are, the happier they are' may look like a simple statement of correlation, but it gives a different implicit message from the inverted statement, 'the happier people are, the wealthier they are'. Coming at the end of a sentence, happiness is implicitly an outcome rather than a cause. This assumption is so normal that when scholars acknowledge the possible causality of happiness, they call it 'reverse causality'.

Here are some of the most significant and common mistakes:

- Confusing self-reports with actual experienced happiness (forgetting that cultural and situational factors like emotion norms, expectations, recent events, and social comparisons always influence reports).
- Reading correlations as stories about one-way causation from factors to happiness (forgetting that correlations may reflect the causality of happiness itself or of some other factor affecting both happiness reports and the variable being considered).
- Interpreting cross-temporal comparisons between happiness reports in the same country as evidence that the same population has become happier (forgetting that we are looking at different cohorts, and that populations move around).

- Inadequate consideration of the difficulty of correlating different kinds of information based on radically different scales (for example, comparing a 0–3 happiness scale with a 0–10 scale, or either of these with an open-ended income scale).
- When a causal pattern is inferred (correctly or incorrectly), extrapolating carelessly to a prediction that the same causal pattern will apply again in other circumstances or for bigger populations (for example, that if some people get happier by getting richer or by becoming more educated, everyone else will be happier if they become richer or more educated, forgetting, for example, that status competition is a zero-sum game, or that not everyone in the crowd can get a better view of the stage if everyone stands up).

A good simple introduction to the need for cautious interpretation of statistical correlations is provided in chapter 2 of Best's *More damned lies and statistics* (2004). Although every statistician and scientist knows that correlations don't in themselves tell us anything positive about causation, this basic rule is frequently forgotten or ignored not only by sloppy journalists but also by many of the most experienced happiness scholars. Elementary interpretive mistakes involving unwarranted causal attribution seem to plague happiness scholarship more than any other scientific domain. This most likely happens because of our strongly ingrained intuitions that happiness is a life outcome, and that it is affected by experience rather than being itself a cause of other outcomes. So, for example, numerous scholars have made the mistake of reading correlations between income and happiness as a story about the effects of money on happiness rather than considering whether the correlation might mean that happiness influences income, or that income and happiness are both influenced by some other factor such as education or health.

Elementary interpretive and representative mistakes are evident, for example, in a classic paper on 'the contribution of marital happiness to global happiness' by sociologists Norval Glenn and Charles Weaver (1981). The analytical bias is evident in the title. The authors were looking at correlations, but are interested in showing how people's happiness with one domain, marriage, might be a causal factor in their overall happiness. There is no sign in this paper of any interest in the possibility that overall happiness, or some more specific aspect such as cheerfulness or work satisfaction, might cause both the marital happiness and the global happiness. Asserting that 'the data from these studies are very strong evidence that the quality of marriage is of crucial importance to the psychological well-being of married Americans' (1981, p 162), they don't pause to consider whether the marital happiness might be largely due to psychological well-being, or whether both might be due to something else, such as learned optimism or strong social networks. This bias matters not just for the sake of academic integrity: the authors are emphatic that the knowledge they are generating 'is important as a basis for public policy decisions concerning the allocation of resource for family-life research and education and for social services and intervention strategies aimed at improving marriages' (1981, pp 161–2). This being the case, is it not astonishing that they failed to consider whether trait happiness or domain happiness might be the cause of the marriage–happiness correlation?

Similarly, Clark and Oswald's equally famous (2002) attempts to promote a 'simple statistical method for measuring how life events *affect* happiness' (my emphasis), widely advertised in popular media, are rendered implausible by the authors' failure to acknowledge the challenges of moving from observed correlations to establishing a reasonable story about causes. They promote the new use of 'happiness regression equations' to measure what they glibly call the 'effects' of key events such as illness, marriage, and unemployment on happiness: marriage brings 'the same amount of happiness, each year, on average, as would having an extra £70,000 income' (Clark and Oswald, 2002, p 1139). Blanchflower and Oswald (2004) are similarly glib in applying the metaphor of purchase to the correlational (but not necessarily causative) relationship between monetary wealth and life outcomes: their slogan 'money buys more sexual partners but not more sex' makes concise and attention-grabbing headlines, but the most elementary enquiry into their evidence would find this interpretively irresponsible.

A recent and more subtle example of the same bias is the otherwise brilliant review of correlations between economic growth and life satisfaction in 140 countries (Sacks et al, 2010). Causality is implied throughout this paper, and it always runs in one direction, from growth to happiness: they start by asking 'Does economic growth improve the human lot?' and proceed to make repeat claims that their correlational data prove that income 'impacts on' and even 'determines' well-being. Yet, in their conclusion they assert that they have not been 'disentangling causality from correlation'. And in a final twist, even while making this denial they reveal their unidirectional causal assumption by saying that 'the causal impact of income on individual or national subjective well-being, and the mechanisms by which income raises subjective well-being, remain open and important questions' (pp 1, 2, 31–2).

Box 8.1 shows several examples from the 2010 Australian Unity Wellbeing Index. There are more examples wherever you look, in journals that publish analysis of survey statistics (see for example Borooah, 2006; Tremblay and Genin, 2008, p 164; Jeffres et al, 2009, p 341).

Box 8.1: False one-way causal claims in the Australian Unity Wellbeing Index

Explanation: Although is it possible that this Index could, over time, produce findings that give strong indications of causality, this report simply uses synchronic information (rather than before-and-after comparisons of the same people) as if it were evidence of the causes of happiness.

Unwarranted (though mainly plausible) claims	What they should have said
Title: 'What Makes Us Happy'	Title: 'Correlates of self-reported happiness'
'The more we earn doesn't just increase our bank accounts, but it increases our satisfaction with health and relationships.' (p 1)	'Our satisfaction with health and relationships correlates positively with our income.'
'Spending time with our loved ones is likely to make us happier, healthier and more productive.' (pp 6–7)	'Happier, healthier and more productive people tend to spend more time with their loved ones.'
'The most powerful two demographic elements are relationships and household income. Both are strongly associated with high and low wellbeing' (p 16)	'Relationships and household income are the elements most strongly associated with high and low wellbeing.'
'Living with your children is good for your wellbeing if you are single and older than 66 years.' (p 20)	'For single people over 66, there is a positive correlation between wellbeing and co-residence with offspring.'
'For people with an annual household income of less than $15,000, an additional $6,000 buys an extra point of wellbeing.' (p 24)	'The difference between an annual income of $15,000 and one of $21,000 is associated with a one-point difference in wellbeing.'
'Household incomes under $30,000 for singles combined with the presence of children, on average, take wellbeing below the normal range.' (p 24)	'Single-parent households with below-normal wellbeing scores tend to have incomes under $30,000.'
'Gambling is not only bad for your bank balance but it is also detrimental to wellbeing.' (p 27)	'Frequent gambling correlates with low wellbeing and low satisfaction with living standards.'

... note also that even the causal claims based on before–after measures, though highly plausible, aren't in themselves warranted by the data, since other causes could have been at work: for example, 'it appears that the presence of an external threat causes the population's wellbeing to rise. This occurred first following the September 11 attacks and reached its maximum about six months after the event' (p 8).

Source: Australian Unity (2010).

One-way causality is sometimes heroically asserted in the full consciousness that this is not warranted by correlational data. For example, Emmons (1999, p 106) argues that although his studies on spiritual strivings and well-being only established correlations, 'I assume, as has previous research on religiousness and wellbeing, that spiritual variables (in this case goals) are causally prior to wellbeing and thus contribute to wellbeing, rather than the converse.' Emmons offers no justification for such an assumption. What he's doing here is confessing to strong bias in favour of finding that religiosity causes well-being. A moment's effort in unbiased lateral thinking should remind us that it is just as plausible that religiosity and spiritual strivings are facilitated by a sense of security that derives from having one's other needs largely met; or, more plausible still, that both religiosity and happiness share common causes in personality types and dispositions. As Lewis and Cruise (2006) have shown, the numerous studies of correlations between religiosity and happiness have been mainly cross-sectional studies, and hence have nothing positive to say about causality. They are in any case mainly studies of university students and have lacked any coherent theory of religiosity and happiness and any consistent methodology that would facilitate assimilation among the studies.

Finally, it is worth noting a recent and unusual example of false causality claims, in which happiness is wrongly assumed to be causal rather than wrongly assumed to be an outcome. Keen to prove that happiness at work is beneficial to other goals that business managers would favour, Jessica Pryce-Jones conducted two one-off surveys that showed correlations between self-reported workplace happiness and length of service, discretionary overtime hours worked per week, and lower number of days' sick leave taken per year. These data, she claims, confirm these as 'outcomes' of workplace happiness (2010, pp 19–20). They do no such thing, but the author's vested interest in these claims becomes clear on her commercial website, www.iopener.com. She's no doubt right to assume that workers' happiness likely has lots of good effects, but it isn't these research findings that tell her this: a *priori* it is just as likely that people simply develop, over time, a stronger sense of happiness at work, and/or that the illness that caused the days off also caused people to feel less happy at work. Reporting on further, more complex surveys, the author's misplaced confidence grows, and soon she is claiming that if all moderately happy workers became slightly happier 'there would be about a 5 percent increase in time on task ... a potential extra 12 days a year. Per person. These results show why being happy at work matters on a daily basis' (2010, p 27). And yet, shortly afterwards, the same correlational data are used to present an equally false causal claim in the opposite direction: 'Hard work leads to happiness. We know that because the numbers tell us: people who contribute the most report that they are happiest at work' (2010, p 31).

The best way of avoiding being misled by false interpretations of surveys is to remember that correlations based on one-off surveys can at best give us negative information about causality: for example, since numerous surveys indicate negligible correlations between education and happiness, and between gender and happiness, we can reasonably infer that neither education nor gender is a strong influence on self-reported happiness. But the stronger correlations between money and happiness, and between marital status and happiness can't in themselves demonstrate that money and being married make people happier than they would otherwise be: without longitudinal before-and-after studies they can only confirm that our causal hunches aren't necessarily wrong. Even long-term before-and-after studies tend to be only suggestive, though they certainly can do a lot more to strengthen our causal hunches than is the case with cross-secctional studies.

Longitudinal studies

So, as George Vaillant, director of one of the most famous longitudinal life-span studies puts it, 'in assessing potential causation, time relationships must be kept explicit. Predictive measures must be clearly separated in time from outcome measures' (1990, p 353). Like several of the other studies exploring possible causal effects of happiness listed above in Box 3.1, Vaillant's Harvard study gave empirical evidence enabling him to make strong claims about how, for example, the role of happiness, or avoidance of 'psychiatric vulnerability', in early life is the strongest predictor of physical and mental health in late life, and that exercise habits in college years were a better predictor of happiness at 65 than health at 65 was (1990, p 355).

Longitudinal studies need not be on a massive scale and/or over a very long period. A nice example of a modest and moderate-length study that tells us much more about causality than cross-sectional studies can do is Frisch et al's (2005) study of how students' perceived quality of life predicted academic outcomes over a three-year period. Note that in all these cases it is happiness that predicts (and most likely plays a significant part in causing) the subsequent benefits, not vice versa. As also discussed in Box 3.1, similarly dramatic findings on the apparent benefits of a cheerful disposition were derived from the Milwaukee nuns' diaries study and the Mills College photo study. These findings are worrying if you have sympathy or empathy with people who aren't of a naturally cheerful disposition. We'll never know whether the gloomier nuns and students might have lived longer had someone identified their pathological lack of cheer and put them through a few courses in self-esteem and joy. The multiplication of the longevity discrepancy with a joy discrepancy does seem a cruel twist on inequality in a cohort who otherwise had exactly equal opportunities and quality of adult life. But it does seem to clash with numerous studies showing little or no correlation between objective health and happiness (for example, Watten et al, 1997; Danner et al, 2001; Snowdon, 2001).

Longitudinal studies give us much stronger hints about causality than merely correlational studies do, but even here there is a need for caution before jumping to causal conclusions and thence to policy prescriptions. Most publications on the 'Whitehall' (now 'Whitehall II') study, which has monitored over 10,000 civil servants' health in the UK since 1967, have painstakingly avoided causal speculations, reporting their findings using the language of 'correlation' and 'association' (Steptoe et al, 2005). But in a rare example of biased misrepresentation of happiness as a cause, a journalist in the *New Scientist* distorted their findings with the unwarranted headline 'Happiness helps people stay healthy', claiming that the study had proved that happiness reduces the risk of heart disease and diabetes (Bhattacharya, 2005).

An even more attention-grabbing example of happiness causality was the claim that winning an Oscar is associated with (and at least partially 'explains') a four-year longevity advantage over less successful peers (same sex, same film, similar age) (Redelmeier and Singh, 2001). The possibility that subjective judgements of a one-off artistic performance might confer not just honour but extra life-years certainly makes for a compelling anecdote. I hate to spoil that story for you, but sadly for the Oscar-winners, it has since been shown that the dramatic finding was an artefact of bad statistical design. It was produced by a rather blatant error of statistical analysis: the researchers had simply correlated the Oscar results with longevity from birth. Instead, they should have measured longevity from the time the selected individuals won their Oscar awards, so as to avoid conferring on the winners an artificial longevity bias (some actors in the sample were dead before the Oscars were even won, and hence before the post-Oscar 'survival race' had started). Re-analysing the same data using the latter method reveals that Oscar winners gained no statistically significant longevity advantage from their wins (Sylvestre, Huszti and Hanley, 2006).

So although these cross-temporal predictive studies carry much stronger hints of causality than merely correlational studies do, and although the direction of causality is from happiness to other life outcomes, they don't provide any guidance for policies or personal life choices. They don't tell us whether individuals can improve health, success, and longevity by training themselves to think more cheerful thoughts or by smiling more, still less whether, if so, everyone's lives would be better in a society where everyone was trained to be cheerful. For that, we need experimental studies (Lyubomirsky, King and Diener, 2005), and there are severe limits on the extent to which they could help us predict long-term outcomes, or the likely mass effects of moderate to large-scale interventions.

Experiments

Another way of learning about causes is to conduct experiments, or observe so-called 'natural experiments', processes that occur without any deliberate experimental design. Conducting psychological experiments on fellow humans is always fraught with ethical and practical challenges, especially if the objective is to learn what makes people happy or less happy. Since experimenters start with hypotheses about what will or won't contribute to happiness, or even what will detract from happiness, there are severe limits to how far an experimenter can go in seeking to manipulate people's enjoyment of life.

Researchers have not been shy of manipulating short-term moods, for better or worse. For example, good moods and associated short-term benefits to creativity and prosocial behaviour, as well as responses to happiness surveys, have been shown to be significantly influenced by such simple techniques as arranging for subjects to find a coin as if by chance, hold a pen between the teeth (to imitate a smile, or between the lips to lower moods by imitating a frown), or to see their national team win at football (Schwarz and Clore, 1983; Schwarz and Strack, 1999). The mood lift derived from coin-finding has also been shown to be more emphatic if it is mysterious (sticker attached to the coin saying 'Who are we? Why do we do this?') rather than explained (sticker attached explaining that this was from the 'smile society', which was dedicated to 'random acts of kindness') (Gilbert 2006, pp 189–90).

When experimenters do try to promote longer-term changes in people's experience, most inevitably focus on trying out uncontroversial, highly plausible ideas on what makes people happy. For example, asking people to pursue, over four weeks, activities guided by 'extrinsic' motivation (money, fame, image) or 'intrinsic' motivation (personal growth, intimacy, community) allowed experimenters to demonstrate that achievements derived from 'intrinsic' motivation had better happiness outcomes for all subjects, including those who were generally extrinsically motivated and had lower expectations that the instrinsically motivated activities would be rewarding (Sheldon et al, 2010).

There are now a growing number of potentially helpful examples of scientists promoting simple happiness-promoting techniques based on experiments at the individual level, such as Robert Emmons' *Thanks!* (2007); Sonja Lyubomirsky's *The how of happiness* (2008); Fredrickson's *Positivity* (2011); and Tal Ben-Shahar's *Happier* (2007), which is based on the runaway success of his Psychology 1504 undergraduate course at Harvard. Though clearly a step beyond non-empirical self-help guides, these texts are inevitably taking a leap of faith in the translatability of findings from laboratory settings or context-specific studies into other real-world contexts.

Discussion points

- All readers of analysis based on correlations between happiness self-reports and other life factors must be aware that they are very likely to read unwarranted causal inferences, even if the text seems plausible and is written by otherwise competent scholars.
- Correlations in themselves can only give us negative information about causes: they can tell us when something is unlikely to be a significant cause of happiness, but not whether it is a significant cause.
- When a correlation is interpreted speculatively as a possible causal link, it is always crucial to consider whether happiness could itself be the driver of the correlation, or whether some third factor may be causing the correlation.
- Stronger pointers towards likely causal pathways can be established through longitudinal studies, or by experiments, or by people's own causal theories.

Key readings

Best, J. (2004) *More damned lies and statistics: How numbers confuse public issues*, Berkeley, CA: University of California Press.
Huff, D.L. (1993) *How to lie with statistics*, New York: W.W. Norton.

Part Two

Social happiness in policy and practice

NINE

Love: fighting philophobia around the world

The day will come when, after harnessing space, the winds, the tides, gravitation, we shall harness for God the energies of love. And, on that day, for the second time in the history of the world, man will have discovered fire. (Pierre Teilhard de Chardin)

Is love an art? Then it requires knowledge and effort. (Erich Fromm, *The art of love*)

The new intrinsic value of intimacy

Social happiness begins with love. Like happiness, love too has been ignored by most modern social scientists. The strong dyadic bonds of parental and romantic love are the prototypes. In their different ways, both matter a great deal for happiness outcomes, yet neither is easy to weave into the planned pursuit of happiness. In the initial euphoria of bringing a child into the world, how many new parents appraise realistically the enormous personal sacrifices that this will entail? In the throes of romantic passion, who pauses to ponder the realities ahead: the lifetime spent in agonising debates over whether the toilet seat should be left up or down? Letting young people be guided by romantic love in making their choice of lifelong partner is a modern cultural experiment that most of our ancestors since the Neolithic Revolution would have found absurd. Everywhere in the world, people are still struggling to come to terms with its revolutionary implications.

Sociologist Anthony Giddens (1992) has argued that the development of the 'pure relationship' – essentially love for love's sake, involving appreciation of one another as unique individuals and based on the unqualified trust that can be learned through child–parent relationships – is a late modern development. Optimism about improving the quality of close dyadic relationships, and liberating them from instrumentalist exploitation, lies at the core of the Enlightenment project of promoting happiness for happiness' sake. It is an ongoing global experiment with very uncertain outcomes: 'No one knows how the ever growing demands for family intimacy can be linked to the new demands for the freedom and self-realization of men, women and children' (Beck and Beck-Gernsheim, 2002, pp 27–8). But in exploring the co-production of happiness through voluntary dyadic unions, one of the saddest lessons is how hard it is to sustain passionate or even cheerful attachment through the trials of domesticity and the inevitably divergent preferences and priorities that couples have (Jamieson, 1999).

When relationships are less voluntary and more survival related, there are more vital matters to argue over, such as whether it is better to spend our last few rupees on alcohol to drown our sorrows, or on a visit to the doctor for our sick child. Disagreements in more instrumentalist unions may matter more, but the quality of the marital relationship may be seen as less vital for happiness. In Bangladesh, for example, researchers found a generational shift: for young women, having a 'good' husband ('does not beat her, quarrel or drink') was salient for personal happiness, whereas for old women even a 'bad' husband was better for happiness than having no husband at all (Camfield et al, 2009, p 83). Thus, paradoxically, even in more 'collectivist' cultures, where relationships matter a great deal for personal happiness, the *mental* aspects of relationships can be given less salience. The primary concern is with material provisioning and physical safety. Significant others, that is, can be significant for diverse reasons: as providers or deniers of basic physical security in one context, and in another as providers or deniers of respect, meaning, and psychic happiness.

Most research linking relationship quality with happiness has been conducted in richer countries, where evidence that has now been gathered for several centuries shows that long-term attachments, on average, make both women and men healthier, happier, and longer lived – especially if the attachments are of the secure, mutually supportive variety (Diener et al, 1999, pp 289–91; Soons et al, 2009; Grundy and Tomassini, 2010). Also, since our happiness tends to wax or wane with that of our spouse, looking after spousal relationships is a basic requirement for the pursuit of happiness (Hoppmann et al, 2011). Self-transcendence is essential for our happiness, but in its primary form – everyday intimacy within families – it is fragile and so is at the same time an increasingly salient source of vulnerability. Love of both the romantic and companionate varieties quickly turns sour, and it is small wonder that people have mixed views about it.

In individuals, the conditions 'philophobia' (fear of intimacy, love, and friendship) and 'erotophobia' (fear of sexuality) have long been recognised as pathologies. These terms can also usefully be applied at higher, social and cultural levels: families, organisations, ethnic groups, and whole nations vary widely according to how much they respect and value the expression of love and sexuality. These two kinds of fear, and the numerous horrors associated with them, have always been strongly associated with other kinds of fear, such as xenophobia, fear of witchcraft, fear of losing property, fear of violence, and fear of divine retribution. These are, thankfully, receding worldwide, giving us unprecedented opportunities to consciously develop a love-friendly ('philophilic', if you like) and hopefully also love-spreading ('philogenic') culture. As open-hearted social and religious movements have insisted since long before the glory days of the hippie movement, love is a potent force for social progress. But it does require cultural systems and social processes that facilitate benign and sustainable forms of attachment. And the incipient research exploring the overlaps and differences between dyadic love and humanity-embracing 'compassionate love' (Fehr and Sprecher, 2009) shows that we are still in the very early stages in our experiments with the 'purification' and spreading of love. It may be premature to herald the global empathy epidemic as the key to global happiness.

Research on marital outcomes hasn't yet clarified whether traditional, parentally guided mate selection or romantic love is a better pathway to marital happiness. Some have found that marital satisfaction levels are similar with either system (Myers et al, 2005). Others have shown that many marriage arrangement processes increasingly occupy a middle ground between autonomy and parental arrangement (Donner, 2002). When parents choose, they don't necessarily prioritise their offspring's best interests over their own financial incentives and status aspiration, and even if they do, there is no guarantee that they will make better choices than those made by the mysterious processes of romantic love. Though Asia is rapidly warming to romantic love, it is highly questionable to claim that arranged marriage is disappearing so fast that 'most Asian people marry for love' (Huang, 2005, p 163). Arranging marriages and the associated negotiation of dowries and inheritances have been and remain a major source of anxiety and family strife in many parts of Asia. Still, it would be smug and naïve for westerners to recommend a quick transition to individualistic 'love marriage', as this is certainly not proven to be a eudaimonically and ethically superior solution.

Love and happiness: ultimate values, but unpopular research themes

But if romantic love remains ambiguous and untrustworthy, no culture can be against love in general. Lindner, exploring policy themes of love, sex, and parenthood at global level, has recently argued that love is clearly 'not just a feeling' but is the most important rallying cry for global social transformation. For her, the concept of 'happiness' is 'weak compared with the potency of love' (2010, pp 9, 97). Alexander Solzhenitsyn's *The Gulag Archipelago* has Shulabin the Bolshevik arguing similarly for an 'ethical socialism' that would reject 'happiness' as a capitalist illusion, and instead promote 'affection' as a uniquely human kind of fulfilment:

> One should never direct people towards happiness, because happiness too is an idol of the market-place. One should direct them towards mutual affection. A beast gnawing at its prey can be happy too, but only human beings can feel affection for each other, and this is the highest achievement they can aspire to.

There is of course ample evidence that 'affection' is not 'uniquely human' and it is hard to understand what Solzhenitsyn meant by this. But the last part, about the nobility of love aspirations, is awkward too: if it is questionable to aspire for happiness, it is just as debatable whether affection is a good life goal. It may well be that both happiness and love are dangerous aspirations, setting us up for endless disappointments and distracting us from the activities and mindsets that would actually make us happy and loving. Still, even if we should sound caution about the pursuit of love, there is no doubt that anyone wanting to promote social progress needs to think pretty carefully about how love and good intimacy can be facilitated or inhibited by social arrangements.

If we're not entirely sure that happiness is the 'ultimate value', then love seems a pretty good alternative. It's more obviously social than happiness, too, although like happiness it has been severely neglected by modern social science. Sociological and anthropological encyclopedias and textbooks tend to ignore love and intimacy altogether, as if dyadic pair-bonding wasn't the basic building-block of society. When you explore the patchy sociological and policy literature on intimacy, you can't help but notice the predominant emphasis on love turning sour, and on intimacy serving as a site of violent abuse. Just as 'well-being' has become a euphemistic rubric for research on illness and suffering, so terms like 'intimate' and 'marital satisfaction' have become glued to literatures on domestic trauma. If love makes the world go round, it also seems to do a pretty good job of keeping therapists, lawyers, and social workers busy. It is largely in these latter, pathogenic roles, that love seems to capture the attention of social scientists.

Regarding dyadic bonds of friendship in general, there has been some progress since 1936, when Dale Carnegie wrote in his Preface to *How to win friends and influence people* that nothing had yet been published on friendship or 'human relations', even though this came second only to health in North Americans' concerns. Despite substantial attention to forms of 'attachment' and to pathological interpersonal desires, dyadic relationships remained undertheorised in Psychology too, and Rubin claimed that 'social psychologists have devoted virtually no attention to love' (1970, p 265). Garth Fletcher's title *The new science of intimate relationships* (2002) rightly implies that the attention to intimacy – mainly by psychologists, therapists, and self-help authors – has hitherto been piecemeal and unsystematic.

Actually, love is not an *alternative* to happiness as the ultimate value: the experience of love is *part* of happiness and is of critical importance to the development of the capability to be happy and to spread happinesss. Like happiness, love matters as an enjoyment, as a component in flourishing, and as a critically important capability and resource. And in every society, the core institution through which this achieved is some kind of family, which is mainly built around (though often departing from) our two main prototypes of love – heterosexual pair-bonding, and parent–infant bonding. From these relationships, the capacity for love may or may not expand. Faith-based agencies and some civil agencies have explicit objectives of spreading love and enhancing people's capacity for love – see for example the Institute for Research on Unlimited Love, which has a mission 'to help people to better understand their capacities for participation in unlimited love as the ultimate purpose of their lives' (Post, 2003, p viii). Every country has some kinds of explicit family policies, some are beginning to develop happiness policies, and some have anti-hate policies, such as those for post-conflict reconciliation and interethnic respect. Sadly, many nations and faith-based organisations also have anti-love policies that are tantamount to pro-hate policies: regulations and biases against homosexual and interethnic intimacy, for example.

Love policing, love policies, and love promotion

We know that every society *polices* love, but who ever heard of 'love policies'? In what ways, if any, are good loving relationships actively promoted? This is the critical point on which we can tell whether a happiness lens might offer significant added value to policy discourse – by making dyadic intimacy, including *positive* intimacy, a core focus of science and policy. As the historian Osterberg puts it in her wonderful review of intimacy-related policies and cultural trends in medieval Europe,

> The majority of Europeans believe that having friends or finding an outlet for their sexuality is something natural and uncontroversial, and hardly a matter for state, judicial, or political interference. (Osterberg, 2010, pp 5–6)

Still, don't imagine for one moment that any country lacks love policies: it's just that they tend to be a lot less explicit than other kinds of policy. Love tends to be seen as too private, too wild, too embarrassing, or too mystical to come under the influence of 'policy'. When couples get married and live happily ever after at the end of fairy tales, we're supposed to nod off to sleep and not develop a lively interest in the details of how this is meant to work out. But the intimacy dimension of happiness is one of the most interesting, tricky, and culturally as well as individually variable aspects of the happiness quest. You don't get happy families without love, and you rarely get happiness without strong emotional bonds and happy families (Soons et al, 2009; Helm, 2010). So if we're serious about happiness policies, we need to think carefully about how our policies influence people's prospects for developing good, sustainable intimacy.

All societies, and many subgroups and doctrines within them, regulate not only who may marry whom, but who may be intimate with whom, when, how, and on what terms. They define some intimacies as good and others as bad, and support these definitions with systems of incentives and penalties that strongly shape the possibilities of love and empathy. Libertarian relaxation of the regulation of intimacy has been rapidly spreading worldwide in the name of freedom, choice, fun, and fulfilment (Giddens, 1992; Beck and Beck-Gersheim, 2002). But even today, few individuals can get through childhood, let alone life, without sometimes feeling that their freedom to be intimate was unduly restrained. The restriction of intimacy remains a leading cause of injustice, violence, suffering, and suicide worldwide (Hatfield and Rapson, 1996; Jankowiak, 2008; Mody, 2008).

So states are increasingly recognising their moral requirement to use legal processes to intervene in the previously private domain of domestic intimacy (Cohen, 2002). Thousands of texts in recent decades have proclaimed an 'epidemic' or 'crisis' of intimacy failure in the modern era (Shumway, 2003; Ridley, 2005). Even the best-intentioned intimacy rules relating to the protection of children from paedophiles can have perverse effects on intimacy (Furedi and Bristow, 2008). Although there's no doubt that modernity has put lots of new stresses on the long-term sustainability of various kinds intimacies it is, however, absurd to deny the horrors of bad intimacy regulation in the past or to neglect the progress that has been made towards better kinds of intimate freedom, respect, and empathy. A more optimistic view has been expressed, for example, in Theodore Zeldin's *Intimate history of humanity* (1994), which notices that 'men and women have slowly learned to have interesting conversations' (chapter 2); in Jeremy Rifkin's celebration of the growth of the *Empathic civilization* (2010); and in Robert Wright's *Nonzero: The logic of human development* (2000), which portrays human destiny as the expansion of love and mutually beneficial cooperation. A classification or inventory of love policies could extend infinitely, but Box 9.1 provides a few indicative examples.

Intimacy matters more today, perhaps, than ever before. Next to ego-focused self-help books, texts offering guidance on intimate relationships are the biggest category in life-improvement literature. With the dwindling of many of the worst threats to our survival, we have unprecedented opportunities for expressing lifelong affections unsullied by exploitative, violent, and unequal structures. It is easier to be nice to one another than it ever was, but it is not yet clear that humanity is performing better in all aspects of intimacy than previously – for example, there is probably less intimate violence, but also less sustained loyalty. If you could strengthen the bonds of romantic and companionate love within the family, and take away some of the painful strife of intimate relationships – lovers' tiffs, marital enmity, parent–child battles, and sibling rivalry – you would seem to have most of the recipe for a very happy society.

Box 9.1: Love rules: policies and techniques for regulating intimacy

- **Cultural regulation of parent–child intimacy:** Jean Liedloff's book *The continuum concept: In search of happiness lost* (1975/1985) is a passionate critique of the insistence in western societies on early physical separation of children from adults, which she maintains goes against fundamental needs for natural growth and condemns westerners to lives of anxiety. Though doubtless exaggerated, and derived from biased contrasts with romantic portrayals of the implausibly pathology-free parenting of 'natural' jungle peoples, Liedloff's argument certainly underlines the important cultural influences of early attachment and contact rules. Furedi and Bristow's *Licensed to hug* (2008) similarly criticises contemporary western paranoias about adult–child physical intimacy.

- **Sex education:** Provided by schools, religious organisations, and community organisations worldwide, sex education is often negative, conservative, erotophobic, and protective: for a passionate critique, see Marty Klein's *America's war on sex* (2006) or Jessica Valenti's *The purity myth* (2009). Formal sex education has responded more to the threats of unwanted teen pregnancy, sexual violence, and sexually transmitted diseases, than to young people's need to learn about sexual pleasures (Forrest et al, 2004). In richer countries, even formerly puritanical organisations now sometimes recognise that education for healthy intimacy is likely to be more effective if it respects and encourages enjoyment, although anyone who encourages young adults to enjoy sex is likely to face hostile media treatment (Simey and Wellings, 2008; Chapman, 2009).

- **Relationship guidance and therapy:** All societies have systems, techniques, and specialists providing guidance on the establishment, maintenance, and repair of intimacy, and on separation if repair isn't a viable option: positive promotion of love is rare. In western countries, many relationship guidance books for women are essentially anti-love and anti-men (Hazleden, 2004); relationship education programmes tend to prioritise at-risk relationships (Gottman, 1999, p 2; Hawkins and Ooms, 2011); and 'family life education' worldwide has the 'primary goal of prevention' (Darling and Turkki, 2009, pp 14–15); and in any case these are rarely evidence based (Gottman, 2000, pp 8–12; Huang, 2009). More positive counselling programmes, such as 'PREPARE', 'RELATE', and 'Great Start' (Holman et al, 2000, chapter 9; Markman and Halford, 2005; Futris et al, 2011), focus on promoting empathy by helping people to understand their own intimate discourse better (see also Tannen, 1991; Scuka, 2005).

- **Workplace intimacy:** Many kinds of organisation forbid any kind of romantic relationship between members of the organisation, even outside of working hours. Some employers that allow intimacy between co-workers encourage or require employees to draw up a formal 'love contract' to protect the company against charges of sexual harassment at the end of a romantic work relationship (Kakabadse and Kakabadse, 2004). Workplace intimacy is on the increase, and constructive guidance is being developed to support it in some countries, such as the UK (Piggott, 2010) and the US (CareerBuilder, 2011).

- **Work–family harmonising:** The gender revolution requires imaginative new approaches to the relationship between work life and family life (Poelmans and Caligiuri, 2008). Policies for parental leave, flexitime, teleworking, and welcoming spouses and offspring to the workplace are important kinds of love policy. They can also promote empathy in the workplace by encouraging people to appreciate their co-workers not just in terms of their one-dimensional workplace functions, but as fully rounded human beings – as spouses, as parents, and as people who care for elderly relatives.

- **Responding to abuse:** Violent abuse by intimate partners is increasingly acknowledged as a public policy and developmental challenge worldwide. Unsurprisingly, it is more likely to be addressed in adversarial ways, emphasising criminal procedures and separation of abusers from the abused rather than restorative justice. Recognising that many victims prefer to continue living with abusers, alternative 'feeling driven', 'affective advocacy' approaches have been developed, based on 'strengths', 'empathy', 'love', 'hope', and 'empowerment' (Strang and Braithwaite, 2002; Mills, 2006). 'Intimate Abuse Circles' aim at sustainable empowerment, reconciliation, and community support for non-abusive relationships, and could become good examples of the transformative power of the social happiness lens. Evidence of these reconciliatory approaches, often especially promoted as culturally appropriate for 'first nation/aboriginal' communities, remains mixed but generally favourable and, surprisingly, a lot of feminist scholars have overcome their initial hostility and are strongly supportive (Belknap and McDonald, 2010).

Domestic intimacy: the bedrock of happiness?

A good starting-point in exploring what kinds of difference a happiness lens might make in various policy domains is to consider all happiness policy as being in some way about close personal relationships, especially within the family. Putting happiness at the centre of policy discourse inevitably means paying more attention to intimacy and the social good of the family than would otherwise be the case, and it is often argued that social policies still pay inadequate attention to the family in many parts of the world (Folbre, 2001; UNESCAP, 2009b). Family relationships are almost certainly more important constituents and causes of our happiness than any other life domain is. Worldwide, in so-called 'collectivist' or 'individualistic' cultures alike, when people are asked what matters for happiness, or what they think about when they consider happiness, they are most likely to mention domestic relationships. They may want and expect different kinds and different expressions of intimacy.

In traditional family relationships in some so-called 'collectivist' cultures such as India, for example, husband–wife intimacy was typically seen as either unexpected or even threatening to the integrity of the family and wider kin group, but the family was still expected to be held together by strong personal bonds, and husband–wife intimacy, though hidden and not idealised, was there nonetheless (Trawick, 1992; Sandhya, 2009). In India, agents of the state frequently connive at appalling maltreatment of those who dare to choose 'love marriage' – for example by registering their deaths as 'suicide' when it is clear that they have been murdered, or by actively assisting in forced abductions of runaway brides – even though legal processes are strongly on the side of people's freedom to choose whom they marry (Mody, 2008, pp 5–7, 9–10, 23–7).

So before we hasten to weep over the breakdown of the family worldwide, we must recognise that the family has always been an instrument of severe oppression even if it has also been a key location for learning the joys of intimacy. If the family can be 'the most decisive shaper of well-being and happiness, the place where our essential humanity – our capacity to reproduce and to be part of the chain of life – finds its purest expression' (Mulgan, 1998, p 128), it can also be a haven for abusers.

Relationships matter in two main ways:

- they matter *constitutively* as the main component in the enjoyable, fulfilling life, and
- they matter *instrumentally* as critical influences on people's ability to flourish in other domains such as school, work, and extra-domestic leisure.

Too often, policies for parenting focus on the instrumental value of parenting, treating parents as the means for bringing up children, rather than also as people whose parental well-being is a valid policy concern. To put it bluntly, in a well-organised society, parenting must be good, and fun, for both children and parents. Not surprisingly, thinking of family life can bring out the extremes of optimism and pessimism in people's evaluations. Consider Tolstoy's radically different takes on family life, in *Family happiness:*

> Now I could see what he meant by saying to live for others was the only true happiness … I believed that our life together would be endlessly happy and untroubled. I looked forward … [to] a quiet family life in the country, with constant self-sacrifice, constant mutual love….

… and in the first line of *Anna Karenina*:

> Happy families are all alike; every unhappy family is unhappy in its own way.

In the first version, domestic bliss is interesting and fulfilling, in the second, it can be achieved only at the expense of interest and fulfilment – happy families are boring, and probably bored too. More generally, the sceptical message of the famous *Anna Karenina* quote is that happiness is itself uninteresting – a claim that Tolstoy no doubt made either with the false bravado of a moody moment or else with deliberate enigma or irony, for in other writings he revealed a passionate interest in happiness as a key part of the meaning of life.

Seen from the perspective of the individual life course, our prospects for happiness begin with the family. From a social perspective, the family is itself shaped by the many other influences that shape our characters and options, and hence our performance as parents. But families, in their diverse forms, are crucial social influences on happiness, and they rely on the various factors that promote or inhibit pleasant and stable relationships between parents. Arguably the earliest modern empirical happiness studies were explorations of marital happiness conducted in the 1920s and 1930s with a view to developing practical strategies for promoting social cohesion and mental health (Angner, 2004). Given the obvious centrality of pair-bonding between adults as the basic building-block of social relationships in modern societies, this shouldn't surprise us. It should remind us that happiness scholarship has from the start been to some extent about social happiness, not just individual happiness, and that it has been driven less by abstract academic interest than by a sense of responsibility for improving society.

Like many of us, Tolstoy retained throughout his life deeply ambivalent attitudes to both happiness and family life. Families, he knew, are the original forge where the possibility of happiness is made, but also where the pathways of much of life's deepest miseries are laid out. But happiness itself, while in some ways quite appealing, was also potentially rather dull, even unfulfilling. Social scientists have tended to follow the sceptical version of Tolstoy: families are devastatingly problematic social institutions, so most social science writing about family life is about *bad* family life. And happiness isn't very interesting anyway, so why write about it or even try to promote it? In books and journals on the sociology of family life, you'll be lucky to find 1 in 50 that isn't primarily about dysfunctionality.

If social happiness research and policy are to flourish, we will complement pathological investigations with more respectful and balanced research on family life, recognising its centrality in the social production of happiness. Before we get too enthralled with the idea of understanding and promoting family happiness, we do need to recognise that the family remains a site of appalling levels of violence and abuse, suffered by wives, children, husbands, elders, and homosexual partners, and that this abuse still receives cultural support and state connivance or neglect in many societies worldwide (Malley-Morrison, 2004; Pinheiro, 2006). We also need to recognise that, even in the absence of abuse, not everyone enjoys family life. George Burns quipped that 'Happiness is having a large, loving, caring, close-knit family in another city': it is of course increasingly likely that key members of our families are geographically separated from us nowadays and, joking apart, we might do well to consider this as a critical malfunction of modernity.

Thomas Jefferson's platitudinous assertion that 'the happiest moments of my life have been the few which I have passed at home in the bosom of my family' may sound more boring than Burns' joke. But it carries an important message that we can't afford to ignore. The research response can't stop at analysing family dysfunctionality. It is a poor show if scientists and policy makers don't try to learn about and build on what goes right with families. If Freud and his followers are right that families can condemn people to lifelong traumas, it must also be the case – since most of us seem to lead reasonably happy lives – that families also do us a considerable amount of good. We could explore examples of good families and prove the sceptical Tolstoy wrong by showing how interesting and diverse they are (Waite and Gallagher, 2004; Martin, 2005; Haltzman, 2009).

The benefits of sustained intimacy

Much of the research on marriage and happiness simply confirms what many of us would expect: that adults who are married or in a long-term relationship tend to be somewhat happier and healthier than adults who aren't. But there are some surprises. One of the most striking is the recent findings from national US samples in the 1980s and 1990s that *divorce brings no happiness benefits, on average, even to those who are in thoroughly unhappy and even violent marriages*: 'if one of the goals of ending a marriage with which one is unhappy is to improve one's emotional wellbeing, this goal is not typically reached' (Waite et al, 2009, p 209). Lots of marriage guidance counsellors, parents of squabbling couples, and religious leaders may have said as much all along, but for the general public this contradicts the common belief that even if divorce may be damaging for children, it does at least bring relief to desperately unhappy couples.

The policy implications of this shocking finding aren't easy to tease out, but it shows how a happiness lens, backed up by empirical research, is a necessary component in applied social research. Knowing that divorce fails to ease unhappiness might make people pause for even more thought before divorcing and, perhaps more importantly, hesitate before entering a potentially disastrous marriage in the first place. It might also raise ethical questions for those in the media who report on the frequent marital shifts of global entertainment celebrities: reports that appear to show famous people slipping happily from one relationship to another may well have played a key role in lowering the threshold level of marital dissatisfaction that triggers divorce (Amato et al, 2007, p 9). Further, given that marital problems are often strongly linked to workplace problems and work–life disharmonies, employers could take note that anything they can do to facilitate the quality of employees' marriages is likely to enhance their employees' productivity and long-term loyalty to the firm (Murphy and Zagorski, 2004). Employers in work forms that pose exceptional challenges for spouses, like the military and long-distance fisheries, know this well and do sometimes come up with strategies for alleviating domestic problems.

To become persuasive, the happiness lens needs to be seen as a way of revealing crucial purposes of our institutions that we might otherwise ignore. The purposes of families and conjugal commitments have in most parts of the world changed almost beyond recognition, even within living memory. Previously a unit of production, distribution, consumption, reproduction, security, and worship, the family today may be none of these things. But families may still hold together

Box 9.2: Surveys of satisfaction with intimate relationships

- The **Locke-Wallace Marital Adjustment Test** has been used for several decades now, in numerous countries. It built on various marital quality schedules and marital prediction tests that had been developed since the 1920s. It included 15 items on marital adjustment (joy in marriage, sex, demonstrations of affection, and so on), and 35 items on marital prediction (addressing childhood factors, relationship history, personality traits, personal happiness, and so on) (Locke and Wallace, 1959).

- The **Rubin Love and Liking Scale** was developed to measure three aspects of love: *attachment* (affiliative and dependent need), *caring* (a predisposition to help), and *absorption* (trusting). Thirteen questions assessed love, and another 13 assessed 'liking', defined as favourable evaluation and respect (Rubin, 1970).

- The **Triangular Love Scale** assesses what Sternberg sees as the three defining components of love: *intimacy*, *passion*, and *commitment* (Sternberg, 1997).

- The **Dyadic Adjustment Scale** (www.mhs.com/product.aspx?gr=cli&prod=das&id=overview) is a 36-item assessment of how couples agree or disagree on everyday matters such as money, household tasks, and friends, and on more abstract issues such as philosophical values and life goals, plus various interactional issues such as sex and quarrelling.

- The **Dyadic Trust Scale** is an eight-item questionnaire measuring interpersonal trust in close relationships, adapted from various previous trust-measuring scales, including perceptions of spouses' honesty, promise-keeping, self-interest, and so on (Larzelere and Huston, 1980).

- The **Relationship Development Questionnaire** was developed for assessment of children and adults with autism spectrum disorders, to assess progress towards the enjoyment of empathic relationships. Depending on the degree of progress that has been made, assessors can rate on the basis of observations at five different levels, from very basic to really excellent relational abilities (Gutstein and Sheely, 2002).

- The **Communication Rapid Assessment Scale** measures various aspects of verbal and non-verbal communication on a five-point scale, rating them as good for communication or destructive (Joanning et al, 1984).

- The **PREParation for Marriage (PREP-M) Questionnaire** was designed for couples considering marriage, although it can also give some guidance on single individuals' preparedness for serious relationships. Its 204 questions collect information on cultural values and expectations (especially concerning relationships, sexuality, and gender roles), personality, life experiences (happiness, parents' marital quality, family upbringing, schooling, violence, sex) (Holman, 2000, Appendix A).

- The **Relationship Quality Follow-Up Study** tracks relationship outcomes and individuals' views on how those outcomes came about. For those still together, it queries respondents on around 100 aspects of relationship experience, and on their the level of satisfaction with specific aspects of the marital relationship such as physical intimacy, love, conflict resolution, relationship equity, quality of communication, and overall satisfaction (Holman, 2000, Appendix B).

- The **Passionate Love Scale** (www.elainehatfield.com/Passionate%20 Love%20Scale.pdf) measures self-reports on romantic love attachments to specific others via 14 questions about the strength of feelings (Hatfield and Sprecher, 1986).

- The **Compassionate Love Scale** was developed as part of a major research effort to raise the profile of self-sacrificial love for others, based on scientific and lay prototypes of love and related concepts. It is intended to be versatile enough to make comparisons between love for people in general, strangers, close others in general, or a specific close other (Sprecher and Fehr, 2005; Fehr and Sprecher, 2009).

because they are essential for quite different purposes, most notably the cultivation of our ability to love and become happy. If these changes aren't acknowledged, we will see the persistence of cultural attitudes and social practices that unduly restrict the scope of people's options for finding love and happiness. These beliefs and institutions may perhaps in the past have been excusable on the grounds that they served some essential function (for example controlling partner choice to keep the peace and prevent fields from being split up too much), but a happiness lens can reveal their anachronisms and help us to optimise attention to other purposes of dyadic bonding and family life: self-transcendence, learning social and emotional intelligence, and developing identity and the sense of meaning in life.

Idealists imagine a better world where the restrictions on love are eased, and where love is based on trust and respect for autonomy. It does seem possible that a safer, more stable world can become not only an autonomy–respecting world but also a more empathic and loving world. We have discussed here mainly the prospect for the prototypical loving bonds within the family to become more intrinsically valued and less exploitative or pathological. Much of the same reasoning can be applied more broadly to friendships, which likewise is good in itself, rather than just good for something else. As C.S. Lewis put it:

> Friendship is unnecessary, like philosophy, like art … It has no survival value; rather it is one of those things that give value to survival. (1960, p 70)

Discussion points

- Love, like happiness, receives less research and policy attention than it deserves. All societies and many of our social institutions have policies and professional specialists for regulating and manipulating intimate relationships. Today the prospects are better than ever for developing policies that are more love friendly, and hence more conducive to happiness.
- Relationships worldwide are rapidly becoming more voluntaristic and less instrumentalist and survival oriented. The happiness implications of these new freedoms, such as the freedom to choose life partners based on romantic love, remain unclear.
- Despite the likely benefits of voluntaristic intimacy and reduction of gender inequalities and gender divisions, lots of social research has shown that modern cultural and socio-economic arrangements can damage the quality and sustainability of domestic intimacy.

Key readings

Fehr, B., Sprecher, S. and Underwood, L.G. (2008) *The science of compassionate love*, Chichester: Wiley–Blackwell.

Fletcher, G. (2002) *The new science of intimate relationships*, London: Wiley–Blackwell.

Gottman, J. (1999) *The seven principles for making marriage work*, New York: Crown.

Institute for Research on Unlimited Love, www.unlimitedloveinstitute. org.

Journal of Couple & Relationship Therapy

Post, S. et al (2003) *Research on altruism and love*, West Conshohocken, PA: Templeton Foundation Press.

Smart Marriages (Coalition for Marriage, Family and Couples Education), www.smartmarriages.com.

TEN

The shape of good hope: cultivating reasonable aspirations

Traditional stories like the Pandora's box myth, Robert Bruce and the spider, and *The Little Engine that Could* remind us that hope has always been seen as a source of private strength. Much less attention has been given to social, collective hope – to the ways in which our aspirations are moulded and sustained through dyadic relationships, networks, political processes, and collective activities (Marmarosh et al, 2005). The popularity of the term 'Hope' in the titles of voluntary organisations and projects worldwide suggests that people recognise this as a key aspect of development. Box 10.1 explores the moral hazards in deliberate manipulation of aspirations at national level by looking at the super-rich Thai King's efforts to persuade his population to be happy with a 'sufficiency economy'.

Box 10.1: Aspiration management in Thailand: the 'Sufficiency Economy' and the 'Happiness Society'

The closest parallel to the Bhutanese 'Gross National Happiness' concept is the Thai government's 'Sufficiency Economy' concept (and associated 'Green and Happiness Society' concept). As in Bhutan, this is strongly identified with a narrative of spiritually inspired thinking from a sacred Buddhist monarch (www. sufficiencyeconomy.org/old/en). King Bhumibok Adulej, recipient of the UN Human Development Lifetime Achievement Award in 2006, is also one of the world's richest royals, yet at the same time a fervent advocate of the financial downshifting of his people.

Having given many speeches on the need for modesty in development, in his 1997 birthday speech, soon after the financial meltdown, the king reminded citizens of his wish that the country should take a 'careful step backwards' towards sustainability via low-risk agricultural diversification and nurturing of community harmony. As in both the GNH rhetoric and Fritz Schumacher's 'Buddhist Economics' concept (1966/1973), the vaguely humanist concept of 'human-centred' development is combined with spiritualism and the metaphor of

---

the 'middle path' in Thailand, focusing on 'well-being rather than wealth' (UNDP, 2007, pp v, xv).

The Thai king is careful to ask that this flexible 'middle path' be generous enough to accommodate his own affluent life-style. Comfortably off with his Crown assets worth some $30 billion, he argues that: 'Sufficiency means to lead a reasonably comfortable life, without excess, or overindulgence in luxury, but enough. Some things may seem to be extravagant, but if it brings happiness, it is permissible as long as it is within the means of the individual' (quoted in UNDP, 2007, p xvii). Given such flagrant hypocrisy, it is hardly surprising that the 'Sufficiency Economy' rhetoric has been sceptically received in Thailand (Tanomsup, 2006). Invidious though it may be for an obscenely rich monarch to advocate voluntary restriction of material aspirations, it is fair to point out that the king is at the same time trying to persuade the poor to inflate their aspirations for empowerment and for social and spiritual fulfilment (Unger, 2009). So he isn't just cynically trying to curb their aspirations: he wants his citizens to be economic downshifters and eudaimonic upshifters.

One of the texts that persuaded me to depart from a normal international development career and engage more strongly with happiness scholarship was *Psychology of aid* (Carr, McAuliffe, and MacLachlan, 1998), a work that pioneered the idea of applying psychological concepts to the complicated relationships and motivations involved in development cooperation. Among their most persuasive arguments was the idea that a key ingredient for good development is realistic hope, and that aid itself may, over time, damage the hopes of foreign donors (by making progress seem cheap and easy) and the motivations of people in aid-recipient countries (by undermining self-help and demotivating even the most senior staff by paying foreigners at much higher rates).

In earlier decades, development scholars did pay attention to hope as an aspect of development and as a public good. Neo-Enlightenment 'modernisation' theorists saw cultural optimism and the collective desire to develop as key factors in development (David McLelland's *Achieving society*, 1961; Alex Inkeles and David Smith's *Becoming modern*, 1974). And more left-leaning social critics, like the Brazilian educationalist and social reformer Paulo Freire in his *Pedagogy of the oppressed* (1972) and *Pedagogy of hope* (1995); Peter Lloyd in *Slums of hope* (1979); and Melvin Rader in *The right to hope* (1981). Less explicitly, Putnam's *Making democracy work* (1993) triggered an explosion of interest in 'social capital' and trust as critical factors, all of which was in some degree about hope – fighting fatalism and promoting optimism about other people and about governance and the future. Overwhelmingly, however, social scientists have always shown more interest in fatalism, cultural pessimism (the 'culture of poverty'), declinism, and alienation than in hope.

These seemingly unremarkable arguments persuaded me that there are three very strong reasons for linking Development Studies with happiness scholarship:

- **Development is fundamentally about hope:** Development agents are all hopemongers. You can't allocate time and money to plans without raising expectations. But hope is fragile, dangerous, and potentially a weapon of exploitation (Drahos, 2004). There are good and bad kinds of hope (the golden mean of optimum ambition is hard to achieve, and repeat disappointments breed fatalism and scepticism), as well as explicit and implicit hope raising (deliberate aspiration raising versus the unintended effects of internationalising social comparisons).
- **Happiness rarely features among the expressed aspirations of development agencies:** Though the agents of development know very well that they are in the business of purveying hope and clarifying the visions and objectives that facilitate hope, they are bafflingly reluctant to mention any aspect of happiness among these visions for a brighter future. You will find references to health, food, hope, empowerment, and justice among their visions and purposes, but it is much rarer to find references to joy or meaning.
- **Engagement in development has intrinsic value:** The *processes* of development – including the nurturing and enjoyment of viable and meaning-giving aspirations – matter as much as the *outcomes*. The social construction of hope is a crucial dimension of development, not just a means to other ends (Gill, 2008).

Hope, trust, and collective self-esteem

Hope has a wide range of meanings, but its core meaning is optimism regarding the future. When self-directed, hope overlaps a great deal with self-esteem. Self-esteem, likewise, is socially produced rather than just coming from inside individuals' heads. More than anything else, it comes from love. A recent social psychology experiment provides evidence in support of the common-sense view that unhealthy fixation on gaining social recognition via conspicuous consumption derives from insecure attachment. Two groups were asked to assign monetary values to a blanket; the group primed in advance with words denoting interpersonal security gave much lower value to the blanket, indicating a lower attachment to objects (Clark et al, 2011).

But hope can just as well be other-directed: we have hopes concerning our offspring, friends, community, nation, future generations, and so on. It therefore also overlaps with trust, in that good motivation and good relationships require a balance between optimism and realism concerning the future dispositions and actions of other people. Both privately and collectively, it is good to be hopeful and trusting, but not naïvely optimistic. As the film *The Social Network* showed, this is a fine line to tread: when presented with prospects for commercial success, the extraordinary creativity that led to the creation of Facebook was very nearly undermined altogether by the trust and optimism that had generated it. But the success of Facebook and other online social networks has now served as a crucial hope-giving and trust-promoting mechanism in the 'Arab Spring' of 2011, playing key roles in supporting popular rebellions and democratisation in the previously fatalistic, low-trust cultures of the Arab world. As Zimmerman argued in a paper on 'learned hopefulness' (1990), social hope is a real form of social power.

Like love, hope tends to be seen as a kind of 'psychological capital' (Luthans et al, 2007), a factor that leads to happiness, via various positive outcomes such as success and health. But in addition to this instrumental value, hope surely has *intrinsic* value too, since living in hope is by default a better way of being than living in despair. Just as feeling positive about relationships and about other people can equally well be seen as part of what happiness is, so too – as I argued in Part One – feeling positive towards the future can be seen as a part of happiness. Social happiness involves learning from other people how to enjoy reasonable aspirations. Provided that optimism isn't entirely unrealistic and hence unsustainable, therefore, it would by default seem better to cultivate hope than not to do so. This has always been the assumption of religious proselytisers who have variously promised this-worldly or other-worldly salvation. As we saw in the Introduction, a lot of the scepticism levelled against happiness policy applies to the promotion of illusory or dubious hope (Ehrenreich, 2009; Ahmed, 2010).

This purveying of positive illusions persists both in religion and in psychotherapy and medicine. In his classic paper evaluating scientific literature on the efficacy of psychotherapies, following many decades of enquiry into placebo effects, Jerome Frank (1968) argued that the most likely mechanism for efficacy in most therapies was via their ability to help people nurture hope. More recently, a normal three-stage process of recovery has been mooted, of which hope is the first ('remoralisation'), followed by 'remediation' and then 'rehabilitation' (Howard et al, 1996). In most branches of medicine there are ongoing irresolvable debates about the ethics of optimism and placebos, since the positive effects of illusions such as homoeopathic 'cures' are fragile and uncertain, only pertaining to the extent that people believe in them.

Along with alienation and anxiety, the loss of hope has often been seen as a critical problem for modernity, to which therapies, religions, and social policies must respond (Scioli and Biller, 2009). Since hopelessness is highly contagious, in caring professions such as psychotherapy and social work the problem orientation frequently generates a culture of pessimism among helpers and their intended beneficiaries alike (Koenig and Spano, 2007). But hope is also contagious, and in some kinds of care practice the generation of hope in others can operate synergetically and recursively, resulting in virtuous spirals (Schwartz et al, 2007; Weingarten, 2010).

Hope, like happiness, has for thousands of years been a favourite theme of theologians and philosophers (Fromm, 1968; Rorty, 1999; Mittleman, 2009). But despite its obvious moral and practical importance it received remarkably little attention from social scientists until the recent and rapid development of a science of hope, optimism, and resilience within Psychology as an important sub-branch of happiness studies (Seligman, 1990/2006; Snyder, 1994). Nesse (1999) provides an excellent overview of the evolution of the capabilities for both hope

Box 10.2: Practical hope-enhancing activities and policies

Solution Focused Brief Therapy (SFBT, or 'Brief Therapy' for short), often interwoven with the reframing approaches of Cognitive Behavioural Therapy, was developed in the US in the 1980s (see www.sfbta.or, and de Shazer, 1985) as a form of therapy emphasising hope and pathways towards solutions, in contrast to traditional therapeutic emphasis on problems. It has a lot of common ground with the 'strengths-based' approaches to well-being advocated by the Positive Psychology movement. Though often focused on individuals, SFBT has often been used with families, groups, and schools – for example the Working on What Works (WOWW) programme for middle schools (Kelly et al, 2008; Selekman, 2010) – and in both individual and group-based end-of-life counselling work (Simon, 2010), the effectiveness of both of which has been positively evaluated.

A team of positive psychologists have trialled a short-term (eight session) **Hope Therapy** intervention designed to improve individuals' ability to identify and pursue realistic goals, based on Snyder's Hope Theory, which introduces to subjects, at the start of the intervention, the concept of hope as derived from synthesis of goal-setting, pathways thinking, and agency thinking, and recognises that these are all *socially* facilitated through role models and intimate support (Snyder et al, 1997). These interventions have produced evidence of significant improvements in hope, life meaning, and self-esteem, and reductions in depression and anxiety (Cheavens and Gum, 2010).

Hope-focused marital enrichment programmes have been found effective in promoting marital harmony, especially when done in groups and combined with forgiveness training (Ripley and Worthington, 2003).

The **Building Family Strengths** programme includes hope (optimism) among a list of strengths that are expected to be found in most families, even highly problematic ones. Other strengths looked for are: communication, contentment, history, humour, resilience, self-esteem, spirituality, unity, and values. The objective is, having identified strengths, to build on these as potential pathways for applying positive psychology principles to improve parent–child relationships (www.clemson.edu/fyd/bfs.htm).

Group-derived Collective Self-Esteem (CSE) has been successfully promoted in many kinds of therapeutic settings, such as Alcoholics Anonymous and Weightwatchers groups (Yalom and Leszcz, 2005). It is particularly promising as an approach in 'tribal reservations', where hopelessness is a common mental health problem but there are good local social resources for supporting collective self-esteem in family life and in faith-based and community organisations, schools, and workplaces (Hammond et al, 2009).

and despair, and how the social and pharmaceutical manipulation of these ought to pay attention to why these dispositions exist.

Collective self-regulation: managing aspirations and delaying gratification

It is a long-standing cliché that happiness derives from narrowing the gap between our hopes and our accomplishments, and that one strategy for doing this is to lower our expectations. In one of the earliest synthesis studies of happiness correlations, Wilson (1967, p 294) found that individuals' happiness correlated with 'modest aspirations' (although this has been refuted by further evidence – Diener et al, 1999, p 283). The anthropologist Marshall Sahlins tried to elevate this to the level of a cultural principle in his famously romanticising portrayal of hunter-gatherers as 'the original affluent society', on the grounds that they kept their hopes simple and modest. I will discuss this below in the section on work and leisure, but for now let us note that what Sahlins celebrated was better described as largely non-voluntary, passive contentment, and certainly not the 'Zen road to affluence', as he put it (Sahlins, 1968/1974).

Happiness policy would be wonderfully easy if all we had to do was dissuade people from being ambitious. There is surely more to happiness than accepting the simplest and least active life that we can get away with. On the other hand, Sahlins' critique of the western pursuit of affluence was fair enough: limitless ambition, coupled with greed and zero-sum status aspirations, are all damaging to our happiness. And so our explorations of happiness policies must start by considering how motives are culturally and socially produced and proceed to some kind of evaluative process that discerns good aspirations from bad ones.

To do this, we must take issue with two implicit assumptions in what we might call the *default grammar of motivation*, namely:

- the concept of happiness as an end-state derived from eventual fulfilment of desires, plans and expectations; and
- the idea of motivation as a largely personal matter.

I have been advocating an understanding of happiness that is *processual*: aspiration and the sense of progress are part of happiness, not pathways towards some goal of completed happiness. In also arguing for a *social* understanding of happiness, I see it as crucial to appreciate the lifelong processes of enculturation and socialisation that shape our motives and expectations. We may strive for autonomy, and our parents and broader culture may help us in this, but our aspirations and our happiness are socially inscribed from before we are born.

In another famous anthropological essay on the relationship between culture and aspiration, the cultural perpetuation of poverty was described by George Foster (1965) as derived in peasant societies from 'the image of limited good': poor, disempowered rural populations, he argued, fail to develop because they put strong moral pressures on one another not to try to rise above their position. This is because they believe that everything of value in life – material and social goods alike – exists in limited supply so that one person's gain must be someone else's loss. Less romantic than Sahlins, Foster saw this cultural pattern as a thoroughly bad thing, preventing people from aspiring to do better.

More recently, the anthropologist Arjun Appadurai (2004) avoided both the romanticism of Sahlins and the pessimism of Foster, and argued that the 'capacity to aspire' is a valuable 'navigational capacity' that tends to be weak among poor and marginalised populations, but can be collectively nurtured as part of an active process of empowerment. For example, far from asking for welfare hand-outs by external agencies, poor slum dwellers in Mumbai organised themselves into a federation that matched its lobbying for housing and sanitation improvements with a cultural–awareness movement encouraging debate about human dignity and the denigration of lower castes. In this context, the previous habit of (moderately) cheerfully accepting their lot was challenged, and gradually replaced with collective aspirations that became increasingly aired in public. Hope is to some extent an independent cultural variable: whereas in most parts of the world destitution is strongly associated with pessimism, in parts of Africa it turns out that optimism about the future is actually highest among the least well-off (Graham and Hoover, 2006).

Box 10.3: The hopeless Hallway Hangers and the hopeful Brothers

In his classic ethnographic study of two groups of adolescent boys in a low-income public housing project in the north-eastern US in 1984, Jay MacLeod (*Ain't no makin' it*, 1987/2009) found strikingly different attitudes to life among the two similarly low-income groups, based on the different ways in which their aspirations had been enculturated. The Hallway Hangers, all white, were strongly countercultural and severely demoralised, lacking any vision of personal or collective progress, rejecting dominant cultural values, and growing up in families long dependent on state welfare assistance, without fathers, and frequently in trouble with authorities. The Brothers, all black, were optimistic about future opportunities, learned aspirational values from their parents and from teachers whom they saw as inspiring role models, and accepted the dominant cultural values.

In 1991, eight years on from his original research, both groups (now in their mid-twenties) remained in poverty, but the Brothers' optimism had all but evaporated as they tried and failed to work themselves into socially and economically superior positions. By then, the Hangers were racialised, blaming black people rather than the class system for their own failure to progress, whereas the Brothers, who had clearly faced racial discrimination, were more inclined to blame themselves.

By 2006, things were looking up for the men in midlife, though most still remained on the lower socio-economic rungs. The Brothers were doing only slightly better, socio-economically, than the Hangers, thus reminding us of the limitations of the optimistic ideology of achievement motivation in the face of persistent class and race barriers. The Brothers seemed slightly happier, but this isn't a clear message of the book, and most Hangers and Brothers alike seem to have developed 'redemption narratives' that explain how their lives have taken turns for the better. The key hope-related messages of the book seem to be: hope is strongly affected by parenting and community culture; hope matters intrinsically (the Brothers were much better off in this respect); it can be naïve to expect hope in itself to be a force for social transformation or even personal social mobility; hope can be nurtured at any stage in life (several of the Hangers ended up cultivating their own sense of hope through personal redemption narratives).

In the chapter on parenting, below, we will be looking at how parents influence their children's aspirational dispositions and capabilities. Psychological research has confirmed the common-sense view that children need to be exposed to enough discomfort to learn the crucial life skill of delayed gratification. Michael Mischel's justifiably famous Marshmallow Study (Shoda et al, 1990) was designed to measure individual differences in self-discipline (specifically the ability to delay immediate gratification in exchange for longer-term goals) and then observe correlations between those differences and life outcomes over many years. Experimenters offered 4-year-olds a marshmallow, telling them that if they could resist eating it until the experimenter came back, they could have two marshmallows. Roughly one third ate the marshmallow immediately and one-third waited 15 minutes or longer and got the reward. Fourteen years later, via a parental questionnaire and Scholastic Adaptivity Tests, the same children were assessed on various criteria. Those who aged 4 had held out the longest were not only still the best at delaying gratification, but were more positive, self-motivating, persistent in the face of difficulties, intelligent, trusting, and happy.

Although causality remains uncertain even in longitudinal studies, Mischel's findings seem to lend support to the dogma of the Greek philosopher Epicurus, who over 2,000 years ago argued that happiness came from self-discipline, and from the ability to delay gratification. This ability is, of course, closely tied up with the propensities to trust other people and to believe in future rewards. Trust and hope need to be supported by collective self-esteem: perhaps more of the kids who ate the marshmallow right away came from families that had failed to help them learn to trust adults or trust the future. Also, although interpreters of the marshmallow experiment tend to emphasise the increased end-benefits derived from temporary self-denial, a different interpretation is possible: if we agree to a processual rather than an end–state definition of happiness, then *delayed gratification potentially becomes intrinsically valuable – an enjoyment in itself rather than just a means to increase future rewards*. This matters: if I train hard in the hope of running a four-minute mile but am hit by a car before I can achieve this goal, I would prefer to have found the training intrinsically rewarding.

Intrinsic and extrinsic motivation – from a social perspective

Complementing research on the ability to delay gratification, another vital area of research and debate in positive psychology has focused on whether different *sources* of motivation bring different kinds of happiness outcome. The key distinction is between '*intrinsic*' motivation (doing things because we find them rewarding in themselves) and '*extrinsic*' (doing things because we expect some later reward, and/or because we believe it will please someone like a parent or a boss).

In a great deal of moral discourse, intrinsic motivation is assumed to be prudentially good and virtuous, while extrinsic motivation is seen as unsustainable and/or damaging to our psyche. These distinctions often overlap and get confused with a different distinction, between 'materialistic' and 'non-materialistic' or 'post-materialistic' values and motivations. It is often argued that we benefit ourselves and others by focusing more on non-materialistic values such as love and happiness than on so-called 'materialistic' values such as money and consumer goods. Happiness promotion is strongly associated with orienting people and policies towards intrinsic goals and post-materialistic values (Kasser, 2002).

The discourse of intrinsic motivation derives mainly from the work of two North American social psychologists whose ingenious experiments demonstrated that motivation is more sustainable if based solely in the intrinsic satisfaction of a task, unsullied by attention to ulterior motives such as payment (Deci and Ryan, 1985). They asked two groups of students to solve puzzles, offering only one. group payment for the correct solution. Both groups were then left to continue working on puzzles if they felt like it. Those who were unpaid continued for much longer, due to their intrinsic interest in the exercise, indicating that payment had adverse effects on the sustainability of motivation.

It's not immediately obvious how this finding ought to be heeded in practice, though it clearly matters in some way. Even if demonetisation continues to gather pace and most of the things we need become 'free', as some futurists predict (Anderson, 2009), we will still often need to reward people for doing things. We can't realistically expect to organise most of our businesses on the strength of unpaid voluntary work. But at the same time we need to stay aware that material rewards (an objective good) may have adverse effects on motivation (a subjective good). So, for example, giving children sweets for doing their music practice, or offering productivity bonuses to staff, may not have the intended benign effects on long-term motivation.

'Be careful what you wish for', goes the argument proposed by psychologists Tim Kasser and Richard Ryan in a much-cited paper on the relationship between motivational sources and happiness (Kasser and Ryan 2001). From an individual perspective, it does seem to make good sense to consider carefully whether the goals we choose are ones that are likely to bring happiness. Particularly, once we recognise that happiness or misery are more likely to come from the process of goal pursuit rather than from accomplishments, then it becomes easy to see that our wishes affect our happiness directly, not just via interpretation of outcomes. The trouble is that we aren't free to choose our own aspirations. As social beings, we can't just wish our own aspirational autonomy into existence: we must accept that our wishes are to a large extent shaped by our ancestral culture, our parents' wishes, and the expectations of people around us.

Since the 1970s, these proponents of Self-Determination Theory have spread a gospel of simplification regarding the choice of motives. They make three highly questionable claims: *that we can clearly distinguish intrinsic from extrinsic motives*; *that intrinsic motivation is better for everyone's happiness*; and *that we are free to choose to be intrinsically motivated*. They're certainly right that it's important to think about sources of motivation. But taking a social perspective on motivation gives us strong grounds for questioning their assumptions about autonomous individual motivation:

- **Because we are socially constituted, all motivation is to some extent extrinsic:** Since the apparently distinct and autonomous self arises through enculturation and through social relationships, starting with our parents, it isn't possible to make neat distinctions between autonomously chosen goals and those chosen for the sake of others, such as parents or teachers or bosses or peer groups. The 'intrinsic/extrinsic' division may help us to get interesting discussions going, but it rests on a belief in the separability of the self and the socio-cultural context that is unrealistic even in highly individualistic western cultures, but even less applicable in more collectivist cultures.
- **The benefits of autonomous motivation are culturally variable:** Even if we can distinguish some kinds of goal as more autonomous than others, it is wrong to assume that autonomous

goals are better for happiness in all cultures. The valuation of autonomy, of social conformity, and of adherence to parental goals varies widely between cultures and between individuals (for a critique from the perspective of South Asian culture, see Iyengar and Lepper, 1999).

- **We can't assume free will in choice of motives:** Once we have introspected, and identified some of our goals as more 'intrinsic' or autonomous, the idea that we are then free to mentally chase away unwanted 'extrinsic' motives relies on a very optimistic belief in will power. We may still choose to follow goals that others have enticed us with, or, in trying to 'be our own scriptwriter' (James, 2002, p 239), we may ironically reject our parents' wish that we should be fully autonomous, self-driven free spirits.

In short, while it is crucial to explore possibilities for improving happiness by improving people's awareness of their motivations, the challenge of developing better motives is at least as much a socio-cultural enterprise as it is about self-help. Psychological scholarship and popular advice on motivation, striving for goals, and self-regulation has so far been aimed overwhelmingly at the individual level, and at pathologies such as addictions, selfish materialism, and unrealistic and frustrated ambitions. All of this matters but, to be effective, policy advice

---

Box 10.4: Tools for studying hope, purpose, and self-esteem

- The **State Hope Scale** assesses current 'pathways thinking' and 'agency thinking' via responses to six statements (Snyder et al, 1996).
- The **Children's Hope Scale** was developed in the 1990s as a positive alternative to the Hopelessness Scale for Children, which had been used in the 1980s. It consists of six questions about life goals, sense of progress, resourcefulness, and sense of self-worth in comparison with others (Snyder et al, 1997).
- The **Work Hope Scale** is a 24-item measure of vocational hope following Snyder's structure of goals, agency, and pathways (Juntunen and Wettersten, 2006).
- The **PsyCap Questionnaire** was developed for workplace usage, with 24 questions assessing workers' sense of self-efficacy, optimism, goal perseverance, and resilience (Luthans, 2007, p 237).
- The **Life Orientation Test** asks 10 general questions about optimism, resourcefulness, and self-esteem (Scheier et al, 1994).

- The **Beck Hopelessness Scale** (Beck and Steer, 1988) assesses pessimistic explanatory styles that are often associated with mental illness.
- The **Meaning in Life Questionnaire** (michaelfsteger.com/MLQ.aspx) builds on many decades of philosophical and psychological work on the acquisition of a sense of meaning and purpose in life to assess these with 10 questions, of which five are about meaning, and five about purpose, all very abstract and about life in general rather than about any specific domains of experience.
- The **Purpose in Life Test** (faculty.fortlewis.edu/burke_b/Personality/PIL.pdf), based on the philosophy of Viktor Frankl, asks 20 questions about individuals' sense of purpose and meaning in life as a whole (Crumbaugh and Maholick, 1964).
- The **Index of Self-Esteem**, though it sounds positive and is in theory neutral, was actually designed as a method for identifying problematically low self-esteem. It consists of 25 statements about the self (niceness, beauty, competence, and so on) and about perceptions of other people's evaluation of the self (popularity, status, likeability, and so on) (Hudson, 1993).
- The **Collective Self-Esteem Scale** measures positive perceptions of the self as a member of a group, including sense of belonging, perception of the group's public esteem, and identification with the group (Luhtanen and Crocker, 1992).

on these issues needs to be culturally embedded and socialised, and addressed not just at the level of individual choices but at higher levels of the family, wider communities and organisations, and broader society.

Discussion points

- Realistic and motivating aspirations are part of happiness and are essential for its sustainability. Hope thus has both intrinsic and instrumental value.
- Hope is always socially and culturally constructed. Trust in the future is closely intertwined with trust in other people. It is both a public and a private good, and can be fostered by group therapy as well as by self-persuasion.
- Development planning is a key mechanism through which hopes are nurtured, yet hope, along with other psychological issues, tends to be given little explicit attention in development discourse.
- Positive psychologists and community therapists have developed a variety of methods for nurturing healthy aspirations. This has been

driven by empirical and theoretical research on the happiness effects of *intrinsic* versus *extrinsic* motivation.

Key readings

Deci, E.L. and Ryan, R.M. (1985) *Intrinsic motivation and self-determination in human behaviour*, New York: Plenum Press.

Mittleman, A. (2009) *Hope in a democratic age*, Oxford: Oxford University Press.

Scioli, A. and Biller, H.B. (2009) *Hope in the age of anxiety*, Oxford: Oxford University Press.

Snyder, C.R. (1994) *The psychology of hope*, New York: Free Press.

ELEVEN

Positive parenting and cheerful childlessness

The soul of a nation is defined by the treatment of its children. (Nelson Mandela)

My father, who had derived such happiness from his childhood, found in me the companion with whom he could return there ... When I was three he was three. When I was six he was six.... He needed me to escape from being fifty. (Christopher Milne, *The enchanted places*)

Family pathology and the 'crisis' in parenting

The happy childhood is one of the bolder promises of modernity – the aspirational belief that we may at last have found the ability to offer most of the world's children an extended period of safety and enjoyment. This is not to assume, smugly, that childhood in the past was entirely unhappy, but for most of humanity's existence parents haven't been able to expect that their children would survive the very short childhood that was on offer, let alone get through it without some extreme suffering. Not only couldn't they assume the safety and happiness of their children, but parents in the past also had to see children as means (labourers, fighters) rather than as ends in themselves. Yet, among the factors blamed for unhappiness in modernity, dysfunctional families and inept parenting are the most common. You don't need to browse long in the literatures on children's rights, family policies, the sociology of parenting, and the cultural history of childhood before one theme appears to recur just about everywhere: a ubiquitous ambivalence towards the goodness or badness of both children and childhood. Though today idealised in many cultures as a phase full of carefree joys, childhood is just as often portrayed as a time of horrors and vulnerability.

There is today a widespread belief that in rich countries childhood and family life are in crisis, and that this is one factor in dissuading people from becoming parents. There are, fortunately, many scholars who question this dogma (Scraton, 1997; Coster, 2007), but there are many state and private business organisations who rely on maintaining public belief in the prevalence of family breakdown and fear of child pathologies. The 'therapeutic state' has developed over the past 50 years a much stronger interest in monitoring the quality of parenting and family life but, like its scholarly advisers (experts in child abuse and neglect, but not necessarily in well-being), it has hitherto confined most of its attention to categories of people deemed vulnerable or potentially criminal. At first glance this might seem like a justifiable use of scarce resources, but there are three very strong counterarguments:

- **We need socially inclusive family policies:** Even if we want to prioritise children with problems, although rates are higher in low-income families the overwhelming majority of cases are from moderate-to-wealthy families not considered 'at risk'.
- **Prevention is better, and generally cheaper, than cure:** Though some degree of targeting is possible in preventive work, the surest approach to prevention is to take more inclusive approaches that seek to improve family life for everyone.
- **Family policy requires understanding of good parenting:** If we want to promote healthy family life, we need to learn from normal and excellent examples, not just from families in trouble.

Whereas folk wisdom and everyday personal memories often emphasise the joys of childhood, scholars, biographers, and therapists have often seen mainly the sufferings and vulnerabilities of childhood, and see there the roots of still more lifelong suffering. As one reviewer of the western cultural history of childhood put it, 'without the image of the unhappy child, our contemporary concept of childhood would be incomplete' (Holland, 1992, p 148). If you browse Google Scholar with 'child' or 'family' as the keyword, you'll quickly see that the most common associated terms are 'problem', 'abuse', and 'dysfunctional', and that even 'child well-being' and 'child health' literature is almost all about suffering and illness. Most of the scholarly and therapeutic attention to child rearing and education addresses childhood pathologies and subsequent adverse outcomes or therapeutic treatments, rather than carefully studying what goes right in childhood and what can be done to facilitate both happy childhoods and good life prospects. Faced with well-intentioned but morbid and anxiety-inducing best sellers like Sue Palmer's *Toxic childhood* (2007) and Oliver James' *They f*** you up* (2002) and *How not to f*** them up* (2010), parents can be forgiven for believing that all the experts are eagerly waiting to document their failures. The default narrative of many psychotherapeutic traditions is that childhood is basically a minefield, something to recover from rather than an enjoyable life phase and a springboard for a happy life. Ironically, this rampant pathologism derives in large part from the idea that childhood *ought* to be 'happy'. It has been argued that this is a 'recent change' in the west, a belief that has put new pressures on parents, social workers, and governments to enforce this ideal by protecting children from anything that looks like harm (Stearns, 2010).

Even those books and journals whose neutral or upbeat titles imply they're not just about toxic childhood still tend to dwell on horrors. The huge annual report on children's 'wellbeing' [sic] in the US, for example is almost entirely dedicated to grim observations on pathologies (Childstats.gov US, 2009). The disingenuously titled *Good Childhood* report in the UK (for which the 'happiness guru' Richard Layard was lead author) is nearly all doom and gloom. The opening paragraph of the press release tells us that 'excessive individualism is causing a range of problems for children including: high family break-up, teenage unkindness, commercial pressures towards premature sexualisation, unprincipled advertising, too much competition in education and acceptance of income inequality'. Another major UK review of evidence on childhood, with a similarly bogus title (*The well-being of children in the UK*, Bradshaw, 2002) had virtually nothing to say about well-being in its 422 pages. The nearest it got to evidence of happiness was in its cover photograph of two cheerful 'Traveller' girls, and even they were chosen not so much because they were smiling and laughing for the camera but because they represented the disadvantaged minorities in whose impoverished and toxic childhoods the authors were mainly interested. So long as even the UK's most famous 'happiness' and 'children's well-being' experts remain as pathological as this, what hope have we of learning positive lessons about *good* childhoods, *good* parenting, and happiness?

So if you spend too much time in the dystopian world of pathological childhood studies, you'll end up wondering whether you just dreamed up the good bits in your own childhood. And you won't want to have children, it'll seem far too risky. Sooner or later, you'll share Benatar's *Better never to have been* point of view, and agree with Philip Larkin's ridiculous 'They fuck you up' generalisations about dysfunctional parenting and the consequent worthlessness of life.

The social conditioning of happiness starts in the family. Most cultural traditions see childhood as the model for innocent happiness, and parenthood as an ideal model of this–worldly and virtuous fulfilment. Yet happiness scholarship in modern societies has repeatedly produced a disturbing finding: parenting, which nowadays is increasingly seen as a life choice freely entered into as part of the pursuit of happiness, appears to be *inversely* correlated with self-reported happiness (Powdthavee, 2009; Keizer et al, 2010). According to most survey self-reports, people who currently have dependent offspring are less happy than those who don't, after controlling for the benefits of marriage, and even those whose children are grown up aren't significantly happier than the rest of the population. Momentary experience sampling of mothers shows that childcare is towards the least enjoyable end of their activity ranking (Kahnemann et al, 2004).

Though these studies have mainly been confined to western societies, similar findings have also come from very different settings where we might expect collectivism, greater stigma of childlessness, cultural salience of the family, and old-age dependency on support by offspring to make a significant difference (Zhang and Liu, 2007). Further, the stress of parenting is probably the strongest explanation for the common finding that happiness is 'U-shaped' through the life cycle, with a significant dip during the parenting years. This is not music to modern demographers' ears: in most rich countries, governments desperately want to persuade people that reproduction is good for them.

As if the midlife dip weren't off-putting enough for the decreasing percentage of us who consider reproducing ourselves, there is also the problem of loss of nerve regarding our capabilities as parents (Deater-Deckard, 2004). Honore argues that 'children are already the target of more adult anxiety and intervention than at any time in history (2008, p 4). Another gift from happiness scholarship that makes uncomfortable reading for parents is David Lykken's argument in favour of denying citizens the right to have their own children until they have either completed a course in parenting or successfully taken a puppy through obedience training (2000, p 121). Essentially he implies we would be better off if the state extended to all citizens its existing parental-capability assessment regime, which is currently applied only where there is clear evidence of neglect or abuse.

Note that this advice, which seems to endorse the standard 20th-century therapist's view that parents are by default a threat to children's mental health, comes from a man who believes that 'happiness is the natural condition of humankind'. Lykken argues that we all hedonically adapt to very good or very bad experiences, returning to a 'set point' that (based on studies of twins raised separately) is more or less genetically fixed: 'Nearly 100% of the variation across people in the happiness set point seems to be due to individual differences in genetic makeup' (Lykken, 2000, pp 6, 58). Lykken therefore believes that most parents have almost no influence on their children's happiness prospects, and sees the moral responsibility of parenting in negative terms, as a requirement not to cause harm. Even so, he still believes that parents require state-regulated parenting licences. *Parenting deficit*, by the communitarian Amitai Etzioni (1993), stops short of the licence argument but makes similar points about the responsibility to avoid causing social harm through irresponsible parenting.

Beyond pathologism ... but is perfectionism better?

Despite what the crisis-mongers say, if we ask children for words they associate with 'family', 'happy' will crop up more than any other. In a recent national survey of young people in England, out of 10 life domains surveyed, children were happiest with family life (only 4% said they were unhappy with it), and the family also came top of the children's rankings in terms of the importance of various domains for happiness (Rees et al, 2010). Even undergraduate students, asked in my lecture to fill out a happiness self-report and then say what aspect of their life had most influence on their self-rating, referred to their family more than any other factor (having, for the most part, rated themselves as 7–9 on a 10-point scale). Note that these results apply to a country that is (according to pathologically biased studies) supposed to be notorious for its dysfunctional families and toxic childhoods (Bradshaw, 2002; Unicef, 2007; Palmer, 2007; Layard and Dunne, 2009). A happiness lens can give us a very different picture from a pathological lens on childhood and family relationships.

But what does it mean to take a 'positive' approach to parenting? One approach is to see parenting as the pathway to future success by instilling in children a sense of ambition and the ability to defer gratitude. Parental promotion of ambition is powerful, but it is therefore also potentially damaging. In early 2011, pushy parenting again loomed large in public debate with the publication of the Yale law professor Amy Chua's *Battle hymn of the tiger mother* (2011), a controversial autobiography boasting of her merciless maternal bullying, dressed up in ethnically chauvinist terms as a form of cultural superiority. Chua boasts of her relentless parenting project that drove her two daughters to academic and musical 'success' by detour of a childhood almost entirely devoid of relaxed leisure or socialisation. Though occasionally capable of mildly humorous self-irony, Chua is largely unrepentant, and whereas the standard 'success' biography tends to emphasise mainly achievements and status, Chua goes further and makes some ambitious claims that her so-called 'Chinese' mothering (and, yes, lots of Chinese people have been vociferously objecting) has definitely given her children a better chance of life-long happiness than more easy-going 'western' approaches do.

You might imagine that a prominent academic who boasts that she never let her children fall below A+ grades in school might herself have done a spot of homework in preparation for her breakthrough text about authoritarian 'Chinese' parenting. But you'd be wrong: apart from its obvious, attention-grabbing crassness, what is also noteworthy about Chua's book is the *absence of any reference to parenting science*. Ignoring the work of thousands of scholars who have studied and analysed the pros and cons of different parenting styles, Chua seems to have been too busy tying her children to their desks to engage in any real-world scholarship herself. And so she writes as if she were the first person to have considered whether authoritarian parenting was a good idea. Chua epitomises the hubris of the attention-grabbing, profit-driven end of the commercial life-improvement book business. Sadly this attitude, though rarely displayed by tenured academics, is all too common in popular authors of texts on life coaching, parenting, and self-improvement, who assume that hard-nosed common sense and a few stories allow you to drive a coach and horses through the scientific study of well-being.

There are various angles from which we might usefully pose ethical questions to Amy Chua:

- **What is success?** While Chua clearly has evidence of her offspring's academic and musical success, and could plausibly argue that this is at least so far attributable in large part to stern parenting, has she really thought through what 'success' means in *ethical* terms? For example, will her daughters sustain through life a warm glow of satisfaction in the kinds of success she has lined up for them, or might they prefer other kinds of achievement, like being a good all-rounder or being socially competent or altruistic? Could they perhaps become success junkies, always hungering for their next fix and never able to relax? It has often been shown that excessive parental insistence on 'success' leads to lifelong suffering from toxic perfectionism and 'performance addiction', no matter how capable and otherwise 'successful' people may become (Burns, 1980; Ciaramicoli, 2004, chapter 10; Holden, 2008; Dychtwald and Kadlec, 2009). There is no doubting Amy Chua's daughters' ability to *delay* gratification; what is worryingly unclear is whether she has left them with any room to *enjoy* gratification.
- **What happens to less able children?** While it's easy for winners to show off their achievements and attribute them to a particular

parenting style, Chua fails to consider the losers, those who inevitably end up scarred for life by the lifelong sense of worthlessness and meaninglessness that this kind of bullying can instil. It's not very likely that they or their parents will be publishing best-selling books about their miserable experiences and regrets.

- **Is hothousing socially responsible?** A few pushy parents may not cause too much social harm, but if everyone behaved like her, how would we cope with the ensuing inflation in standards? She argues that all truly 'Chinese' parents in the US would give their children a severe row if they ever came home with any grade below an 'A'. Truly 'Chinese' parents won't let their kids take part in school drama productions or attend social events or sleepovers because this will detract from homework and music practice. So what would society be like if all kids had to get A grades and no one went to parties? Chua may on her terms be a 'successful' mother, but her social irresponsibility is worryingly callous. What she seems not to have understood is the vitally important ethical distinction between *motives* (in this case, the pursuit of status and esteem) and *purposes* (just as profit can be a motive for business but not its ultimate social purpose, it is similarly implausible to claim that status is a good life purpose for anyone, even if we acknowledge that it is sometimes a good motivator).

But we mustn't pin too much blame on one pushy mother. Chua is responding to a wider cultural belief in the US that normal parenting has gone horribly wrong. Social scientists, authors of parenting and self-help guides, and popular media alike have fostered this belief. If childhood is a place of enchantment, in which we invest so many of our retrospective hopes for humanity's happiness, it is noteworthy that modern social scientists seem reluctant to put this to the test by researching children's happiness. If parenting really is believed to be one of the most significant components in a fulfilling life, it is strange that it seems so beset with woes. The two are not unconnected. While no one could seriously expect childhood and parenting to proceed without trouble, one of the most perverse outcomes of modern social and psychological science, and of media coverage of parenting, has been to pathologise both childhood and parenting.

Good-enough parenting

Whether or not the doom-mongers are even half right about the prevalence of childhood psychopathologies, we clearly need to base our guidance for parents and social workers on a combination of knowledge about what goes right as well as wrong. There is little doubt that most people involved with children could probably do a bit better at facilitating good childhoods, but it is doubtful whether pathologising childhood is a good way of encouraging such improvement. I sympathise with Frank Furedi's fury, in *Licensed to hug* (Furedi and Bristow, 2008) and *Paranoid parenting* (2001), and with similar US-focused critiques (Glassner, 1999; Stearns, 2003) concerning the perverse outcomes of dwelling excessively on parental responsibilities and on the possible adverse outcomes of childhood abuse and neglect. A minority of individuals clearly do need to be prevented from doing silly or horrid things to children, or helped to recover from childhood traumas by talking about them. But the majority also need to be protected from rampant pathologising of childhood and child rearing, and reassured or inspired with examples of good child rearing.

There is therefore a real need to defend the overwhelming majority of good-enough parents against the slurs of the predominantly anxiety-provoking scholarly literature on parenting. We also need to put parenting in the broader context of the full range of influences on enculturation. Few psychological researchers are more relevant to social happiness policy than Urie Bronfenbrenner, key figure in human ecology, parenting, and school improvement research, who in the 1970s and 1980s tirelessly promoted socio-ecological approaches to upbringing (see, for example, Bronfenbrenner, 1979). To understand human behaviour we must go beyond the level of the individual person and look at the environments and levels of influence on the development of our capabilities. Here's what he had to say on the relationship between self-help and parenting:

> Witness the American ideal: the Self-Made Man. But there is no such person. If we can stand on our own two feet, it is because others have raised us up. If, as adults, we can lay claim to competence and compassion, it only means that other human beings have been willing and enabled to commit their competence and compassion to us – through infancy, childhood, and adolescence, right up to this very moment. (Bronfenbrenner, 1977)

Perhaps the most promising strand of parenting advice from the perspective of both children's and adults' happiness is the common-sense idea of 'good-enough parenting', an attitude promoting intuitive, non-perfectionist parenting as advocated, for example, by the psychiatrist

Donald Winnicott (1965). Winnicott believed that most parents have a 'sound parental instinct' and insisted that child development will follow a healthy course if only parents and supportive communities can provide an adequately 'facilitating environment' (or, more physically, a 'holding environment') that allows natural growth to occur. In other words, children's growth will be fine if it is not inhibited by either sheer negligence, abuse, or unnaturally pushy parenting.

The concept of 'good-enough parenting' remains normal currency in social work and clinical nursing, and it underpins legal procedures for child protection. Practitioners have considerably more difficulty identifying this than they have recognising either 'bad parenting' (a concept they normally fall back on) or 'good parenting' (Taylor et al, 2009). It probably has more use as a general reminder to attend to intuition and natural development than as an assessment label. In their key text *Studies in the assessment of parenting*, which like nearly all the literature on this topic is about the assessment of parenting of children who have been harmed or are at risk of harm, Reder et al define the purpose of parenting as 'to facilitate the child's optimal development within a safe environment', and note that it is composed of three core elements: *care* (meeting needs, protecting from harm); *control* (authoritative boundary setting); and *development* (enabling children to realise their potential) (Reder et al, 2003, p 5). Any of these three can be sources of anxiety, but pathological assessments are much more likely to focus on deficiencies in the first two. As for the realising of potential, for most parents this is a double-edged sword: the highs of parenting come as children's capabilities develop and they flourish academically or in sport or the arts, but any parent of an anxious disposition is faced with the ever-present possibility that they aren't doing enough to help their children reach their potential. Self-realisation is multifarious and open-ended, so 'enough' can never really be 'enough' and there are endless trade-offs between the domains in which a child might be expected to reach their potential.

In the US, Ellen Galinsky asked over 1,000 children about how they evaluated the parenting skills of their own parents. Most said that 'being there for me' was what mattered more than anything else: they were much less concerned about parenting skills than about the basic need for them to be present and attentive when it mattered (2005). Jim Taylor, in a diatribe against consumerist damage to family life in the US, argues that although parents primarily want their children to be happy, they focus instead on the consumer goods they can provide for them, as a result of which 'happiness is one of the most neglected family values in twentyfirst-century America' (2005, p 177). Addressing the gap between popular media exaggerations of the problems of children with working parents, Galinsky noted that most parenting studies have found that the employment of both parents is not in itself a damaging factor for parenting. She also found that although media concerns about absentee parents typically focus on the working mother, most parents and experts don't believe it matters whether it is the mother or the father who takes primary responsibility for childcare. She found that parents and children are more likely to complain about the inadequate parenting of fathers than of mothers. The leading expert on fathering, Michael Lamb, notes that in western countries there has been a dramatic shift towards much more social policy attention to fathers (1976/2010, pp 11–12).

Box 11.1: Positive parenting interventions

- The **Video-feedback Intervention to Promote Positive Parenting** is a short-term intervention that has been used in both clinical and non-clinical settings in various cultural contexts in Western Europe and the US. Normally used for remedial or preventive work, it tends to be used for mothers with problems such as anxiety or eating disorders, or parents with adopted, pre-term, or behaviourally problematic children, and is designed to give parents strong visual cues about the early development of secure attachment (Juffer et al, 2007).
- **Triple P – Positive Parenting Program** ® was developed as a response to child abuse and children's behavioural problems and mental illness, and is rapidly becoming influential worldwide, though mainly in rich countries, as an evidence-based support strategy for non-clinical application. It is a multi-level set of support systems ranging from basic advice that can be delivered either direct to parents (for example via web or TV) to more advanced training that can be delivered to couples, and consultations and collective learning via carers and large organisations. There is now a substantial body of evidence on effectiveness at individual and population levels (www.triplep.net; Sanders, 2008; Hartung and Hahlweg, 2011).
- The **Couple CARE for Parents** programme combines relationship education with lessons on parenting and positive couple adjustment to parenthood. At least four controlled trials have found that the approach prevents deteriorating relationship adjustment across the transition to parenthood (Halford et al, 2010).
- '**Theraplay**' is a therapeutic approach to remedial parenting that has been developed in the US since the 1960s to promote good parenting and healthy

attachment through play-based attunement and empathy strengthening, inspired by Winnicott's and Bowlby's research on intuitive parenting and secure attachment. It is mainly applied in clinical work with vulnerable or disturbed children, especially at younger ages, but the principles and practices are just as applicable to all kinds of children (Booth and Jernberg, 1979/2010).

Most theoretical and empirical literature on assessment of parenting, as well as assessment tools associated with training and communities of practice, has been developed for clinical applications or legal processes in cases of parenting breakdown. Some research, however, has been developed more neutrally or positively, to promote understanding of adequate or optimal parenting (for positive examples, see Moore and Lippman, 2005, and Proctor et al, 2009; for more comprehensive overviews of clinical applications, see DeCato et al, 2002, and Reder et al, 2003). Box 11.2 gives examples of some of the assessment methods that could be used without a clinical or pathological lens, to promote good parenting among people who are not already in trouble or deemed 'at risk'.

Box 11.2: Tools adaptable for non-pathological parenting assessment

- The **Strange Situation Procedure** is a classic, simple way of assessing the security of children's attachment to parents, developed by Mary Ainsworth in Uganda in the 1960s by observing children as they are exposed to mildly stressful situations (for example an unfamiliar room or person) and two short separations from their mother or father. Tolerance of unfamiliarity, and behaviour during separation and reunion, give important cues about confidence and relations to parents (Ainsworth et al, 1978).
- The **Bethlem Mother–Infant Interaction Scale** is used to monitor seven aspects of interaction: eye contact; physical contact; vocal contact; mother's mood; routine; risk to baby; and baby's contributions to interaction (Kumar and Hipwell, 1996).
- The **MacArthur Story Stem Battery** is a collection of story stems and associated suggestions for props and actions designed to elicit children's narratives that researchers hope will reveal insights into their life experiences, particularly family life and parenting. Examples include 'spilling juice' (targeted at children's perception and experience of authority) and 'climbing the rock' (to assess both mastery and attachment) (Emde et al, 2003).

- The **Youth Happiness with Parent Scale** has an overall happiness measure, plus items on 11 domains: Communication, Friends and Activities, Curfew, Household Rules, School Work, Rewards, Discipline, Chores, Alcohol, Drugs, and Illicit Behavior (DeCato et al, 2002).
- The **Parent–Adolescent Relationship Scale** is an eight-item scale (with shorter options) for self-report by adolescents. Developed from a review of several hundred assessment tools used since the 1950s (see DeCato et al, 2002), it focuses on identification with parents (identification, admiration, and enjoyment of their company), and on perceived parental supportiveness (praise, criticism, help, and so on) (Hair et al, 2005).
- The **Sibling Inventory of Behaviour** comprises six scales for assessing mothers', fathers', and siblings' self-reports, looking at: empathy/concern; companionship/involvement; rivalry; conflict/aggression; avoidance; and teaching/directiveness (Volling and Blandon, 2005).
- The **Parental Locus of Control Scale** is a 47-item self-report questionnaire addressing: parents' sense of efficacy, of responsibility, of children's control of parents' life, fatalism, and control of children's behaviour (Campis et al, 1986).
- The **Family Assessment Clinician-Rated Interview** was developed as a fairly simple assessment of family situations related to high levels of anxiety, as an alternative to self-reports and complex, lengthy behavioural observation procedures. It has subscales for 'Family Warmth/Closeness', 'Parental Involvement/Protection', and 'Parental Expectations for Child' (Ehrenreich et al, 2009).

One-child parenting and non-parenting

Before leaving the theme of parenting, it is worth pausing to remember that we now live in an era of unprecedented personal choice over whether or not to become a parent, and over how many children to have. Since this is understood as a decision that is vital for our happiness, we need to think about how it is influenced by broader social and cultural contexts. All societies and most individuals, whether they are aware of it or not, have policies relating to human fertility. Often a great many decisions and attitudes aren't necessarily guided by those policies – witness the powerlessness of governmental and religious pro-natalism in many parts of the world, and the only marginally more impressive performance of anti-natalism. Nonetheless, few factors influence happiness as much as fertility, and it is plausible that couples' and individuals' fertility decisions are to some extent influenced by policies as well as economic factors, cultural attitudes, and information. Fertility choice has become uniquely liberating, but also uniquely problematic, in the modern era. Sometimes we naïvely believe fertility choice to be a matter of individual preference. It is, however, intrinsically social – strongly shaped by cultural upbringing and by relationships and socio-economic forces. This matters in some way for everyone's happiness, but equally a 'happiness lens' can enrich the way we explore fertility decisions.

The world's most dramatic experiment in state-led control of fertility was China's one-child policy, which was introduced in 1979 to urban populations and still officially applies to over one-third of China's population. Though still apparently widely supported in China, and believed to have had dramatic impacts on population growth, it has been widely criticised on various grounds, including inefficacy, human rights abuses, gender disparities and infanticide on account of son preference, the '4-2-1 problem' of one adult having to support two parents and four grandparents, and the grounds of possible psychosocial ill-effects. Though benefiting in some ways from higher parental investment, and hence better living conditions and survival rates, only children in China may suffer lifelong costs of growing up in one-child families and in communities of so-called 'little emperor' only children (being hyper-parented and spoiled, lacking sibling competition, developing unrealistic aspirations), according to anthropologist Vanessa Fong, who conducted longitudinal case studies of five Chinese families (Fong, 2004, 2007).

Fong does take care to note, however, that many of these problems are co-produced by broader cultural and socio-economic factors such as generational shifts in values, and changes in job markets and educational norms. In other parts of the world, many researchers on only children have argued, and found evidence, against popular myths concerning loneliness, being spoiled, lack of ambition, and so on (Siegel and Uviller, 2006; Pickhardt, 2008; Sorensen, 2008). Veenhoven and Verkuyten found no evidence that only children were any less well adjusted, happy, or popular than other children in adolescence (1989). As these authors note, however, it is not only popular myths that spread beliefs about the troubles of only children: research on families and siblinghood has traditionally taken the multi-child family not only as the norm, but as a desirable norm. In any case, whatever knowledge we may have of the advantages and disadvantages of siblings in the past is everywhere becoming less germane as the multi-child family norm wanes and the single-child 'beanpole family' norm takes over (already 50% in countries such as Portugal and Italy).

Throughout most of humanity's history, in most societies, childlessness has either been involuntary (because of infertility or lack of a spouse) or chosen as a religious role, or perhaps both. After the demographic transition of modernity, untold millions of people worldwide are choosing childlessness voluntarily and explicitly as a strategy for leading a flourishing life. Typically this is done in the name of personal freedom and fulfilment, and sometimes other justifications are brought in, such as poverty, lack of time, or the need to avoid overpopulating the world. Sometimes the degree of voluntarism is ambiguous, and justifications are increasingly invented – and no doubt believed in sincerely – as age progresses and the likelihood of lifelong childlessness increases.

Both men and women have three main voluntary pathways to childlessness: not becoming a parent in the first place, having children adopted, or waiting until the children grow up and leave. Although rates of childlessness haven't increased everywhere, voluntary childlessness is rapidly increasing in all countries and is likely to go on increasing. The more upbeat term 'childfree' has clearly paedophobic overtones, though not all advocates of childlessness proudly announce their dislike of children. In fact, most tend to say they love other people's children very dearly (May, 1997, p 204). But, as an appealingly empowering term, 'childfree' may well come in time to replace the term 'childless'. The happiness implications of this for non-parents, and for humanity in general, will continue to develop as a crucial theme in happiness policy discourse.

Finally, we must resist the medicalist and individualist-gynocentric biases in research on childlessness. Although choosing not to reproduce has for many decades been heralded as a liberating new capability, childlessness has tended to be medicalised and assumed by default to be involuntary. Another persistent bias has been to treat childlessness (voluntary or not) as a women's issue – implicitly, that it's only really women who are childless (see for example May, 1997; Gonzales and Jurado-Guerrero, 2006; for a discussion of this bias, and an antidote, see Keizer, Dykstra, and Poortman, 2010). Fertility choice is of course normally a dyadic, social issue: couples choose whether or not to become parents and those choices emerge from socio-cultural contexts rather than just from individual happiness pursuits.

Discussion points

- The structures, processes, and purposes of families have changed dramatically almost everywhere in the world, posing new threats (particularly rising divorce rates and breakdown of family caring) as well as many new opportunities for happiness. The key policy challenge is to adapt cultural attitudes and the social regulation of intimacy to meet these new contexts.

- Most research, policy, and practice relating to family life, sexuality, intimacy, and parenting remains problem oriented, promoting remedial or – at best – preventive actions. But, particularly in richer countries, there are many promising signs of explicitly positive and socially inclusive approaches, promoting virtuous forms of intimacy without sacrificing freedom and enjoyment.
- In the coming years, as family structures and processes continue to change and there are more only children and more voluntarily childless people, our knowledge about the relationships between family experiences and happiness will need to be updated, as will our strategies for promoting healthy upbringing.

Key readings

Conoley, C.W. and Conoley, J.C. (2009) *Positive psychology and family therapy*, London: Wiley.

Juffer, F. et al (2007) *Promoting positive parenting: An attachment-based intervention*, Hoboken, NJ: Lawrence Erlbaum.

Martin, P. (2005) *Making happy people: The nature of happiness and its origins in childhood*, London: Fourth Estate.

Positive Parenting Program® website, www.triplep.net.

TWELVE

Schooling for joy

There is nothing inherently good about education, schooling, or learning. (Harber, 2004, p 7)

Only to an authoritarian mind can the act of educating be seen as a dull task. Democratic educators can only see the acts of teaching, of learning, of studying as serious, demanding tasks that not only generate satisfaction but are pleasurable in and of themselves. (Freire, 2000, p 90)

The changing purposes and evaluations of schooling

Universal standardised schooling is arguably the world's most ambitious social experiment. It is still rapidly evolving and constitutes just a brief phase in the history of enculturation, whose purposes and benefits remain unclear and endlessly debatable. Evidently, we wouldn't continue investing in schooling if we didn't believe it to make useful contributions to social quality and personal well-being. But it is troubling for both educationalists and happiness scholars that the research evidence in most countries suggests that years of formal education show at best very weak correlations with self-reported happiness, after controlling for other variables such as health and class (Ross and Van Willigen, 1997; Hartog and Oosterbeek, 1998; Feinstein et al, 2006; Michalos, 2007). More worrying still is that programmes specifically aiming to improve social and emotional outcomes in schools, even those specifically labelled 'positive', are so strongly focused on pathologies that they go under the generic label of 'prevention science' (Hoskyn, 2009). It is as if the imaginary ideal school were merely trouble free and therefore able to focus on academic attainments, and all efforts to deal with social and emotional issues were just damage-limitation exercises.

Similar levels of interest in toxicity, and disinterest in happiness or even in normal enjoyment and satisfactions, are evident in the literature under other psychosocial pedagogy rubrics such as 'school psychology' (Clauss-Ehlers, 2009; Gilman et al, 2009; Peacock et al, 2009), 'school climate' (Peterson and Deal, 2009), 'school social work' (Kelly et al, 2010), 'behaviour education' (Hulac et al, 2010), and 'school-based mental health' (Christner and Mennuti, 2008; Macklem, 2011). Small wonder that a plea has gone out to use positive psychology to produce 'authentically happy school psychologists' (Miller et al, 2008). If you are already a specialist in one of these areas, you may be thinking 'So what? With limited resources of course we have to prioritise remedial work.' My point here is not to devalue these approaches, but to make people aware that pathologism pervades psychosocial work in schools in a way that is not true of other non-academic aspects of schooling: it is much rarer for research and guidance on music, sports, or drama to prioritise remedial work, for example. Between them, the overemphasis on academic test scores and the pathologism of psychosocial work in schools seem to indicate a dire need, worldwide, for a happiness perspective to be applied holistically across the whole school rather than marginalised to a few 'fun' activities.

Inspiring as it may be that within such a short space of time nearly all the world's nations have managed to institutionalise the education of nearly all of their children in this way, it is also deeply worrying that a model developed during the Industrial Revolution to keep children out of trouble while their parents worked and to prepare them for the world of work has so dramatically failed to adapt to the very different priorities and needs of the modern era. Most disturbing of all is the absence of systematic mainstream attention, in any country in the world, to schooling's influence on pupils' happiness or on their prospects for leading happy lives. In a few richer countries, we have very recently begun to see the first signs of state interest in 'social and emotional' aspects of learning processes, but progress has been patchy, outcomes remain very uncertain, and the dominant emphasis is on manipulation of those processes not for the sake of happiness, but for the sake of 'success', 'character', and 'spirituality' (Lantieri, 2001; Zins et al, 2004; Elias, 2010) as well as, less explicitly, for the maintenance of control and order in the classroom (Gillies, 2011). Of all the policy themes addressed in this book, schooling is without a doubt the one on which the happiness lens has made least impact.

Because universal schooling has been so readily accepted as a marker of civilised modernity, its relationship with children's well-being and life prospects has been inadequately explored. Although lots of literature does acknowledge school shortcomings and harms, the predominant approach worldwide is to assume it to be in principle good, and to look for good outcomes (Harber, 2004, p 1). But happiness has rarely featured in the outcomes assessed (Thin, 2009a). Harber's critique rightly notes that far too much supposedly evaluative literature on schooling policies, qualities, and techniques fails to base itself on explicit clarification of what schools are for. Fair point. But schools obviously have to be multipurpose institutions, and if there is to be some kind of ultimate purpose, it had better have something to do with happiness. Harber favours 'peace and democracy' as the two main purposes (2004, p 136). In a similarly impassioned plea for schooling with a clearer sense of values and social purposes, Terry Wrigley's *Schools of hope* (2003) argues for a core emphasis on social justice and the empowerment of disadvantaged people. Even Brian Matthews, in *Engaging education*, though explicitly keen on schooling for happiness, picks as his main aim that 'education should enable pupils to ...question society and to play a part in changing it' (2006, p 11).

Peace, democracy, justice, and empowerment are important themes, but could they really serve as the ultimate purposes for something so fundamental as schooling? These are surely *compensatory* objectives, not *ultimate* ones: they sound very appealing when they are missing, but they are interim goods that tell us nothing positive about the goodness of life. We could live in miserable boredom in peaceful and democratic societies, and schools highlighting only these values could seriously short-change pupils in terms of both their school enjoyment and their life prospects. I don't want my children *only* to emerge from 12 years of schooling as peaceful and democratic, I want them to be happy throughout their school years and to emerge with capabilities to be happy throughout their lives, and to spread happiness to others. Other common school purposes are similarly lacking in ambition: filling heads with knowledge, keeping children out of trouble, preparing them for employment – all of these are useful instrumental objectives, but not ultimate values.

Once happiness is established as an important purpose of schooling, it should become a lot easier to conduct sensible discussions about the purposes of specific uses of school time and resources:

- Playtime breaks can be defended against policy makers who have been restricting them in favour of academic test-preparation (Doll, 2010).
- Physical exercise instruction is approached differently if it is geared explicitly towards happiness or pleasure, rather than seeing it as merely instrumental for fostering health or competitive success (Wright, 2004; Pringle, 2010).
- Field trips, museum- and zoo-based learning can be justified both for their intrinsic fun and for the important contributions that enjoyable experiential learning make to academic study (Csikszentmihalyi and

Hermanson, 1995; Falk and Dierking, 2000; Pumpian et al, 2006; Buys and Miller, 2009, Sickler and Fraser, 2009).

- The multiple benefits of music for enjoyment, sociability, school ethos, and school–community links can be appreciated and promoted (Garner, 2008; Green, 2008; Ofsted, 2009; Thin, 2011b; Institute of Education, 2011).
- Activities intended to promote social capabilities such as tolerance, empathy, and cooperation can be justified both in terms of the intrinsic enjoyment and value of the activities, and in terms of personal life outcomes, academic benefits, and social outcomes (Hammond, 2006).

There are good arguments for combining pathological/clinical approaches with more optimistic and eudaimonic approaches to upbringing. Since schools are for everyone, the objectives of schooling can't be confined to a harm-mitigation approach, although in bad schools it may sometimes look like that. In many countries, most parents would say that two key objectives for schooling are to contribute to the happiness of childhood and to improve children's chances of thriving in later life. Too often, however, these happiness themes are in practice crowded out by 'excellence' themes – particularly performance on narrowly defined academic test scores – and by the idea that schooling is an 'investment' that should bring 'returns' in the form of better prospects for well-paid employment.

Just as the case for economic growth in rich countries would not be weakened even if someone could plausibly demonstrate that it correlates only weakly with happiness, so too we much resist the temptation to conclude that if schooling doesn't correlate with happiness it doesn't matter. But it would be equally wrong to conclude that these findings are irrelevant for policy. Economic growth and education clearly do matter, so, if they aren't correlating with happiness, there may be something wrong with them that we should try to fix.

Critical investigations of possible adverse effects of schooling are a top priority in contexts where the rush to get all children into school has outpaced poor-country governments' ability to ensure minimum standards or even basic safety of pupils. By treating schooling, in effect, as if it were an intrinsic good (which it clearly isn't), most promoters of schooling have wished away the need for justification. It has been too easily forgotten that if the quality of schooling is poor, or if prospects for translating learning outcomes into well-being are poor, then the prospects of happiness in childhood or adulthood are not going to be improved through school attendance.

As Nel Noddings convincingly argued in *Happiness and education* (2003), in all countries, rich and poor, there is inadequate attention to the ways in which school can or could give children a better chance of happiness during and after their school years. Scholarly critiques of schooling may be entirely right in identifying a wide range of harms that schooling does to children, but entirely wrong in their failure to balance these critiques with complementary and comparative recognition of benefits. And those who do research the benefits may be entirely right in their verdicts on good outcomes, such as knowledge and employment prospects, but entirely wrong in their neglect of happiness effects. In addition, the effects of happiness on children's and teachers' performance at school have yet to be substantially researched in anything but the negative mode that explores the ill-effects of unhappiness.

So it is important to consider carefully the ethical justifications for schooling. Many children perhaps enjoy school more than they would enjoy alternative ways of spending their childhood, but it is for all children in some senses a 'tax on childhood', paternalistically imposed on children, against their will, by parents and governments. Schooling involves deferred gratification on the promise of lifetime rewards to individuals and nations. Though often associated with suffering, school life can (and clearly should) bring direct enjoyment to pupils. But this function is not routinely assessed, even in rich countries (Thin, 2009a; Soutter et al, 2010).

In the UK, there are incipient signs that children's happiness at school may become part of formal national assessment. But this is yet to progress substantially beyond rhetoric. For example, in the set of indicators for the UK Department of Communities and Local Government's 'New Performance Framework for Local Authorities and Local Authority Partnerships' (www.communities.gov.uk/publications/localgovernment/nationalindicator, 2007), whereas the adult section includes adults' own perceptions of various indicators of the quality of life, the section on children has an 'enjoy and achieve' section, hinting that children's enjoyment is going to be taken seriously, but that has no indicators of enjoyment and 37 indicators mainly about 'achievement' in formal academic tests, plus a handful about participation in activities. Astonishingly, even when explicitly assessing 'satisfaction' with school, happiness can still be ignored: based on 7,000 school inspections, the UK school inspectorate Ofsted published a report on *Parents' satisfaction with their schools* (2006) that had nothing to say about parents' views on their children's happiness at school, or on their beliefs about schools' contributions to their prospects for happiness. Even the report on *Pupils' satisfaction with their schools* (Ofsted, 2005b) similarly neglected happiness, focusing instead on children's views on the quality of provision and on their sense of academic achievement.

Emergence of a happiness focus in rich-country schooling

In western countries that have now enjoyed the luxury of being able to afford universal schooling for over a century, there is also the luxury of being able to critique schooling, questioning its values, purposes, quality, and even its right to exist. Happiness and the desire for holistic, non-stressful development of children's social and emotional capabilities are often cited as reasons for either home-schooling or sending children to 'community' schools or 'alternative' schools such as Steiner-Waldorf or Montessori schools (Albert, 1999). Few scholars who question the value of schooling, however, discuss how schooling might be improved by taking pupils' happiness seriously or by evaluating the long-term happiness effects of schooling. The sociologist Stanley Aronowitz's book *Against schooling* (2008), for example, is largely an opinionated rant against educational militarism in the US, without clear recommendations for better forms of upbringing, or evidence that children in general fare badly in schools. Like self-declared 'anti-happiness' authors, he isn't plausibly bent on abolishing his declared enemy: despite his attention-demanding title, he clearly wants schooling to improve, rather than stop.

Aronowitz declares confidently that 'at the turn of the 21st century, our [US] collective sense of wellbeing has never been more precarious' and that there is generalised anxiety about the future and lowered expectations of what schooling should offer children (2008, pp ix, xiii). It may well be true, as he argues, that in the US schools are overly based on discipline, privilege, and credentialism, teaching children to become virtuous citizens, to accept their social class, and to learn to work for a specific capitalist kind of economy, rather than facilitating creativity and social mobility. But reimagining education (which may well involve some degree of de-schooling) requires much more persuasive proposals based on evidence of better forms of upbringing. It also requires a clearer sense of what kinds of life outcome really matter, and what forms of upbringing can make a difference to those outcomes.

Still, in western countries there have now been several decades of debate and research on the purposes and methods of schooling, introducing teachers, parents, and pupils to happiness-related concepts and approaches such as 'emotional intelligence', 'affective education', 'values education', 'emotional literacy', 'character education', 'resilience education', 'cooperative learning', 'learning for life', 'whole child education', 'school climate', and, most recently and most influentially, 'social and emotional learning'. Although assessments of pupil happiness or satisfaction, or of emotional literacy outcomes, are massively outweighed by assessments of other issues such as academic test scores and progression to employment, there are at least incipient signs of eudaimonic and hedonic criteria being deployed in educational assessments in rich countries. A major review of over 300 studies of school-based Social and Emotional Learning initiatives involving over 300,000 children from kindergarten to eighth grade in the US has found these to be 'among the most successful youth-development programs offered to school-age youth', confirming that they fit well with routine educational practice and improve participants' academic performance by 11 to 17 percentile points, in additional to the many other benefits to well-being and social responsibility (Payton et al, 2008).

A study of teachers in Italy, the Netherlands, Poland, Spain, and the US found that in all samples there was among teachers a strong emphasis on 'social intelligence', despite the dominant focus on cognitive qualities in western educational assessment practices (Harkness et al, 2007). The John Dewey tradition of schooling for freedom and democratic citizenship has seen a new lease of life in a proliferation of texts on education for citizenship, democracy, happiness, and the 'good life' (for example Noddings, 2003; Stradling, 2004; Siegel and Uviller, 2006). Affective education, aimed at strengthening children's social and emotional competence as part of the broader agenda of providing a 'rounded' education, has a mixed history in richer countries but has been increasingly emphasised in recent years (Goleman, 1995; Lang et al, 1998; Puurula et al, 2001).

In the UK, the campaign for emotional literacy took off following a 1997 conference on 'Emotional Development and the School Curriculum' (Antidote, 1997). Education inspectors by 2005 were already routinely monitoring schools and nurseries to assess their performance in fostering pupils' emotional and social development (Henry, 2005; Ofsted, 2005a), and the Education and Inspections Act 2006 made substantial provision for promotion of well-being that went well beyond traditional academic responsibility: local education authorities in England and Wales were henceforth required to provide facilities for recreation and social and physical training 'for the improvement of their well-being' (see also Ofsted, 2007). The 'happiness' value of physical education in English schools, rather than just its physical and social spin-off benefits, has been championed by

Wright (2004). Not only private schools, but also some local education authorities are now making substantial investments in 'happiness classes' (*Daily Telegraph*, 2007).

Partly, this trend is a backwash from widespread concerns about the damaging effects on children of frequent academic testing (see for example McNess et al, 2003). It has also responded to a new theme in school effectiveness literature that casts doubt on the contributions of education to lifelong happiness (Gardner and Oswald, 2002; Persaud, 2006). More positively, it responds to many rather obvious confirmations that, if pupils are happy, they also study better (Brezovsky, 2002). Maxcy argued that while in principle it is important to have a 'humanistic' school 'climate' that is happiness promoting, we can't deliberately create an atmosphere of happiness in a school – 'school happiness like personal happiness tends to happen without artificial stimulants or incentives' (1988, p 32). Frank Furedi, whose objections to paedopathologising and paranoid parenting I agreed with above, links these attitudes with the call for state-sponsored happiness schooling, to which he therefore also objects (Furedi, 2006a). However, work in European countries has demonstrated cost-effective methods of assessing pupils' well-being that could enable education authorities to monitor school performance in facilitating physical and emotional well-being, regardless of the extent to which they actively promote pupil happiness in a direct way (Engels et al, 2004; Huebner et al, 2004; Konu and Lintonen, 2006).

Box 12.1: School-based promotion and assessment of happiness

Positive Education (such as the **Penn Resiliency Program** and the **Strath Haven Positive Psychology Curriculum**) is the most explicitly happiness-oriented school experiment so far. It invites teachers, pupils, and parents to adapt empirical findings from Positive Psychology into various techniques and approaches for happier learning and for learning about happiness. So far, high-profile case studies have mainly come from well-resourced private schools (Brunwasser et al, 2009; Morris, 2009; Seligman, 2011).

EdVision (http://edvisionsschools.org) is a US programme developing the ability of small schools to facilitate highly personalised, project-based and pupil-directed learning strategies, with a view to enhancing hope, autonomy, and other life skills. There is also a strong emphasis on the autonomy of the school, and on building a democratic school climate. Results of comparison studies and before–after

---

self-reports are already showing excellent progress in facilitating autonomy, engagement, belonging, and motivation (Newell and Van Ryzin, 2008).

The **Whole Child Initiative** is an approach to school improvement promoted in the US since 2004 by the Association for Supervision and Curriculum Development, with an emphasis on warm social environments among pupils, teachers, and families. It has promoted use of a five-point 'Learning Compact' for health, physical, and emotional security, active engagement in learning, personal caring relationships, and preparation for employment in a global environment (www.wholechildeducation.org).

The **4-H Positive Youth Development** programme is the largest youth development organisation in the US (www.4-h.org), enabling young people to participate in extracurricular activities focused on science, prosocial community work, and health. Benefits such as prosocial behaviour and reduction of drug taking and risky sex have been observed by repeat interviewing of 6,000 adolescents from 45 states since 2002, focusing on relations between positive life goals and civic engagement, and by controlled comparisons with participants in other extramural programmes (http://ase.tufts.edu/iaryd/researchPositive4HAbout.htm).

GoodSchool.dk (www.godskole.dk) is an online tool for evaluating children's well-being and academic performance at school, developed by Danish positive psychologists Hans Henrik Knoop and Svend Erik Schmidt. Pupils log on to self-evaluate and can observe the findings on their own or with teachers and fellow pupils.

Big Picture Learning (www.bigpicture.org) was founded by US educational reformers Dennis Littky and Elliot Washor in 1995, and has now spread to over 100 schools in several countries. It aims to promote and assess personalised, self-directed, and community-linked learning in schools. Initially targeting 'at-risk' children from ethnic minorities, the programme has been encouraged by positive evaluations to address whole school populations (Levine et al, 2001; Littky and Grabelle, 2004).

The **Jigsaw Classroom** approach to team-based classroom learning (www.jigsaw.org) is based on the simple recognition that cooperative, socially intelligent learning can be strengthened by ensuring that the participants in teamwork each make unique contributions. It responded to a perceived epidemic of competitive behaviour and attitudes in schools in the US. Group project participants are each given a different part of the problem to work on, so that each develops and offers a part-solution and, in the process, learns about the value of cooperation, as well as developing self-esteem, and respect for participants (Aronson and Patnoe, 1997; Aronson, 2004).

The **Building Hope for the Future** programme was a five-week intervention to promote hope, life satisfaction, self-worth, mental health, and academic achievement in middle school students, going beyond the level of the individual mind to include key players in the social environment – parents, teachers, and school peers. In an 18-month follow-up, improved hope, life satisfaction, and self-worth were observed (Marques et al, 2010).

The **RULER Approach** (http://therulerapproach.org) was developed by positive psychologists at Yale University, focused on helping pupils to: Recognise emotions in themselves and others; Understand the causes and consequences of emotions; and Label, Express, and Regulate emotions. Studies have indicated significant benefits in academic performance, reduction in behavioural problems, improvement in school climate, and better social skills.

For further examples (albeit mainly remedial and preventive ones), see: Rathvon, 2008; Clauss-Ehlers, 2009; Peacock et al, 2009; Macklem, 2011.

Few people have had more influence on western schooling systems in recent years than the psychological journalist Daniel Goleman, whose 1995 book *Emotional intelligence* has sold millions of copies. Goleman was a co-founder of the Collaborative for Academic, Social and Emotional Learning in the US, which has been helping North American and European schools to introduce emotional literacy courses and monitor the emotional experience of pupils. In the UK, Goleman's influence is evident in the government's *Social and Emotional Aspects of Learning* (SEAL) programme, which encourages schools at all levels to incorporate promotion of social and emotional capabilities throughout the curriculum (Department for Children, Schools, and Families, 2005). Consistent with the downplaying of happiness in schooling systems, even this programme has paid remarkably little attention to happiness or even pupil satisfaction. It was justified, and has been evaluated, on the grounds not that it would enhance happiness but that better emotional capabilities would enhance academic success. This is eerily reminiscent of the 'social capital' movement in international development, which similarly got its values backward by seeing social goods mainly in terms of their instrumental use for 'the economy' (Thin, 2002, chapter 5).

The SEAL programme is described by Carol Craig (Director of the Centre for Confidence and Wellbeing and Chair of the European

Network of Positive Pychologists) as a 'mass psychological intervention' based on a 'feel good' ethic similar to the self-esteem movement in the US. She subjects it to several ravaging critiques, accusing it of lacking a serious evidence base; of raising unrealistic expectations of teachers' psychotherapeutic capabilities and psychological knowledge; of reacting too hastily to ill-founded beliefs in a national 'depression epidemic'; and of naïve deployment of questionable concepts such as 'emotional literacy' and 'self-esteem'. Craig concludes by arguing, reasonably enough, that 'teachers' contribution to young people's wellbeing is first and foremost as teachers, not as surrogate psychologists or mental health workers' (Craig, 2009). Ecclestone and Hayes similarly argued vociferously against the mainstreaming of psychotherapeutic approaches in schools in their book *The dangerous rise of therapeutic education*, which goes further and argues against any 'prioritisation of the emotions in learning', in favour of traditional, knowledge-focused lessons (2008).

But these critics seem too hasty in appearing to condemn out of hand any efforts to persuade educationalists to pay serious attention to those crucial life skills that give us emotional rather than merely academic or vocational capabilities. 'Happiness lessons' may well not be the ideal way to promote emotional well-being, but like it or not, teachers have responsibilities not just for children's knowledge but for their happiness. With or without explicit happiness policies, schools affect children's well-being for better or worse, and the quality of children's emotional and cognitive experiences are inextricably intertwined. Simply relying on teachers' own intuitions regarding children's emotional development is not a responsible approach to schooling.

A much more sympathetic response to the Layard/Positive Psychology view that schooling can be improved through happiness lessons is offered in the British educational philosopher Harry Brighouse's book *On education* (2005), which argues that schools can be significantly improved by taking happiness seriously, applying lessons from Happiness Studies, and actively promoting happiness (broadly conceived as 'flourishing') through both curricular and extra-curricular changes. Without going into much detail on specific evidence for specific changes, he puts forward persuasive common-sense arguments for including attention to happiness in traditional school subject lessons, in new kinds of classes on family life, leisure, and work (arguing against the tradition of steering children towards ambitions for paid employment). Schools mainly facilitate flourishing, he argues, by building children's sense of autonomy and civic engagement, and much of this can be done through extra-curricular activities and through the school ethos. Reviewers have reasonably pointed out weaknesses in

Brighouse's confusingly inconsistent and weak conceptual treatment of happiness and flourishing (White, 2006; Warnick, 2009), but the arguments nonetheless look strong enough to provoke useful debates about whether schools can actively promote happiness, how, and under what kind of rubric.

Box 12.2: Tools for assessing happiness in schools

The **Students' Life Satisfaction Scale** is a seven-item global life satisfaction self-report measure for children in grades 3 to 12, eliciting views on general statements like 'My life is going well' and 'I would like to change things in my life', rather than any specific life domains (Huebner, 1991).

The **Multidimensional Students' Life Satisfaction Scale** is a 40-item questionnaire on young people's experiences of various life domains (school, family, friends, self) (Huebner, 1994).

The **Student Engagement Instrument** is a 35-item self-report structured on six factors: teacher–student relationships; control and relevance of schoolwork; peer support for learning; aspirations and goals; family support for learning; and extrinsic motivation (this last one involving two negative items: reliance for motivation on rewards offered by parents or by teachers) (Appleton et al, 2006).

The **Quality of School Life** was developed in Scotland to expand school assessment to include the role of schools in facilitating 'non-intellectual' goods; it consists of 56 items organised in 14 domains, including academic issues such as curriculum, attainment, and teaching, plus personal needs, school ethos, relationships, and environmental factors (Karatzias et al, 2001).

The **Quality of Life Profile – Adolescent Version** is a 54-item questionnaire developed in Canadian schools for health applications. It is grouped in nine subdomains: Being (physical, psychological, and spiritual); Belonging (physical, social, and community); and Becoming (practical, leisure, and growth). On each item separate importance and enjoyment ratings are collected (Raphael et al, 1996).

The **High School Survey of Student Engagement** (http://ceep.indiana. edu/hssse/index.htm) was developed in 2003 by Indiana University's Center for Evaluation & Education Policy and has now covered over 300,000 individuals in 40 states in the US. Assessments are grouped under three headings: Cognitive/ Intellectual/Academic Engagement; Social/Behavioral/ Participatory Engagement; and Emotional Engagement (Yazzie-Mintz, 2010).

The **Comprehensive School Climate Inventory** (CSCI) (www.schoolclimate. org/programs/csci.php) is widely used in the US to assess 12 essential aspects of school climate in four broad categories: safety, teaching and learning, relationships, and the institutional environment. No questions ask directly about happiness, but some assess feelings concerning safety and resolution of arguments.

Schooling in non-western countries

Almost all the world's research on happiness in school, and on schooling's effects on happiness, has been conducted in rich western countries. In non-western countries, educational ambitions and evaluations are much less likely to be linked with happiness concerns. This is partly due to poverty and the higher parental priority of basic needs provision and basic schooling (Bennett and Grimley, 2000, pp 101–2). But it would be wrong to assume that, as non-western countries get richer and post-materialist values begin to take hold, parents and teachers will quickly begin prioritising happiness. Even in the moderately rich Asian countries, mainstream schooling largely proceeds as if neither pupil happiness nor prospects for lifelong happiness matter, although in recent years substantial numbers of academic articles on schooling and happiness have begun appearing (not yet translated into English) in Chinese and Japanese journals. Dundes et al (2009) have found that East Asians studying in the US are mainly guided by their mothers in their educational choices and ambitions, and that happiness is low on the priority list, as compared with success in cognitive tests and subsequent earnings and status. This kind of attitude has often been reported in East Asia, and in China in 2001 the controversy surrounding Zhou Hong's autobiographical text on bringing up his daughter to be happy rather than successful by other criteria (*I'm mediocre, I'm happy*), and the contrastively popular reception of a best-selling book celebrating academic ambition (*Harvard girl*), showed that in contemporary China the idea of educating for happiness has little popular appeal (Eckholm, 2002; cf Chua, 2011). With educational ambitions so completely unhinged from concerns about personal happiness, and educational competitiveness so prone to inflation, it is small wonder that in China educational achievement is negatively correlated with life satisfaction (Solnicka et al, 2007, p 539).

But let us be clear: the shortage of research and policy based on evidence of pupil satisfaction in poorer countries is not for want of funds. There has for many decades been plenty of aid-funded and local government-funded business to be found for researchers willing to explore other aspects of educational systems. The reluctance to conduct research on schooling and happiness betrays institutionalised disrespect, even in the world's supposedly child-friendly agencies, for the feelings and opinions of children. This contradicts both pedagogical and humanitarian values. What explains this baffling lack of researchers' and policy makers' interest in something so obviously of both intrinsic and instrumental value as pupils' happiness, educational motivation, and enjoyment of schooling?

The key culprit seems to be the dominance of the 'human capital' metaphor in justifications of educational investments since the 1960s. Unlike a happiness-aware approach to schooling, which would surely start by appreciating and assessing the immediate expected contributions of schooling to children's happiness, the 'human capital' approach implicitly instrumentalises childhood and devalues children's well-being, treating childhood as an 'investment' in favour of adulthood instead of as an intrinsically valued life phase. Policy makers have listened eagerly to economists' often extravagant claims about measurable 'returns to education', treating schooling merely as a means to achieve a restrictive set of measurable outcomes (Colclough et al, 2009). Hanushek's (2008) review of evidence on schooling, gender equity, and economic outcomes rightly criticises the prevalence of misplaced confidence in economists' ability to infer causation from correlations between such simple items as years of schooling and subsequent earnings. Yet he too displays narrow economism by arguing for 'quality' (measured solely as cognitive attainment) on grounds of 'payoffs' (measured as income and economic growth). Relying on the 'human capital' metaphor, he treats children as vehicles for parental and/or state investments, ignoring both the intrinsic value of an enjoyable childhood and the instrumental value of schooling in facilitating lifelong happiness. Small wonder that economics is still commonly known as the 'dismal science'.

It is not just economists, though, who in practice take this dismal view of schooling. Even Bhutan, with its long-standing and loud-hailed commitment to a national 'Gross National Happiness' policy, has come nowhere near integrating happiness considerations systematically into its education system. In its periodic nationwide assessments of performance in education it pays no attention to the happiness or satisfactions of pupils, teachers, or parents (Government of Bhutan, 2002). A one-off study of education, part of a wider 'national happiness' research effort, briefly explored statistical evidence of pupil and parent satisfaction with schooling, and of links between education and happiness more generally (Wangdi, 2008). Beyond that, Bhutan conforms to the global pattern of taking pupils' subjectivity largely for granted when assessing their schooling.

In China, it is at first glance tempting to read signs of happiness policy into the government's efforts to promote new approaches to 'quality' and 'creativity' in schooling. These heavy-handed and ill-fated policies were knee-jerk reactions to many years of obsession with test scores that have seen millions of children forced by parents and teachers into absurdly long hours of rote learning. State efforts to reduce homework and cramming have been strongly resisted by teachers and parents (Niu, 2007). But in any case, there is no sign that an interest in happiness has played any direct role in educational reform attempts. Ironically, efforts at reducing competitive cramming by pupils have been targeted at the promotion of creativity not for its intrinsic value but in order to produce adults who can compete better in the global marketplace.

Perhaps schooling promotes happiness without needing happiness policies or evidence of pupil satisfaction. But in Asia and the rest of the world there is inconclusive evidence concerning happiness–education correlations. Several studies, like the above China example, have found negative correlations. Veenhoven's (1984) comprehensive review of happiness studies worldwide found some evidence that in poor countries more educated people tended to report higher levels of happiness or life satisfaction, but he also noted a lack of evidence for common claims that schools *cause* greater happiness (for example, through character building), and noted that schooling can foster discontent in poorer countries by promoting unrealistic aspirations. Meinert's ethnography of schooling in Uganda since 1997 shows that there remains widespread faith in the benefits of universal schooling in Uganda, but that many also suffer deep disappointments because of frustrated ambitions, particularly among boys whose hopes of lucrative jobs had been unrealistically raised (2009, p 15). Causality can be researched through longitudinal studies, like the Gansu Survey of Children and Families (Zhang, 2011), which is studying the development of rural children's welfare outcomes and relationships among education, health, and psychosocial development. We shall have to wait to learn what this, and perhaps other longitudinal studies, can teach us about the links between schooling and happiness in countries that have universalised schooling much more recently and rapidly than in the west.

Consistent with the 'human capital' approach discussed above, Boissiere's review of factors influencing outcomes of primary schooling in poor countries defines 'desirable outcomes' as 'completing primary school with the acquisition of basic knowledge and skills' (Boissiere,

2004, p 1). This adult–centred approach implies that, for adults, it is enough that their children satisfy the aesthetic requirement of a childhood spent in school and the instrumental requirement that they acquire capabilities for later life. By contrast, a child–centred approach sees childhood as an inherently valuable period of life (Ben–Arieh, 2006, p 7). In that perspective, schooling then becomes important for the part it plays in facilitating good childhoods, not just good adulthood. Or, with reference to the above classification of influences on well-being, it becomes important for its *direct* influence on pupil well-being, and for its *indirect* influence on childhood well-being more generally. As Leanne Johnny points out in her review of children's voice in education policy (2006), Article 12 of the UN Convention on the Rights of the Child holds that young people have a right to participate in matters affecting them, yet this participatory principle has proved difficult to implement in schools worldwide.

There is, to conclude, no reason to suggest that happiness is any less relevant as an educational issue in poorer countries than in richer ones. While no one has a right to happiness, if all the world's children have a right to schooling, they also have a right to have their happiness given careful consideration by anyone who has a role in the provision of their schooling. They are, as Spring puts it in his global review of schooling, 'entitled to school practices that promote their health and happiness' (2007, p 38).

Discussion points

- Research and policies on schooling worldwide have paid little attention to happiness either as an outcome of schooling or as an aspect of educational processes. Even the growing diversity of work on 'psychosocial' or 'social-emotional' aspects of learning tends to be pathological and remedial rather than aimed at promoting the happiness of all pupils.
- A happiness perspective in school research and practice would respect the intrinsic and instrumental value of pupils' happiness; enquire into how schools promote or inhibit lifetime happiness; and introduce the serious study of happiness into the school curriculum.
- Western countries have recently been introducing happiness themes and positive psychological experiments into schooling, though often in a piecemeal manner. Mainstream policies and evaluations remain excessively focused on academic performance, in-school pathologies, and labour market outcomes.

- In non-western countries, even in richer ones and in programmes and evaluations funded by aid donors from western countries, there has been little formal attention to happiness as an aspect or outcome of schooling. Cost and lack of expertise are not the main deterrents: there are cheap and simple methods for happiness promotion and assessment that could comfortably be included within the rapidly increasing investments in schooling.

Key readings

Gilman, R., Furlong, M. and Huebner, E.S. (eds) (2009) *Handbook of positive psychology in schools*, London: Routledge.

Newell, R.J. and Van Ryzin, M.J. (2008) *Assessing what really matters in school*, Lanham, MD: Rowman & Littlefield.

Noddings, N. (2003) *Happiness and education*, Cambridge: Cambridge University Press.

Schuller, T. et al (eds) (2004) *The benefits of learning: The impact of education on health, family life and social capital*, London: RoutledgeFalmer.

Spring, J.H. (2007) *A new paradigm for global school systems: Education for a long and happy life*, London: Routledge.

Stradling, J. (2004) *Educating for the good life*, Cresskill, NJ: Hampton Press.

THIRTEEN

New gender agendas: feel-good feminism for fun and fulfilment

Are not women of the harem more happy than women voters? Is not the housekeeper happier than the working-woman? It is not too clear what the word happy really means and still less what true values it may mask? (Simone de Beauvoir, *The second sex*)

The 20th-century disdain for happiness is well exemplified by the history of feminism. Whereas George Eliot complained in *Mill on the floss* that 'the happiest women, like the happiest nations, have no history', and John Stuart Mill in *The subjection of women* (1869) argued that women's 'real path of success and happiness' lay in liberating them to pursue hitherto male-dominated activities, de Beauvoir – like many feminists of the 20th century – preferred to keep feminism and happiness apart. Happiness was a deceitful promise used to legitimise injustice, and women should instead pursue justice for its own sake. Some people find it necessary to keep the pursuit of justice and the pursuit of happiness in separate compartments, and the dominance of their voices over much of the last hundred years is nowhere more evident than in the history of feminism. But if the pursuit of gender justice is to be appealing and effective, it has to persuade people – women and men – that it will bring happiness, and that the process will be enjoyable.

The potentially radical influence of a happiness lens is nowhere more compelling than in the policy theme of gender reform. Yet nowhere are the moral quandaries of happiness policy more evident than in efforts to link gender reform to happiness. Most happiness scholars have steered clear of offering advice to gender reformers, and most modern feminists have avoided happiness themes like the plague.

Gender reform studies and campaigns are rarely based on claims that women are in general unhappier than men, or that changing gender arrangements would make women or men happier. It would be comforting if we could clearly demonstrate that happiness (or even just women's happiness) increases with every advance towards gender justice. But because this has been hard to demonstrate in the face of lots of contradictory evidence, the typical response of the gender reformer has been simply to proceed without reference to happiness, as if it were irrelevant to ask whether reform improves happiness. There has been even less attention to the equally intriguing question of whether efforts to promote happiness might help in the fight to promote gender justice and reduce gender-based harm. Is unhappiness not a key cause of bullying among adults, as we know it is among children? If so, might happiness policies not be an effective part of efforts to achieve social justice?

Feminists have good reason to be worried about the threats posed by happiness studies to feminist assumptions about injustice. Feminism has always emphasised the sufferings of women, and has generally had a reputation among both women and men for being puritanical and anti-fun − a reputation challenged by various renegade and populist 'fun feminist' and 'sex-positive feminist' movements (Braithwaite, 2002; Queen and Comella, 2008). Yet worldwide, despite all the adverse discriminations they face, women have a cunning habit of confounding feminist expectations by not only living longer than men but also reporting levels of enjoyment and life satisfaction that are equal to or better than men's (Diener, 2003). In one study, out of 51 countries surveyed, women reported higher happiness levels than men in 48, and were generally happier with their sex lives and with their partners than men were with theirs (Nielsen Wire, 2008). Despite numerous persistent forms of workplace gender inequity, women typically report higher work satisfaction than men do (Clark, 1997), and part-time women workers tend to be happy with both their work status and their work–life balance (Warr and Clapperton, 2010, p 82). You could go through many hundreds of texts under 'gender' or 'women' and 'mental health' rubrics without finding any reference to these intriguing findings. They are of course not uncontroversial, but they surely merit discussion because they do at least remind us that not all gender inequities work against women, as feminists have tended to assume. Often men's unfair access to jobs, money, and power doesn't afford them more enjoyable or more satisfying lives. Indeed the pursuit of 'masculine' success often shortens men's lives and makes them more miserable and unhealthy (Courtenay, 2000). Why, then, would women want to copy men?

On the other hand, just because women tend to lead long and happy lives doesn't mean that we should be complacent about the appalling prevalence of gender-based violence and gender inequalities in access to education, jobs, land titles and so on. When seeking moral justification for gender justice, 'the key seems to lie ... not in what people want, or in what they possess, but in what they do' (Annas, 1993, p 284). That is, women may be satisfied and have all the goods and rights they need, but their agency may still be impaired by gender norms that prevent them from flourishing in ways that they are theoretically capable of. A different argument against too close a linkage between gender reform and happiness is that both may be raising unrealistic aspirations. It has been observed in Bangladesh and India that women beneficiaries of apparently successful 'empowerment' interventions by NGOs have heightened levels of anxiety that can end up depriving them of both happiness and sense of agency (van Kempen, 2009). A different version of the worrisome aspirations argument is the claim that unhappiness is rising in rich countries because of the false happiness promises of modernity:

> The feminist revolution in the West has raised women's expectations of wellbeing beyond possible attainment in the short period since the movement was launched. (Lane, 2000, p 323)

It is of course naïve to expect the social upheavals of gender reform to proceed without tears. But if there have been trade-offs rather than only positive synergies between justice and happiness – if modernity's radical rethinking of gender relations may have been damaging to happiness – it is best that we try to understand how this has happened, rather than pretend that it doesn't matter. In a review of evidence from General Social Surveys in the US, plus some European multi-country surveys, the economists Stevenson and Wolfers (2007) have argued that while men in richer countries have actually been getting slightly happier, women's happiness has either flatlined or declined from an earlier position of greater happiness than men's. Alan Krueger has similarly found that while men are spending more time than before on activities they enjoy, the reverse is true for women in the US (Krueger, 2007). If so, this isn't really the kind of 'gender equalisation' that feminists had in mind. Antifeminist backlashers are already gleefully using it to justify conservative arguments: feminism, rather than inept governance and continued gender-inequalities, then gets blamed for causing women's anxieties and their excessive workloads, the dysfunctional family, and both women's and men's role confusions. Perhaps it does so in part because the movement hasn't in general been 'about happiness' (Mohler, 2009), but as feminist journalist Susan Faludi clearly demonstrated, the tactic of blaming feminism for women's unhappiness has been cynically deployed in the US throughout the past century (1991/2006, chapter 4).

Another compelling gender-and-happiness story comes from Russia. This is one of the few countries in the world where women tend to report themselves significantly less happy than men. Since female disadvantage doesn't correlate systematically with inequality in women's and men's self-reported happiness, there must be other factors behind women's unhappiness in Russia. The story becomes much stranger when you notice gender inequality in life expectancy: *Russian women live on average 12 years longer than men* (75 vs 63 in 2010). Men die younger, mainly due to alcoholism and stress, both of which tend to be associated with lower happiness levels. Who, then, fares better: the women, who have much longer but slightly less happy lives, or the men, who are perhaps happier (or maybe just say so out of bravado) but die 12 years younger? No doubt a great deal of the disparity in happiness scores is attributable to the fact that a high proportion of the women surveyed are suffering in extreme poverty, having lost male bread-winners and loved ones. This is an important reminder of why the rethinking of gender must be approached holistically and not as a competition to see who can bring about the quickest wins for women.

It is extraordinary that the United Nations, following the lead of the Nobel Prize winner Amartya Sen, has institutionalised the idea (in its Gender Development Index – see for example Dijkstra, 2006) that a five-year longevity gap in favour of women is desirable worldwide. Not only is this repugnantly unfair to men (turning highly suspect assumptions about 'natural' longevity into a moral value), but it ignores the fact that long years of widowhood are not generally ideal for women's happiness. So is male longevity disadvantage necessarily just an embarrassment, the recognition of which would undermine the case for gender reform? Not at all. Though the reasons for premature male mortalities are many, culturally highly variable, and no doubt underexplored, a common pattern worldwide is for male gender roles and gender identities to play a significant part. Propositions for gender reform ought to be given a massive new impetus if it becomes more widely recognised that culturally constructed gender arrangements are sending many millions of men to an early grave every year. If women seem to hold important 'secrets' of how to be happy despite adversity, and therefore have much to teach men about how to enjoy life, it may be just as instructive to note that they have much to teach men about how to stay alive.

A happiness lens can help us to address three kinds of bias that persist in gender reform policy, and in some but not all variants of gender scholarship, namely: *negativity*, *gynocentrism*, and the *neglect of feelings*. Between them, these seriously constrain the purposes and effectiveness of gender reform, if we agree that its purpose ought to be to facilitate better lives for everyone:

- **Negativity:** This has two connected forms – *gender-disapproval*, and *abolitionism*. Gender reformers tend to treat gender as a source of problems and unfairness, something to fight against rather than a cultural resource to work with. This is unrealistic: whether we interpret it as largely biological or as largely cultural, gender difference is a source of a great deal of what is most enjoyable and interesting in life. Naturalised assumptions about gender inequalities do often need to be challenged, but promotion of endless discomfort with gender identity is hardly a recipe for happiness.
- **Gynocentrism:** Ironically, *gender studies and gender reform are often gender blind and hence inept and socially irresponsible.* Among researchers, policy makers, and social movements alike, gender themes worldwide remain unrealistically seen as a female domain – by women, about women, for women. This will continue so long as women and men see gender campaigns primarily in terms of tackling female disadvantages. Because we are a sexually dimorphic and strongly interdependent species, a humanist approach to gender reform requires us to address both female and male disadvantages and to see both of these as equally worrying for both women and men.
- **Neglect of feeling:** Despite the common belief that women are more interesting and eloquent on the subject of emotions than men are, gender theorists pay remarkably little attention to how women (and men) actually feel about the various bad gender arrangements that are being criticised. Feminists tend to rail against inadequate access to resources or justice, inadequate power vis-à-vis men, inadequate choice, and so on, without any evidence of women's unhappiness or domain dissatisfactions. Gender progress is evaluated with regard to 'objective', readily observable interim goods, rather than subjective progress towards happiness.

One poignantly ironic outcome of all three biases has been a tendency of gender reformers to assume that because 'male' privileges are unfairly denied to women, smashing this barrier will make women's lives better. Some areas of male cultural traditions are clearly better for both women and men: comfortable trousers and sensible shoes are better for health and mobility than tight skirts and high heels, for example. But are women really advantaged by joining and emulating male competition for power, money, and prestige? To be socially responsible, feminists require plausible theories, preferably supported by evidence, of how the changes they propose would improve the lives of everyone. They will do no one any favours by ignoring the evidence of female happiness in situations of disadvantage and assuming that removal of disadvantages will make them happier still. Instead, female happiness could be celebrated and examined as an extraordinary achievement, and hence offering justification for promoting more 'feminine' approaches to life. That would be a truly 'radical' approach to gender reform.

These three kinds of bias, I should stress, are collective, institutionalised biases. As individuals, women tend not to show any of these three feminist biases. They have a positive, hopeful outlook: though women's aspirations can be blighted, women still want to live well, not just to avoid harm. They are sociocentric and convivial, wanting to engage in positive relationships with men as well as women. They are certainly very interested in feelings, and in many cultures, including western ones, are believed to be more naturally empathetic than men are (Strauss, 2004). Women are not only very interested in love and happiness, but in many ways and in many parts of the world they are expected to be more expert in these matters than are men (Fischer and Manstead, 2000). In western countries, both sadness and happiness 'are stereotypically associated with girls and women' (Kelly and Hutson-Comeaux, 2000), and several psychological studies have found women more disposed to emotional self-disclosure and/or to more frequent expression of happiness than men are (Alexander and Wood, 2000). And women would like men to care more about emotions: based on survey of 5,000 women in the US, Wilcox and Nock (2006) found that male emotional investment mattered far more for women's marital happiness than equality, and that housewives were significantly happier with their marriages, on average, than employed women.

The association of femininity with respect for emotional experience is so widely accepted that when the social psychologist Hofstede promoted the multicultural study of cultural values in workplaces worldwide (1999) he labelled cultural contexts as 'masculine' or 'feminine' according to the extent to which employees' goals reflected 'masculine' values such as earning high wages, being recognised for achievements, making a career, having challenges, or 'feminine' values such as good working relationships with superiors and colleagues, pleasant environment, and good quality of life.

Building on this somewhat overambitious concept, Arrindell and Veenhoven (2003) found that national average scores for self-reported happiness and longevity (combined as 'Happy Life-Expectancy') correlate positively, among rich countries but not among poor countries, with high scores for cultural 'femininity'. Thus, happy life-years are lower than expected in rich 'masculine' cultures (for example Japan, Austria, Venezuela) where political/organisational values emphasise material success and assertiveness, and higher than expected in rich 'feminine' cultures (for example Sweden, Norway, the Netherlands) that prioritise welfare, interpersonal relationships, and sympathy and concern for the weak. Arrindell and Veenhoven speculate that part of the causal pathway between cultural 'femininity' and happiness may be stress reduction, particularly the reduction of work stress. Other possibilities include the macro-level effect of feminine values in providing better gender flexibility, hence more choice in employment, marriage, parenthood, the possible benefits of multiple social roles in themselves, and the more diffuse benefits of a caring social system.

This kind of evidence is vitally important as a complement to the frequent finding that women's multiple gender disadvantages don't tend to be reflected in gender inequalities in happiness. It reminds us that gender matters for everyone's happiness and life expectancy, and that therefore we need more holistic, less piecemeal and partisan approaches to gender reform. The feminist philosopher Alison Jaggar has argued that promoters of 'feminist ethics' often saw this as challenging 'masculinist' biases in western thought, by paying more attention to things that matter to women, including: 'culturally feminine traits like ... connection, sharing, emotion ... process, joy, peace, and life'. Possible ethnocentrisms aside, it is noteworthy that her argument in favour of increased ethical recognition for happiness and love is a *feminist* claim on ethical discourse (Jaggar, 1992/2001, p 530). I agree strongly with her ethical position, but I find it hard to imagine how she saw the promotion of happiness and love as typical of feminism. Heterosexual love and parental love have awkward status within feminism as issues to worry about rather than values to uphold, although some feminists have, of course, had a lot to say about love, emotion, and relationships. Happiness, on the other hand, has never been a prominent feminist concern.

Strong moral objections have often been made to happiness policy on the grounds of the 'happy oppressed woman' dilemma, which is a version of the Marxian 'false consciousness' argument. People may be genuinely happy despite, or even because of, their positive illusions about the moral acceptability of their objectively bad situation. Since poor and oppressed people tend to adapt to their adverse situations, what matters is that policies afford people equitable opportunity to achieve good lives, rather than (only) making people happy. It is certainly essential for any promoters of happiness policies to consider the moral hazards posed by hedonic adaptation, and to remember that development policy is about good societies as well as enjoyable lives (Nussbaum, 2000, chapter 2; Annas, 1993, p 282).

Nonetheless, these moral hazards are an absurdly lame excuse for keeping happiness indicators and happiness considerations out of the policy process. Neglect of happiness itself poses a serious set of moral hazards. Remember, the happiness lens is an insistence on ethical transparency: anyone who claims to work for social justice while rejecting or neglecting happiness (and consequently treating subjectivity as irrelevant and unreliable) must surely be suspected of paternalism, blind dogma, and downright empathy failure. And moralisers do neglect happiness – most of the time, in most parts of the world.

My proposal here is that gender reform can become not only more constructive and more effective, but also considerably more radical, by seeing the promotion of love and happiness as central to its mission and its strategies. But if gender scholarship and gender policy are happiness blind, are happiness studies and happiness policies reciprocally gender blind? Here, the picture is more mixed. Certainly, it is standard practice for happiness survey analysis and other happiness studies to offer gender-disaggregated information and analysis. Still, the literature on happiness has so far tended to generalise for all human beings, and has had remarkably little to say either about gender differences in happiness levels, appraisals, conceptions, and pathways, or about the ways in which different kinds of gender arrangement may influence the happiness of women and men. To my knowledge, no major monograph or collection of essays on happiness or positive psychology has yet devoted a whole chapter to gender relations or gender reform.

To situate happiness within the broad field of gender reform, it may help to identify some plausible if vague objectives and principles that most reformers would agree on:

- Gender reform is about promoting *wisdom* (especially by increasing gender-awareness), *well-being* (better lives, especially for women and girls), *justice* (fairer societies), and *conviviality* (better relationships, especially cross-gender ones).
- Everyone (not just women) can benefit from better gender arrangements.
- Feelings matter, and must be assessed within domains as well as holistically: to study subjective well-being, that is, happiness, we must ask people how they feel about domains of experience (paid work, care work, housework, intimacy, leisure, and so on), and about their lives as a whole.

- Enquiries into fairness and inequality should include (without being restricted to this) assessment of the distribution of happiness – how happily people live, and for how long.
- Since gender reform is fundamentally about relationships, and since love is a core value in good relationships, we must also look for positive synergies between love and any changes we may hope for in gender arrangements.

Table 13.1 presents a plausible starting-point for analysis of how gender reform might enhance the goods that all humans have reason to value. The intention here is to pave the way for new variants of happiness-focused gender reform by situating both Happiness Studies and Gender Studies within the broader arena of the goods we ultimately have reason to desire. The point is not to suggest that wisdom, well-being, conviviality, and justice are best seen only as outcomes: they are also all important means to achieving other goods. Rather, the point is to render more transparent our implicit theories about how changes in gender arrangements should translate into better lives.

Table 13.1: Gender reform and ultimate values

	Wisdom	Well-being	Conviviality	Justice
Deficits addressed	Attention deficits due to androcentric or ethnocentric worldviews	Ill-health and unhappiness	Mistrust, discord, disparagement	Undeserved inequality (especially female disadvantages)
Gender theory	Collective wisdom increases through improved awareness of gender, and complementing knowledge of/about men with knowledge of/about women	Women's (and men's/children's) lives improve through gender awareness and gender justice	Love, trust, respect, and empathy increase by reducing gender segregation and prejudice	Society gets fairer as female disadvantage is minimised
Modern social experimentation with gender	Gender awareness: making people think about gender and discuss gender options in detached and critical ways	Gender freedom: increasing personal autonomy and well-being by challenging the restrictiveness of biological sex, gender roles, and gender identity ascriptions	Gender mingling: challenging the universality of gender segregation, so as to promote gender harmony	Gender justice: challenging the unfairness of gender inequality
Critical questions	How realistic are reformers in promoting the belief that gender is culturally constructed and hence changeable? Are male privileges really as advantageous as they appear?	Is feminism too pathological? Does it treat all gender difference as bad? Could it be enriched by exploring good lives, good relations, and good gender?	Where feminism promotes animosity, mistrust, and new segregations, is this just a transitional problem? Does co-education lead to better cross-gender relations?	Does attention to female disadvantage entail inattention to male gender-based disadvantage?

Discussion points

- Feminists largely forgot to theorise happiness in the 20th century. Yet feminist challenges to injustice and to masculinist attitudes in many domains of life can and should benefit everyone, including men. The happiness lens could have a radical influence in reviving feminism, but it will be resisted by those who see feminism as an essentially gloomy, win–lose struggle against injustice.
- There is clear evidence that the pursuit of gender justice and women's empowerment can lead to new sources of unhappiness in both women and men. This moral hazard must be addressed by careful attention to the happiness outcomes of interventions.
- Despite their many unfair disadvantages, women's self-reported happiness in most countries of the world is higher than men's, and they live longer. This paradox implies under-recognised strengths and hidden advantages enjoyed by women. By seeking to appreciate these, gender reform efforts can become more *positive*, pay more attention to *feelings*, and include *both women and men* as participants and intended beneficiaries.
- Reported happiness is lower than expected in so-called 'masculine' cultures that emphasise material success and assertiveness. The unhappiness of both men and women is strongly linked with bad gender arrangements, both as a cause (for example of domestic violence) and as an outcome (restrictions on both men's and women's freedom to flourish, failure to develop cultures and institutions supporting equitable work–life harmony for both sexes).
- So far, efforts to make feminism and gender reform appeal to younger generations have tended to be confined to the marginal appeal of 'fun feminism' in the 'sex-positive' movement.

Key readings

Gerson, K. (2010) *The unfinished revolution: How a new generation is reshaping family, work, and gender in America*, New York: Oxford University Press.

Held, V. (2005) *The ethics of care*, Oxford: Oxford University Press.

Lynch, K., Baker, J. and Lyons, M. (2009) *Affective equality: Love, care and injustice*, London: Palgrave Macmillan.

FOURTEEN

Working for happiness, happily working, and work–life harmony

Work is much more fun than fun. (Noel Coward)

Workplace happiness: prioritising process over products

From the biblical envy of the placid contentment of the 'lilies of the field' ('they toil not, neither do they spin') to Bentham's insistence that 'love of labour is a contradiction in terms', work has tended to be portrayed as antithetical to happiness. Browsing the section titles of Keith Thomas's *Oxford book of work* (1999), you learn that work can be defined as 'intrinsically unpleasant', as 'physical compulsion', and as 'economic necessity', but also as the 'creator of civilisation', as 'the distinguishing human attribute', 'the pleasures of occupation' or 'a remedy for grief', and even as 'the only sure route to human happiness'.

The covers of happiness books (like this one) are far more likely to show people at leisure and play than people at work. Yet the study of workplace happiness is one of the most advanced and long-established branches of happiness scholarship. The scientific study of work satisfaction has been going on for more than 50 years in many countries. Just as wider society has been debating the meaning of prosperity, so in the workplace there has been substantial rethinking of what a 'good' job or a 'good' company is, going well beyond the routine scrutiny of basic pay and conditions. Though touted as radically new in the 1980s for emphasising that 'the first concern of the company is the happiness of people who are connected with it', the Japanese 'total quality management' guru Kaoru Ishikawa (1985) was reiterating a long-standing focus of managerial interest, albeit one that has tended to be subsidiary to profit and productivity.

Work can be our most significant source of meaning, our best opportunity for 'flow' or for social engagement, or a necessary evil endured for the delayed rewards bought with the pay. Consider one of the standard 'light bulb' jokes of the 1980s:

> How many hairdressers does it take to change a lightbulb?
> Six. One to change the bulb, and five to stand around
> gasping 'You're doing a lovely job there Gary'.

It turns out that in UK work satisfaction surveys, hairdressers are happiest (http://news.bbc.co.uk/1/hi/business/4296975.stm). Perhaps this is attributable to the intrinsic merits of the occupation, or to the self-selection of happy people to that kind of job. But in light of considerable research on the importance of workplace relationships and sociality for both job satisfaction and happiness (see for example Shirom, 2002, pp 257–9; Waddel and Burton, 2006; Blustein, 2011) it seems more than likely that it has a lot to do with the social climate of the workplace.

Perhaps if we could all relate to each other like the six Garys we'd all be happy at work. I count myself lucky to have spent 23 years doing fulfilling and enjoyable work with the same university employer. Yet in all those years none of my managers, nor even the university's army of 'human resource' specialists or mental health committees, has ever thought to ask me about how happy I am with my work, whether I enjoy some aspect of my work or workplace more than others, or whether my work harmonises well with the rest of my life. We just muddle through without considering the possible benefits of workplace happiness research. Although probably everybody would prefer to enjoy work and to find it meaningful, and although most employers would prefer their workforces to be happy at work, it is still only a small proportion of workers and employers that pay systematic attention to workplace happiness.

Some companies are today making the happiness of the workforce a core principle of operation, such as the John Lewis Partnership in the UK, whose constitution insists that its 'ultimate purpose is the happiness of all its members, through their worthwhile and satisfying employment in a successful business' (www.johnlewispartnership.co.uk): for it, profit has a function, but only insofar as its profits are used in support of 'activities that are consistent with its ultimate purpose'. In other words, the 'ultimate purpose' of the business is not profits, nor its services to customers (which most people agree are extremely good), but the *social processes whereby employees can enjoy their work and sustain a sense that their work is meaningful and good.*

There is a superficial echo of this kind of happiness promotion in many businesses, but just as customers should beware of commercially motivated happiness promises, so should workers. Tony Hsieh, founder of the Zappos shoe business in the US, reached No 1 in the *New York*

Times with his auto-hagiographic book *Delivering happiness* (2010). The Zappos mission statement reads: 'Zappos is about delivering happiness to the world.' Judging from Hsieh's book, the company shows some signs of quirky, happiness-related workplace policies, such as encouraging all staff to read books (particularly those recommended by Hsieh) and to participate in development of a common 'culture' (he insists that all staff are 100% committed to the ten 'core values', which include such items as 'Create fun and a little weirdness' and 'Family spirit' – a hint, here, of the ultra-pushy parentalism that Hsieh says he experienced in his own family upbringing). Judging from Hsieh's own account, the overwhelming emphasis of the business has been on the obedience rather than the happiness of workers. Hsieh autocratically relocated the whole company from San Francisco to Las Vegas at six months' notice. 'Embrace and drive change' is one of the core values, which seems to suit Hsieh but presumably played havoc with the family life of a lot of his employees. Hsieh is also proud of pleasing customers at all costs – boasting for example of his environmentally irresponsible marketing strategy 'happiness in a shoebox', which includes offering free shipping to all customers, and back again, even on multiple returned items. Workers, customers, and trees alike: beware any employer who promises 'fun and a little weirdness'.

Another US clothing magnate, Jack Mitchell, has similarly written best-selling books called *Hug your customers*, and *Hug your people*, respectively insisting that his business culture succeeds by metaphorically and literally embracing customers and workers alike. The hugging and enforced emotionalism may, of course, not travel well. In Scotland I suspect that most employees would prefer to be slapped about the chops with a soused herring than hugged by their boss. It is far from self-evident that making happiness an explicit objective of management is going to make the workforce happier. But certainly the idea that work should be fun and that business relationships can be warm and friendly is one that could catch on. As the leading researcher on workplace 'flow' argues, 'happiness and business [...] are inextricably linked. Fundamentally, business exists to enhance human well-being' (Csikszentmihalyi, 2003, p 21).

But this crucial social responsibility of employers to generate well-being via workplace happiness is easily forgotten in the pursuit of profit or of some other not necessarily well-being-focused goals, like technical excellence. Even when it is remembered, it still begs large questions about whose well-being can or should be prioritised by businesses: that of workers (and within workforces, the managers or the heavy lifters, the try-hards or the do-wells, young or old, and so on), or the customers, or the shareholders? So even this guru of positive psychology is extraordinarily pessimistic about work, claiming that 'most work is either so dull and uninspiring that doing one's best still means using less than 10 percent of one's potentiality, or is so stressful that it sucks the worker's life energy dry' (Csikszentmihalyi, 2003, p 30).

Even in work-loving cultures like the UK and North America, vocational and industrial/organisational psychology has tended to be pathological or defensive in orientation, and has become detached from mainstream psychology, just as to some extent work has, in modern societies ,detached itself from the rest of life (Quick and Tetrick 2002; Blustein, 2008). Yet we shouldn't forget that the world's most work-loving country, the US, where workers take half as much holiday as Europeans and spend much longer each day working and commuting, is also the country that produces and consumes most self-help and life-coaching instruction and has given us the 'Positive Psychology' movement. It's debatable whether US citizens work more because they find their work more enjoyable and meaningful, or whether some other factor forces them to work long hours, and to recover by reading self-help books in their brief hours of leisure.

Time affluence and autonomy

In his essay 'The original affluent society' (1974) – one of the most celebrated and controversial anthropological essays of all time – Marshall Sahlins proposed that hunter-gatherer societies might offer a most appealing model for a good society based on a supportive culture in which ample leisure time is assured by minimising people's desires. Leaving aside for a moment the question of whether Sahlins mustered reliable empirical information on hunter-gather labour (assuming they even have such a concept) to back up his claims, and just supposing he was at least half-right that hunters and gatherers have more free time than most other people in the world, is this a reliable sign that their lives are better?

Many people believe that free time is a good indicator of well-being, that in general more of it is better (see the discussion of Goodin et al, 2008, at pp 208 et seq below), and that differential ability to enjoy free time is a significant and rising form of inequality (Jacobs and Gerson, 2004). But are hunter-gatherers really happier sitting around doing nothing for most of the day than they would be if they could find meaningful work to do? Sahlins seems too quick to believe the all-too-common myth that humanity's natural preference is for idleness.

For lots of people worldwide, work is no doubt mainly a miserable experience, tolerated only because it provides income for life's necessities. And Sahlins was no doubt right to remind us that both the agricultural and industrial revolutions do seem to have required many people to work longer hours of hard and/or dull labour than they would have freely chosen. But some people enjoy gruelling or even very mundane tasks. In *Useful toil: Autobiographies of working people from the 1820s to the 1920s*, Burnett notes that

> One of the most remarkable characteristics in much of the writing is the uncomplaining acceptance of conditions of life and work which to the modern reader seem brutal, degrading and almost unimaginable ... most of those who experienced such conditions are not, in their writings at least, consciously discontented. (Burnett, 1974, p 14)

Still, the absence of discontentment doesn't signal that people in that era derived happiness from their work. Often, the feeling that we are working for pay and hence for deferred rewards gets in the way of the here and now. There is a common belief that we are 'naturally' disposed to idleness, and hence expend effort only reluctantly (Gini, 2003). And there is the problem that in many societies since the agricultural revolution, the masses have yearned to emulate the 'idle rich' elites, and so are unlikely to associate work with well-being. Even when working conditions and the match between the job and the worker are excellent, 'for many people, enjoyment is undermined by powerful negative stereotypes about work' (Nakamura and Csikszentmihalyi, 2002, p 91). Many of these people nonetheless report themselves as 'happy' overall because they see other aspects of their lives as more significant for their overall sense of self, and sufficiently compensatory to offset the ill effects of work.

One expected outcome of technological progress was that we would be able to get away with a lot fewer hours of work. Compared with 100 years ago, hours of paid employment have reduced dramatically in most countries, though not to the extent predicted by futurists in the early to mid-20th century (Lee et al, 2007). There is of course a significant 'downshifting' or 'semi-retirement' movement (Drake, 2001; Clyatt, 2007), but it hasn't resulted in major reductions in average hours of paid work. Although downshifting may often facilitate happier and more meaningful lives, despite the exuberant promises of a new rash of self-help books it doesn't necessarily follow that if you 'work less' you will 'live better', or that by leaving a job you will 'get a life'

(Jones and Ghazi, 1997): it is unrealistic to expect to find what one meaning-in-life philosopher has called 'superlative meaning' without working for it (Levy, 2005). Nor should we consider it paradoxical to regard meaningful work as a core component in happiness or 'human flourishing' (Hinchliffe, 2004). Some argue that citizens ought not just to have a right to work, but a 'right to *meaningful* work' (for a critique, see White, 1997, pp 30–5).

Technology-facilitated reductions in unpaid domestic work have been far less dramatic than many predicted, although the kind of work has shifted from drudgery to childcare and eldercare. Another, more interesting and more complex outcome, though, has been that instead of trying to minimise the number of hours we work, people are upgrading their aspirations regarding the quality of working life. Increasingly, particularly in richer societies, where people know they could survive with little or no paid employment, we are learning to expect work to provide us with some of our most rewarding experiences and with our overall sense of self-esteem and purpose in life.

Arguably, the idea of combining work with happiness is as revolutionary, and as unique to the modern era, as the idea of choosing marriage partners on the basis of romantic love. These two massive global social experiments have in common the idea that autonomy is good for happiness: work, and marriage, is good if we get to choose. Not only is it becoming more common worldwide to see work as a matter of personal choice, ideally leading to passionate dedication, it is also increasingly expected that we ought to be able to tailor our work throughout our lives to dovetail with a variety of other, non-work passions.

So instead of simply shaping our working lives around linear career paths laid out for us by employers, an increasing number of us (particularly women, but many men too) are working out our own 'kaleidoscope careers' (Mainiero and Sullivan, 2006) and, at later ages, developing 'encore careers' that tend to be more 'purpose-driven' and fulfilling than previous careers (Freedman, 2008). These options are partly pushed by job insecurities, by the pace of change, and by difficult work–family trade-offs; but they are partly also encouraged by pull factors, such as new opportunities, and ambitions to work flexibly from a variety of locations, with or without corporate employers, to adapt to new livelihood options, and to make our own job designs to suit our changing preferences and capabilities.

Employers, for their part, are increasingly feeling obliged to facilitate the happiness of the workforce, rather than just facilitating their productivity and abiding by minimal labour standards. The happy workforce requirement is seen both as *intrinsically* good and hence morally required, and as *instrumentally* good and hence required for sound rational management. Well-established though this kind of thinking now is in modern workplaces, it would be naïve to see it as the dominant global norm. Even in richer countries and in very secure companies, it is, as Jessica Pryce-Jones notes in the Prologue of her book *Happiness at work*, often downright awkward and embarrassing trying to get people to discuss workplace happiness (2010, p viii). Also, United Nations agencies are yet to show any substantial interest in happiness at work and even the International Labour Organisation's 'decent work' agenda remains focused on pathologies and minimal standards.

'Work' as a social and experiential rubric

Conversations about the relationship between work and happiness aren't helped by the fact that 'work' doesn't refer to a specific kind of entity or activity, but is a loose label used in quite different ways, depending on how societies are organised. For many people, 'work' signals the kinds of place, activity, and time allocation that are least voluntary and least life-enhancing. To the extent that it is the opposite of autonomy, work can hardly be expected to be an intrinsically enjoyable activity in autonomy-respecting cultures.

'Business' has similarly problematic connotations for happiness research, since it is often taken as a shorthand for 'for-profit' and even for 'selfish, greedy, only for-profit' organisations, in contrast to state and civic organisations, which exist to promote public goods. Hence 'mixing business and pleasure', or work and leisure, have generally been seen as unrealistic combinations. Yet there has always been a countervailing discourse that work is a key source of dignity and meaning in life, and that businesses should facilitate the happiness of workers, customers, and the general public. These more benign views of work and businesses are likely to increase, the more work is seen as optional rather than driven by necessity.

With the debatable exception of hunter-gatherer societies, most of humanity since the Neolithic era has to some extent compartmentalised experience and time into work and leisure (Veal, 2004). Often, this has involved perceiving work to be about the production of necessities, and leisure to be about the enjoyment of rewarding time off. Reproductive activities, particularly the care and enculturation of children, have never quite fitted into either of these categories. In general, happiness has been more commonly associated with non-compulsory activities pursued in discretionary time. Increasingly, however, people are recognising that 'work' isn't just a means to facilitate the pursuit of happiness, it is part of happiness, an essential core component of what we think of as the good life. This is more than just the sense that our purpose in life must involve some kind of dignified employment: it also consists, at least in richer countries, in the idea that work itself should be enjoyable, and that we should be able to integrate this well with opportunities for the enjoyment of other, non-work domains.

Increasingly, the happiness of workers and customers is being invoked as a core concern in discussions of the quality, the ethics, and the sustainability of our businesses, and of the associated challenges in family and community life, and in our relations with the material environment. Advertisers have always promised happiness to prospective customers, of course, but in ways that no intelligent person could have been expected to take seriously. All participants in consumerist societies are complicit in the agreement that businesses need to deliver not only enough customer satisfaction to sustain goodwill, but also enough dissatisfaction to rekindle the yearning that will motivate future purchases. Even self-help books and psychotherapy sessions, clothed almost entirely in the promise of happiness, must also at the same time encourage dissatisfaction if they are to enjoy repeat custom.

If, as customers, we expect to get the happiness we pay for, as workers we are likely think of our pay as 'compensation' for happiness opportunities forgone. Employers have always expressed some degree of interest in the happiness of workers, at least as an instrumental good in the interests of productivity. Only recently has this begun to be a core concern and a key criterion for the evaluation of company performance. Nonetheless, business ethics and human resource management are arguably the most advanced and long-established areas of applied Happiness Studies.

For several decades, businesses have been studying the happiness of workers with a view to making workers happy, productive, and loyal. Over 40 years ago, the sociologist Mary Robertson opened an article on 'The pursuit of happiness at work' by saying that the theme of the happiness or satisfaction of workers had been 'in the managerial repertoire for a long time' and had 'been the subject of innumerable attitude surveys' (1969, p 47). Those studies have become considerably more numerous in the past four decades, and various aspects of worker satisfaction and work–life harmony are now routinely monitored in the regular workplace surveys that feed into national and international business-ranking systems such as Fortune 500 and the AON Hewitt Best Employers Study Around the World (Box 14.1).

The main UN organisation charged with assessing business (and government) effects on well-being is the International Labour Organisation (ILO). Although the ILO focuses on (violations of) workers' rights, its 'decent work' agenda is at least hinting at paying more substantial attention to the enjoyment of work and to work–life harmony. It is, however, so firmly embedded within the pathological 'human rights' tradition that most of this work still looks at adversities and unfairness rather than at happiness and satisfactions. Many of its 'decent work' reviews focus not on job satisfaction but on the basic challenges of ensuring sustainable, safe, healthy, and adequately remunerative employment. 'Decency' of work has a range of meanings, implicitly ranked in a hierarchy, with enjoyment attended to only once more basic and vital criteria are met.

Regardless of any final resolutions to debates about whether job satisfaction, workplace happiness, or work–life balance are good for productivity, the happiness of workers is such a vitally important intrinsic good that we ought routinely to require employers to promote and monitor it, and to use the findings as key information when choosing or evaluating employers.

Researching and publicising workplace happiness

From a happiness perspective, one of the most encouraging developments in recent years has been the proliferation of public surveys of the quality of working life, steering our attention towards organisational performance in facilitating the well-being of workers. In contrast with national happiness surveys, which sceptics can claim may have little or no effect beyond occasional flurries of media attention, the organisational happiness surveys that are increasingly widely publicised seem very likely to have real effects via the reputations organisations have with employees, prospective employees, and customers. Some examples are in Box 14.1.

Whereas surveys tend to give mainly numerical information on workers' perceptions and satisfactions, and are restricted to the issues that the surveyors have decided to investigate, ethnographic studies can provide a much richer portrayal of working life. They give observations of how relationships and attitudes unfold. They reveal the cultural history of the workplace. They allow respondents to tell their own stories of how their working day goes, how it relates to their broader activities, their lives, and aspirations.

Box 14.1: Surveys exploring subjective experience of work

The **World's Most Admired Companies** survey covers 44,000 workers in 34 countries (2010) and has been conducted five times since 1991, reviewing working conditions and trends in workforce and quality of work, with increasing emphasis on subjective experience of psychosocial risk, participation, decision-making, and work–life balance (www.haygroup.com/ww/best_companies/index.aspx?id=155).

The **AON Hewitt Best Employers Study Around the World** survey assesses employees' perceptions of the 'intangible' benefits of employment, including advancement and learning opportunities, clarity of role expectations, flexibility, work–life balance, recognition, and being treated with respect (http://was2.hewitt.com/bestemployers/pages/index.htm).

The **Great Place to Work Institute/Fortune** survey of large US companies emphasising the importance of trust, cooperation, and a 'positive' working environment (www.greatplacetowork.com).

The **European Working Conditions Survey** measures 20 aspects of job satisfaction via 100 questions or via a shorter 20-question version (www.eurofound.europa.eu/ewco/surveys/index.htm).

The **Gallup Workplace Audit** covers various features relating to the intrinsic enjoyment of work, such as clarity of role expectations, fit between skills and tasks, workers' perceptions that good performance is recognised and praised, workers' sense of being able to influence management, and workplace friendship (Harter et al, 2002).

The **US General Social Survey** includes questions on how much overtime work people do; whether they see this extra work as mandatory; whether they feel 'used up at the end of the day'; whether they find their work stressful; how many hours per day they have for relaxation and enjoyment outside of work; whether they enjoy good fringe benefits; and whether their 'main satisfaction in life comes from work' (www.norc.org/GSS+Website/Browse+GSS+Variables/Subject+Index/).

Workplace ethnographies are usually conducted by anthropologists or sociologists who spend long periods – from weeks to years – observing, interviewing, and participating in workplace activities so as to develop a strong sense of how things really happen. Ethnographic approaches are subject to the personal preferences of ethnographers and to the cultural biases of the disciplines of anthropology and sociology. Two overwhelming biases dominate ethnographic and sociological literature on work:

- **Limited attention to good, safe, dignified work:** There is a predominant focus on the underclass and on unpleasant and low-status work, such as boring factory work, hard labour, and prostitution (for recent examples, see for example Montgomery, 2001; Johnson, 2002; Ehrenreich, 2002; Marchevsky and Theoharis, 2006; or see Michael Glawogger's devastating ethnographic films of dangerous and dirty work – for example *Working Man's Death*, 2005).
- **Disinterest in the joys of work:** Ethnographers tend to show more interest in the ills and injustices of the workplace than in the enjoyment of work. Compared with surveys, ethnographic studies have in practice had a great deal less to say about job satisfaction, worker happiness and positive aspects of business culture and work–life harmony, although to be fair there has been considerable, if rather ad hoc, ethnographic attention to positive phenomena such as worker resilience, workplace solidarity, dignity, and occasional fun.

Slightly more positively, Randy Hodson's *Dignity at work* (2001), without referring to happiness, reviews scores of ethnographic workplace studies that provide some insights into how workers make their working day at least bearable and dignified if not actually fun. Arguing that dignity and self-fulfilment at work are essential components in a good life, he focuses mainly on the obstacles that make it hard for people to achieve a sense of self-worth through work, particularly those that are socially created: abusive management, overwork, limits on autonomy, and incoherent approaches to employee involvement. But he also critiques the sociological tradition that overemphasises workplace pathologies and worker passivity in the face of them, and takes care to analyse and exemplify the strengths through which workers make working life better: resistance, citizenship, creation of autonomous and idiosyncratic meaning systems, and the development of solidarities and good social relations. George Gmelch's *Behind the smile* (2003), which allows 21 men and women who work in the Barbados tourist industry to speak of their work experiences, shows still more interest in workers' dignity and enjoyment. Contradicting many critical and pathological studies of North–South tourism, these workers all spoke of their enjoyment and satisfaction with their jobs, commenting favourably on both environmental aspects, such as the pleasure of working outdoors, and also the social aspects, such as the enjoyment of tourists' company and the satisfaction of helping others to enjoy good leisure and exercise.

Understanding different people's experiences in various kinds of work has also been greatly helped by publications and media portrayals that allow people to speak for themselves, with varying degrees of editorial selection and analysis. Probably the most famous oral history publication on the theme of work is Studs Terkel's collection *Working: People talk about what they do all day and how they feel about what they do* (1974). Based on over 100 interviews with North Americans in a very wide variety of jobs, both low status and high status, manual and intellectual, and letting them all tell their own stories, this collection gives a really balanced portrayal of what people like and don't like about work, and about how even when work doesn't seem to go very well for people, they seem to find a way of making it bearable and meaningful.

In the same year, the British historian John Burnett produced his less acclaimed but just as remarkable collection *Useful toil*, based on diaries and a few rare biographies of working people from the 1820s to 1920s. Though (unlike Terkel) Burnett chose to focus on people in low-status occupations, he nonetheless expresses admiration for the protagonists' 'uncomplaining acceptance of conditions of life and work which to the modern reader seem brutal, degrading and almost unimaginable' (1974, p 14). But he also notes that work was not their 'central life interest' and that it was thought of as something 'to be endured rather than enjoyed'. They were 'probably glad enough to have it at all, and to expect to derive satisfaction or happiness from it was an irrelevant consideration' (1974, p 15). Aspirations for fulfilling work may have become more widespread since then, but in the UK at any rate this way of thinking about work would still seem normal in the 21st century.

Probably the most positive and influential multimethod research on work and happiness has been Mihaly Csikszentmihalyi's iconic book *Flow* (1990), and his several follow-up publications (1997; 2003; 2006). He used a mixture of methods, including interviews, experience sampling, and short thumbnail biographical sketches, to capture people's descriptions and self-analysis of what it feels like to achieve, through work, a sense of total positive involvement in the job at hand. This has inspired a lot of attention to the experience of flow, and to related concepts such as 'engagement', 'energy', and 'creativity' in the workplace (Moeran, 2007; Cook, 2008; Ross, 2009). A rightly celebrated more recent example is Matthew Crawford's (2009) *Shop class as soulcraft*, an auto-ethnographic (pun unavoidable) celebration of the 'psychic satisfactions' of useful manual work in a motor repair shop that explores the connections between flow, sense of achievement, and the satisfaction of witnessing other people's appreciation of your work.

Table 14.1: Influences on happiness at work

Objective conditions	Subjective perceptions and individual responses
Pay: Levels, inequalities, variability/reliability, and transparency	Perceived adequacy, fairness, and reliability of pay – whether we see it as a fitting reward for the work we do, and in relation to what other people are paid
Working time: Length of working day, week and year	Perception of working time as about right, too much, or too little
Flexibility of working time and location	Perceived ability to make use of flexibility available so as to ensure work–life harmony and integration
Job fit: The match between our work and our capabilities	Perceived fit between work and capabilities, interests, and aspirations
Society and culture: Workplace social structure, relations, habits, attitudes	Enjoyment of good social relations; mutual respect within and between hierarchical levels; perception of the social environment as supportive, trusting cheerful, interesting, and so on
Personal/professional growth: Opportunities for autonomy, dignity, and growth in the job, and for recognised sense of achievement	Workers' sense of autonomy, dignity, achievement
Security: Safety, stability and predictability of the job	Feelings of safety, job security, confidence
Freedom: Objective autonomy	Perception that one is free or compelled to work (in general, or in this particular job, or on specific tasks)

Temporal and spatial autonomy: harmonising work and other domains

Leaving aside for the moment the question of how people might enjoy and derive meaning from their work, at the most basic level people need to consider what time allocation and what location of work would be optimal for their well-being and that of their families. A core concern is that in general, although people in richer countries work shorter hours than they did 100 years ago, the promise (or threat) of massive reduction in work time hasn't materialised. There is considerable evidence that people in richer countries are experiencing more time pressure and more unpleasant commuting than previously. There are also different but not unrelated concerns about temporal and spatial flexibility, about the extent to which employers can and should give their workers freedom to choose their own work times and the location from which they work.

Time spent on the job varies widely in rich countries and is clearly not just a matter of personal choice but is strongly influenced by the policies of business leaders, unions, and governments. For example, Alesina et al (2005) found that the average US citizen works 46.2 weeks per year, while the French average just 40 weeks per year, with the difference explained mainly by European labour market regulations. It would seem that the French are better off in this regard, given that so many people say they would prefer to work shorter hours. But to understand whether the US or the French approach to work is more sensible, or to make similarly evaluative comparisons between the working time of men and women, young and old, or different social categories, we need to know a lot more about how people experience their work and the balance between work and other life domains. Further, we need to know whether the people who do little or no work are happy, as it is already clear that in all countries non-voluntary unemployment is one of the most adverse influences on happiness. It is also clear that lots of people feel compelled to work very long hours: the ILO survey *Working time around the world* found that over 600 million people worldwide work more than 48 hours a week: for example, 50.9% of workers in Peru, compared with 18.1% in the US. Many are compelled to do so to make ends meet, while hundreds of millions more live in poverty because they have too little paid employment (Lee et al, 2007).

In their ground-breaking book *Discretionary time*, Goodin et al propose that free time should become the key 'measure of freedom' and as well as serve as a new 'currency for egalitarian justice', given that 'virtually everyone agrees that more time would be better' (2008, p 3). They note that although there are conflicting reports of trends in free time worldwide, in richer countries at least, although people are today much better off financially and temporally than they were in the early years of the Industrial Revolution, 'people's subjective sense of time pressure has become increasingly urgent' (p 69): we are 'better off but busier' (p 76). They also note that regarding domestic 'work' (that is, time that people spend on activities seen as non-voluntary) supposedly labour-saving technological advances haven't reduced working hours, although it may be that for many the allocation of this time has shifted from uninteresting chores towards more rewarding aspects of domestic labour, such as childcare and shopping. Welfare regimes have enormous power to influence the distribution of discretionary time, particularly between women and men. Indeed, particularly for gender reformers, their argument makes it abundantly clear that unequal access to free time is in richer countries a more serious and persistent problem than unequal access to careers and income.

As well as the absolute amounts of time spent at work, the flexibility of working arrangements is also critical for happiness: the ILO report recommended not only stricter controls over maximum working hours, but also that all countries should consider family-friendly approaches such as flexi-time, emergency family leave, and provision of high-quality part-time work. While these concerns do seem well-directed towards people's well-being, it is regrettable that the ILO is yet to develop a more direct interest in assessing the happiness of workers. This and another major ILO labour review, *Decent working time* (Boulin et al, 2006), ignore work satisfaction altogether, in stark contrast to reviews in the for-profit sector, which have been taking work satisfaction and workplace happiness seriously for decades. Much more encouraging is the strengthening ILO interest in work–life harmony, and particularly the need for policies encouraging flexible integration between work and family life. Another major ILO study, *Reconciling work and family responsibilities* (Hein, 2005), provides a superb overview of trends in work–family conflict and responsive policies and practices worldwide, from government policies and legislation to specific workplace and community-level policies and practices, such as informal care arrangements, parental and carers' leave arrangements, lactation breaks, work-time and workplace flexibility, time banking, and improvements in the provision of high-quality part-time work.

The concept of family-friendly practice is not as ambitious or as socially inclusive as happiness-friendly workplace practices, but it is an important step in that direction, and in any case the organisations that promote such policies are very likely to be interested more broadly in the happiness of their workforces. Many businesses recognise that 'family-friendliness' has low priority for many employees, and that other kinds of adjustment are needed if they are to facilitate the happiness and loyalty of workers. For example, the Korean firm Cheil Jedang organised a benefit points system, using a 'cafeteria approach' to give workers a wide range of options for work-related benefits (childcare, gifts, holidays, use of leisure facilities, tickets to cultural events, and so on) (Beck, 2000; Kim and Kim, 2004). Good approaches to work–life integration can be socially inclusive, as well as holistic.

Discussion points

- There is a long tradition of research and policy development relating to workplace happiness, making this one of the most substantial domains of applied happiness research. This research seems likely to have real influence on practice via the incentive of organisational reputation – more so than is ever likely to be the case with national happiness surveys.
- Ethnographic workplace research enriches our understanding of workers' subjective experiences, but to be useful it will need to complement the existing corpus of mainly pathological research on unpleasant and low-status work with research on work enjoyment. Recent research has begun to pay positive attention to the dignity of workers, and research on 'flow', 'engagement', and 'creativity' is becoming increasingly influential.
- Research on discretionary time (or 'time affluence'), temporal flexibility, and work–life harmonising shows the importance of temporal autonomy in the facilitation of enjoyable and creative work, and good lives in general.

Key readings

Cameron, K.S., Dutton, J.E. and Quinn, R.E. (2003) *Positive organisational scholarship*, San Francisco: Berrett-Koehler.

Cook, S. (2008) *The essential guide to employee engagement*, London: Kogan Page.

Csikszentmihalyi, M. (2003) *Good business: Leadership, flow, and the making of meaning*, Harmondsworth: Penguin.

Goodin, R.E. (2008) *Discretionary time: A new measure of freedom*, Cambridge: Cambridge University Press.

Hodson, R. (2001) *Dignity at work*, Cambridge: Cambridge University Press.

Linley, P.A., Harrington, S. and Garcea, N. (eds) (2009) *Oxford handbook of positive psychology and work*, Oxford: Oxford University Press.

Reeves, R. (2001) *Happy Mondays: Putting the pleasure back into work*, New York: Basic Books.

Warr, P.B. (2007) *Work, happiness, and unhappiness*, London: Routledge.

FIFTEEN

Shopping for happiness: corporate happwash and consumption ethics

I have learned to seek my happiness by limiting my desires, rather than in attempting to satisfy them. (John Stuart Mill)

You can never get enough of what you don't need to make you happy. (Eric Hoffer)

Corporate happwash and the market's hidden heart

As is well known, Adam Smith argued in *Wealth of nations* that the 'hidden hand' of the market allowed people to promote social happiness by pursuing their own self-interest as consumers and producers. In *The theory of moral sentiments*, by contrast, he emphasised humanity's natural interest in other people's happiness, which we promote for no other reason than the joy of considering it. Any serious debate about the ethics of business and consumption turns on these two quite different mechanisms for happiness promotion – the mechanical synergies between self-interest and virtue achieved through the market, and the enlightened self-interest of deliberately promoting other people's happiness. This latter theme, the 'heart' which motivates us to cherish other people's happiness, is all but entirely hidden in discourses on ethics of consumption and business.

We've all heard of 'corporate greenwash' – the accusation of implausible or tokenistic claims to environmental responsibility. Other variants like 'bluewash' (use of the UN flag to gain respectability) and 'sweatwash' (claiming to avoid the use of sweatshop labour) similarly echo the well-known Tom Sawyer vignette in which he persuades other children to pay for the privilege of doing his punishment exercise of whitewashing a fence. In that example, everyone's a winner: the fence painters, genuinely persuaded that whitewashing is an enviable task, are as happy as Tom. We might also consider the concept of 'corporate happwash' – marketing or seeking reputational gains by using implausible promises of happiness. Examples include the classic

'Happiness is a cigar called Hamlet', more recent insidious efforts to promote smoking in Africa by linking it to music and happiness (Patel et al, 2009), or the labelling of the sugary drink 7Up as 'Seven Happinesses [*qu xi*]' in China, echoing Coca-Cola's efforts to link its products with happiness in China and elsewhere since the 1920s, but also recalling 7Up's own promotion in the 19th century as a lithium-based mood-booster in health spas (Healy, 2002, p 47). Even prospective buyers of spare parts for cars ('complete Honda happiness') and fabric softeners (Nihon Lever: 'Happiness is a soft blanket') are advised to expect more than mere satisfaction. Indeed, there can be few products that haven't at some stage been sold via explicit or subtle happiness promises.

But as well as the obvious examples of blatantly misleading advertising, should we not also consider the more insidious threat of those who implicitly claim moral high ground for their organisations, whether or not they are profit motivated and whether or not the promises are fully explicit? Is it not implausible and ethically questionable to research, advocate, or evaluate so-called 'ethical business' or 'ethical consumption' without paying explicit heed to happiness? Most research and advocacy under these labels makes exactly this mistake. 'Ethical' typically doesn't mean 'we're doing our best to promote sustainable happiness for as many people as we can', it means 'we've taken some actions to avoid, mitigate, or compensate for, possible harms'. It is still rare to find substantial attention to happiness in research or policy texts on 'ethical' (or 'green', or 'sustainable', or 'eco-friendly', or 'fair trade') consumption or investment, or even in texts on corporate social responsibility (CSR).

Unless they deny that happiness matters, business moralisers and critics of consumerism are simply doing implicitly what unethical advertisers do explicitly: making false or unfounded promises of happiness. It is hard to improve our understanding of which kinds of production, distribution, and consumption make us better off over the short or longer term, but this is no excuse for shirking empirical investigation. And even if you doubt the value of empirical happiness research, that still leaves a lot of scope for rational and open debate on what kinds of benefit are valued and prioritised, and why. Even if you profess a 'deontological' ethical code that emphasises rights and rules, rather than a 'consequentialist' ethic that emphasises ends such as happiness, there is still room for happiness in the discussion of what justifies rules and how you persuade people to follow them (Barnett et al, 2005). Claims of betterment that lack any link to empirical research on well-being are therefore at best severely negligent, if not fraudulent, and are by no means restricted to the commercial sector.

In the 1970s, environmentalist organisations falsely claimed that a ban on DDT would improve the lives of malaria-prone Africans: over 100 million have died needlessly, thanks to this irresponsible campaign. In many countries it has become routine practice for both for-profit and non-profit promoters of so-called 'organic' food to make false claims that it tastes better and is safer than food grown with the aid of added chemicals. Any organisation of any kind ought to be required to make use of the best available evidence when making any claims about well-being enhancement.

A major strand of happiness research has begun to address these failings by generating and publicising new understandings of relationships between the desires whipped up by advertisers, ensuing consumption practices, and happiness. The idea of feel-good asceticism − a modern variant on the ancient Epicurean ideology of achieving happiness by keeping our wants moderate − is in principle sensible and appealing, both to our self-interest and to our social and environmental conscience. Unfortunately, too much of this research has (paradoxically, despite its strong links with 'positive psychology') been unduly puritanical and pathological − obsessed with the 'dark side of consumerism', to the neglect of the many happiness benefits facilitated by consumption under capitalist systems. Though many declinist scholars and soap-box moralisers would like us to believe that materialist consumption, or modern urban capitalist life in general, is bad for our happiness, the evidence is overwhelmingly against them (Veenhoven, 2008b).

Purchasing power, worldwide, has never been better. Shopping is in this sense easier than it's ever been. Yet if the labour of earning money is seen as problematic, choosing what to spend it on is becoming an ever-increasing source of anxiety. If the 'consumerist society' is by definition focused on producing, selling, and buying things we don't need, this keeps us entertained and creative on the one hand, but also anxious and environmentally destructive on the other. *Caveat emptor:* not only do we the buyers, as we always have done, have to be wary of fraudulent marketing, we are increasingly conscious of the minefield of moral dilemmas that bedevils shopping. We have become 'political consumers', and much of the moral crusading previously done as voters or as social protest movements we now do as consumers (Micheletti, 2003, pp 9, 14).

But consumption and anti-consumption activists have, as Stearns' excellent global history of consumerism amply demonstrates, always been associated with some downright unsavoury and chauvinistic name calling and guilt peddling (Stearns, 2001, especially chapter 6). There is a slippery slope from consumer concern to an epidemic of consumption anxiety that can quickly lead to apathy and scepticism. As consumers, we are becoming increasingly worried about our endlessly debatable responsibilities to ourselves, to other people, to future generations, to the environment, and to the welfare of animals. Even if we were to cut through these worry knots by deciding just to consume selfishly, there are plenty of happiness scholars eager to discourage consumerism by tell us that even *thinking* about shopping can be bad for our well-being (Frank, 1999; Kasser, 2002; Schwartz, 2004; Hamilton and Denniss, 2005; James, 2007).

Campaigners for environmental, animal rights, and human rights causes have for many years tried to sow doubt and guilt in the minds of consumers, but it is perhaps even more troublesome that we now have happiness promoters telling shoppers that we are our own victims. Anxious types would be better off, perhaps, just leaving the buying to someone else, although this is no guarantee of peace of mind because many of our peers want us to be fellow shopaholics and treat us with contempt if we under-shop.

Older readers may remember a wonderful 1978 hit by Wreckless Eric called 'Take the K.A.S.H.', which had the chorus 'it's the sweetness of the radish makes the bell ring on the till'. Though some merchants may believe this principle, that customers buy things because they like them, we must also bear in mind the crucial distinction between the wanting ('appetitive') and the liking ('consummatory') emotion systems, with their quite different neurological bases (Kringelbach and Berridge, 2010). Both of these, I have argued, are components of happiness. Really, it's the *wanting system* (the temptation of the radish), and not the *liking system* (its sweetness) that is mainly responsible for what we buy. Advertisers know this very well, so their interest focuses much more on our motivations than on our satisfactions. If I'm right that motivations are part of happiness and not just a pointer towards happiness, then anyone who whets our appetites, thereby making us more motivated than we might otherwise have been, seems to be doing us a favour, provided that they aren't fraudulently promising us sweet radishes that turn out to be sour.

However, to this we must add two other worries. First, they might be stoking an interest in things to which we will never have access – indeed, any advertisers who target anyone other than the very poorest exploit this by tempting the moderately well-off into conspicuous consumption. Second, they might be inviting us to buy stuff that would invite moral censure – and they might do so quite cynically, in the knowledge that a judicious amount of guilt makes the radish seem all the sweeter.

Commerce, purposes, and motives

Nowadays, for a large proportion of the things we might want, we are likely to need to earn some money. If being motivated is part of happiness, in this sense we work because we are happy. We work because we are happily anticipating at least the consequent rewards in the form of delights bought with our earnings, if not also anticipating the intrinsic enjoyment of the work itself. No motivation, no work. The stresses and moral dilemmas of shopping may make us miserable, but the promise of shopping is a crucial driver of modern motivation, and hence a major cause of happiness. Work may be, as even the happiness-sceptic Robert Lane concedes, 'the market's principal contributor to both happiness and human development' (1991, p 235). It achieves this magic not just through the intrinsic joys of work and the satisfactions that purchases bring, but also through the idea of purchasing power – the motivating belief that we turn ourselves into sovereign consumers and expand our choices through paid work.

Still, even if all businesses were to become ultra-happy workplaces, their net contribution to happiness could be negative if the forms of consumption they promoted were sufficiently harmful. Many people now believe that the capitalist merry-go-round of marketing, getting motivated, working, buying, and experiencing the hedonic effects of both our work and our purchases is a destructive treadmill. You probably won't have much trouble thinking of a friend or an acquaintance whose line of business you find ethically problematic (and quite likely they themselves do too), or whose consumption habits seem very obviously harmful to themselves and/or to others. That person almost certainly believes fervently in goodness and happiness and in the importance of helping other people towards better happiness prospects. Have you ever wondered whether, in conversations about business ethics, a happiness lens might be more persuasive than other kinds of ethical argument, such as the more common 'business case' (it pays to be nice in the long run), or fundamentalist arguments such as 'you're abusing people's natural rights', or 'that's against Christian doctrine', or 'gut feeling' arguments like 'that's just not right', or 'you're wasting your life'?

The ethics of marketing and consumption are at the heart of social happiness policy. With the application of a happiness lens to these two reciprocal activities we see particularly starkly how this forces new kinds of holism (treating customers as whole people rather than just as buyers), as well as new kinds of transparency, inviting sellers and customers to clarify their ultimate *purposes* rather than just the proximate *motives* of engaging in transactions. Distinctions between purposes and motives ought to lie at the heart of business and consumption ethics (Duska, 1997). We have always known, for example, that the motive of advertisers is to sell. But when we ask what purposes it serves or what social value justifies the existence of this immensely important commercial and social institution, we have often been left without an answer (Phillips, 1997, p 109). Today, however, there are an increasing number of businesses, especially those set up with explicit social missions and based on principles such as sustainability, social equity, and co-ownership, that make explicit recognition of the idea that businesses exist in order to spread happiness (Reeves, 2007).

Customer satisfaction or customer happiness?

There are two puzzlingly contradictory philosophical and empirical assumptions that lie behind the argument for introducing happiness information into these debates:

*   On the one hand, *the customer is always right*, so their subjective opinions on their own experience is vital information. People are wise, and consumers are sovereign and best placed to choose their own routes to happiness. Customer feedback complements money and purchasing power as a source of information on economic value. Just as governments increasingly agree that they need to look beyond purchasing power to find whether people are better off, so it is no longer good enough for businesses to take an interest in their customers' money. They need to understand their customers' subjective experiences, and in doing so they take an important step towards empathy.
*   On the other hand, *the customer is often a right idiot*. People are easily led into making choices that are bad for their well-being. This may happen because they mispredict what will make them happy, or because their *wanting* system makes them choose things (often addictively and passionately) that their more 'rational' *liking* system tells them aren't in their best interest. Andy Warhol's quip that 'buying is much more American than thinking' could now be said of most people just about anywhere. And just in case we do pause to think before buying, the young science of neuromarketing is springing into action, deploying the latest brain-scan technologies to help advertisers understand our feelings better than we do (Lawton and Wilson, 2010; and see www.neurosciencemarketing.com).

From a prudential perspective, the discipline of consumer ethics is about the considering whether it is good for people to be left utterly free to make their own mistakes, or whether we need at least some degree of protection by restricting or nudging our potentially damaging choices (like alcohol and tobacco). From a virtue perspective, business ethics is about encouraging marketers to promote the common good and restraining their ability or desire to promote damaging forms of consumption. But if, as argued in the previous chapter, business leaders have been developing a serious interest in the happiness of their workforces, it is much harder to discern a similar interest in those responsible for advertising and customer service. Modern businesses have long been promising happiness to their customers. Advertisers understand very well the pull of happiness promises, and what we might call 'corporate happwash' has a much longer history, and no doubt much more profound influences on all of us, than the more talked-about corporate greenwash.

Businesses are often thought of as being nicer to their customers than they are to their employees. Despite his apparent optimism about the market's contributions to workers' happiness as quoted above, Lane quickly follows this up with insistence that 'market forces systematically undermine worker satisfactions and learning in order to advance the interest, not so much of owners but of consumers. Consumers may not represent a ruling class, but they are sovereign and those who work are their subjects' (1991, p 235). This is a naïve theoretical point of view, perhaps reflecting 'customer is always right' rhetoric and not based on serious empirical verification. In practice, business leaders and business researchers have hitherto shown very much more substantial and sincere interest in employee happiness than they have in customer happiness. The substantial interest in evidence-based happiness policies in the workplace contrasts with the cynical exploitation of people's aspirations that we see in false promises of happiness in advertising. While the happiness of workers may be seen not only as a company asset but also as a business goal in its own right, the happy customer has traditionally been seen as an idiot whose short-termist hedonism is easily exploited by profiteers.

Advertising regulators, and the ethical codes of marketers, have so far been remarkably lenient on fraudulent happiness promises. In most countries, you're not allowed to make just any old unverified health promises to your customers, but you can get away with patently absurd promises of happiness. Yet lots of people believe that advertisers aren't just guilty of mild deceitfulness in their false promises about the benefits of their specific products; more seriously they also poison the psychic and social environment by creating unrealistic wants. For this, the guilt is collective. Barbara Phillips has even argued, persuasively, that it misses the point to blame advertisers in general: we need to look at the overall economic and social system for which we are all responsible (1997). As the critics of capitalist consumerism never tire of pointing out, the whole system thrives by spreading dissatisfaction and fostering irresolvable anxieties about status and consumption (Scitovsky, 1976; Frank, 2000; Kasser, 2002; Schwartz, 2004; Perelman, 2005; James, 2007). A key theme in arguments for new policies deriving from happiness scholarship has been the call for more careful restrictions on advertising as part of governments' responsibilities for promoting their citizens' happiness (for example Offer, 1996; Shah and Marks, 2004). But if the critics of capitalism are right, this kind of regulatory interference would only tinker with the superficial manifestations of much more fundamental systemic problems.

Still, even if their assessment of the veracity of happiness promises has been negligible, there are some signs of good companies not only looking at their 'social responsibility' but also going beyond 'customer satisfaction' to promote a more holistic and lasting relationship with customers by addressing 'customer happiness' (Martin, 2000, chapter 5), or the 'consumer well-being' or 'personal flourishing' that businesses may or may not facilitate (Gibbs, 2004, p 5; Bragues, 2006; Sirgy, Lee and Rahtz, 2007). Students in business schools are increasingly being exposed to the emergent concept of the 'Experience Economy', based on the idea that to thrive in business you need to understand not just your customers' desires but also their actual experiences in using your products and services. And, with explicit recognition of the influence of happiness scholarship, businesses are using, for example, a new customer emotional experience measurement system called 'Emotional Signature', which assesses, for example, the extent to which customers not only are 'satisfied' but actually derive 'fun' or 'delight' from their engagement with the business (Shaw, 2007, pp xix, 107–12), and more generally emphasising the need to move beyond mere 'customer satisfaction' to promote 'customer delight' (Goodman, 2009, chapter 9). There is also an explicitly social component to this trend: the concept of 'Customer Relationship Management' is now in widespread use as a standard rubric for practical and moral discourse in business management.

Whether or not they make explicit promises to consumers that their products lead to happiness, businesses, as much as governments, must recognise that happiness ought to have a central place in the justification of their existence and the assessment of their performance. While many businesses have recently begun to take social responsibility seriously, at least as a public relations exercise but often more substantially than that, the emphasis in the corporate social responsibility movement has been on minimising and compensating for harm rather than on facilitating happiness. Yet happiness is extremely prominent in advertising. An obvious focus of attention for the CSR movement might be to take the happiness promises seriously and punish offenders like Hamlet Cigars who promise happiness when they know that their products do more harm than good.

Commercial businesses are for many of us the biggest influences on our prospects for happiness. By advertising, promising happiness or domain satisfactions as they do so, they make us want things or services. We then commit large amounts of our time to earn money and then to go shopping. Believing that more purchasing power and a bigger range of commodities will make us better off, and so 'maximising' our purchases rather than 'satisficing', we are confronted with the 'paradox of choice' (Schwartz et al, 2002; Schwartz, 2004). The products and services may or may not provide us with the promised satisfactions, and neither we nor they put much effort into evaluating this, still less into checking whether, even if we are satisfied, our lives in general have gone better than they would have done without those goods and services. More importantly, perhaps, businesses provide us with work that, if enjoyable, can be a major part of our life happiness. But if work is alienating or damaging to our health or relationships, or if it simply takes up too much time, it can make us unhappy. Businesses also affect the quality of our lives by influencing the social environment, the built environment, and the natural environment, for better or worse.

How well is the 'corporate social responsibility' movement performing in helping us to understand these various crucial influences on our well-being? At a global level, concerning the huge multinational companies, many of which have far more important influences on people's happiness prospects than most national governments do, you will find that the United Nations-led World Business Council for Social Development (WBCSD) barely concerns itself with business effects on happiness. Instead, the reports and indicators associated with WBCSD focus mainly on extremely indirect and uncertain potential influences on long-term future happiness via climate change, to a lesser extent on current environmental influences, and on meeting minimum obligations for workers' rights. Even job satisfaction, which has been a key area of research on business management for five decades, is barely mentioned. This is consistent with the apparently systematic neglect by UN agencies of happiness and satisfaction as indicators of progress or of social responsibility. It's not just the UN that side-steps questions of how businesses influence happiness: you have to search long and hard in the burgeoning scholarly, business, and governmental literature on CSR worldwide to find any references to happiness or related concepts. Dominated by noble-sounding principles such as human rights and sustainability, and by harms such as pollution and abuse of workers, the CSR movement is so far largely agnostic concerning people's experiences and evaluations.

If it's wrong for advertisers of sweet drinks, cars, and tobacco to exploit our longing for happiness, in their defence it can at least be said that most people targeted by these adverts are not exceptionally vulnerable people, and most probably are well aware that the happiness promises relate at best to short-term trivial pleasures and aren't meant as sincere pointers towards really good lives. The same can't be said, however, of the happiness promises of the vast self-help, coaching, therapy, and religious businesses: they tend specifically to target vulnerable people, and though they may not promise happiness there can be no doubt that their customers are expected to believe that the services they buy should make their whole lives go substantially better. The self-help and self-esteem industries trade on the endless regeneration of self-doubt and dissatisfaction, as Stout has forcefully argued in her critique of US school-based self-esteem promotion in *The feel-good curriculum* (2001, p 16), and in this regard they are just as guilty as any other businesses that knowingly trade in false happiness promises.

Stout's anger is directed at the overtly commercial interests of shallow self-help advisers, but arguably it is the more insidious, less clearly commercial profiteering by religious leaders worldwide that is most in need of exposure. In the case of religious services, these expectations even extend beyond this world, to the belief that payments or services to religious institutions will translate into rewards in an afterlife. There are of course lots of coaches, therapists, and religious leaders who have no reason to wilt and squirm under the ethical scrutiny of the happiness lens: they may have studiously avoided making even implicit promises of happiness, they may not have tried to benefit from vulnerable people, or if they have done so they may have linked their work with the best available scholarship on what really does make people's lives go well.

In general, however, it is to be hoped that a major outcome of the current surge of interest in happiness studies and in public debate about happiness will be that all of these businesses become subject to much more careful evaluation and self-regulation than has hitherto been the case. Just as we can expose frauds who deliberately fake 'faith healing' for financial gain, so we could at least begin a process of public questioning of the morality of religious organisations that profiteer from promises of heavenly rewards (Dawkins, 2006, pp 358–60; Larrimore, 2010). We might still accept that for some people the belief in afterlife rewards is a positive illusion that can deliver this-worldly happiness benefits, but we would become less likely to accept doctrines that use promises of other-worldly rewards to legitimise unfair and avoidable this-worldly suffering. Though clearly much broader than mere commercial organisations, religious organisations do nonetheless take the form of businesses that people either buy into or don't. They ply their trade on the basis of doctrines that can quite legitimately be scrutinised under a happiness lens, and they can't legitimately hide behind the claim that customer happiness will be delivered only after the customers die. As innumerable critics have pointed out, psychotherapic movements have always had a lot in common with religious movements, and both have been strongly resistant to scientific scrutiny. But there are worrying signs of new anti-science conspiracies between religionists and therapists that are not likely to do any favours to customer happiness (Morrall, 2008; Helminiak, 2010). As with all therapeutic promises, religious ones must stand or fall on whether this-worldly consolations and benefits are actually experienced. If the public discussion of the verifiability of happiness promises were to become more normal, it might become a bit harder to exploit people in this way, and we might see real progress towards socially responsible religious and therapeutic practice.

Discussion points

- Most 'corporate social responsibility' research, advocacy, and reporting continues to undermine its own plausibility by failing to enquire into happiness or consult people about their subjective evaluations.
- Capitalist marketing has become so endemically corrupted by false and often fraudulent happiness promises that happiness researchers and promoters have all but lost sight of positive links between businesses, consumption, and happiness.
- Happiness scholars have made useful critiques of 'materialism' but have focused excessively on its dark side (insatiable greed and unsustainability). Unrealistically puritanical critiques neglect or deny the many benign forms of materialism, and generate consumption anxiety that can turn to scepticism.
- Critiques of materialism also risk detracting attention from many *non-materialist* happiness promises and consumption habits that also damage happiness – for example, the many forms of insincere or

false marketing by religious proselytisers, therapists, social reformers, electronic gaming companies, and self-help businesses.

Key readings

Bauman, Z. (2004) *Work, consumerism and the new poor*, Maidenhead: Open University Press.
Micheletti, M. (2003) *Political virtue and shopping*, London: Macmillan.
Schwartz, B. (2004) *The paradox of choice*, New York: Ecco.

SIXTEEN

Geronto-eudaimonics: late-life thriving for all

There may come a time when not being able to run a marathon at age five hundred will be considered a profound disability. (Harris, 2010, p 14)

Valuing and sustaining the late-life bonus

Of all the global social experiments we've reviewed, none raises more interesting and challenging happiness questions than our unprecedented experiment in life extension. Even if much of happiness scholarship appears simply to rake over age-old conversations about the good life, the same could not possibly be said for geronto-eudaimonics, the study of happiness in old age. This has been one of the richest and most inspiring veins of happiness enquiry, because the mass-scale enjoyment of old age is a radically new invention. Traditionally, most gerontological research has been pathological (Bowling, 2007, p 2; Stirling, 2010, p 4), although there have been many significant exceptions, building up to a clear recent trend towards positive and balanced approaches (see for example the readings at the end of this chapter).

The late-life bonus is one of modernity's greatest gifts, even if it also poses the difficult new ethical and practical challenges that still dominate much research and policy discourse on the 'burden' of expanding populations of old people. Cultural life-course maps and visions of the good society or the good life that don't assume a large percentage of the population over 65, and that don't assume that individuals should expect to live into their 80s, are already outdated. The life-expectancy revolution has been one of the most persuasive drivers of happiness scholarship and of happiness policy experimentation. For the first time in human history, it now seems possible that the majority of humanity can live for several decades beyond the end of their child-rearing years, and not only that but live well in communities and networks of peers who can all enjoy the greatly expanded life-style opportunities of the modern age. Cross-cultural gerontological studies of the possibilities for successful (and unsuccessful) ageing are among the most promising contributions of happiness studies to social development policy.

Have you ever wondered whether the bonus 30% extra 'free' on your chocolate bar was really worth having? Globally, the average life expectancy gain over the past 50 years has been 20 years – a bonus of roughly 25–50% in most countries, depending on your starting-point. The quality of the age bonus has always been of interest, but recently, researchers and age-care practitioners have begun taking an interest in not just 'active' or 'disability-adjusted' life expectancy, but also 'happy life expectancy' (Veenhoven, 1996; George, 2010). Though mostly due to physical public health improvements, some of these gains are also due to the effects of increased happiness on health (Guven, 2009; Diener and Chan, 2011). So to sustain the old-age bonus and keep medical costs at affordable levels, we will need to sustain old-age happiness, which of course we want to do anyway. But ageing in later life is often wrongly assumed to be a minus sign in our happiness accounts, as if there could be nothing good about getting older. Even champions of the joys of old age tend to betray residual gerontophobic prejudice by reassuring old people that they don't look old, or boasting that they don't feel old.

In fact, for most people late life isn't dominated by fear of ageing and of death. One of the more inspiring findings from happiness studies has been the comforting recognition that self-reported happiness in most cultures doesn't seem to decline in old age. Indeed, in many countries self-reported happiness is U-shaped over the life cycle, rising slightly in later life after a midlife trough (Diener et al, 2003, p 211). Public and scholarly interest in happiness has received a great deal of its support from the growing awareness of the radical new life possibilities afforded by our global social experiment in life extension. In stark contrast to the pathological social science of families, childhood, old age, and relationships, there is a wealth of gerontological writing celebrating the joys of old age, and reminding us that it is possible to age and even to die 'well' (Baltes and Baltes, 1990; Vaillant, 2002; Bowling, 2007; Bury and Holme, 2009).

Happiness lessons from the elderly

Just as men can derive important lessons from women's ability to be happy despite their manifold disadvantages, so it may well turn out that the young and middle-aged can learn valuable happiness lessons from old people's ability to thrive despite their declining health and loss of friends, money, and employment. In fact, those lessons might help both happiness and longevity.

In many countries, old men report slightly higher happiness levels than old women, reversing the discrepancy of younger age groups (see

Box 16.1: Modelling the good life in old age

Kidahashi (2010) has identified five different 'positive' models of the good life in old age, drawing mainly on research in Japan and the US, though arguing that these ideal types are found in 'most developed countries':

- **Traditional Golden Years:** Ideal of a long and leisurely non-working retirement, with an emphasis on relaxation.
- **Neo-Golden Years:** This is a revised, more active version of the traditional golden years, with emphasis on new forms of 'self-fulfilment' and 'self-development'.
- **Second Career:** A strong emphasis on revised kinds of work orientation in the 'third age'.
- **Extension of Midlife Career:** Here the key objective is to extend midlife work as long as possible, though in reality individuals often fail to maintain midlife status and are often obliged to find 'bridging' employment.
- **Portfolio Life:** This approach combines moderate 'work orientation' with 'third age life perception', the objective being to achieve a new balance between such elements as paid work, voluntary work, learning, and leisure.

Ann Bowling (2007) has noted that approaches to the well-being of the elderly vary widely according to which aspect or model researchers and practitioners focus on, including: Objective indicators; Subjective indicators; Satisfaction of human needs; Psychological characteristics and resources; Health and functioning; Social health; Social cohesion and social capital; Environmental context; Idiographic approaches (looking at factors that people say are important to them).

Several contributors to Mollenkopf and Walker's *Quality of life in old age* (2007) also emphasise, in additional to psychological, medical, and living condition perspectives, the importance of a *life span perspective* in appreciating the relation between old-age experience and the expectations and plans developed over the life span. Numerous researchers and carers have noted the importance of life course and life narratives in facilitating or inhibiting old-age happiness (Grimm and Boothe, 2007; Hatch et al, 2007).

for example Inglehart's 65–country study, 2002). Often this is because socio-economic support systems haven't adapted to ensure protection of old women, especially those living in poverty. It may be in part because the unhappier men have died of coronary disease (something they might have avoided if they had learned from their wives and sisters about how to cope with stress – see the findings on social happiness epidemiology from the Framington Heart Study in Christakis and Fowler, 2010). And a third factor is that old women are much more likely to suffer spouse bereavement than old men are (a discrepancy that can be reduced when changes in gender arrangements facilitate reduction in marital age differences and when progress is made in protecting men from the 'masculinist' life-style causes of premature mortality that are having such devastating effects in Russia, for example).

So, in addition to win–win outcomes from gender reform, it may well turn out that 'age-friendly' policies and practices are of benefit to everyone (WHO, 2007). Happiness in old age is a triumph of mind over matter, of positive attitude over declining life conditions – the ability to keep our spirits up, savour our accomplishments and memories, and retain a sense of hope, satisfaction, and meaning despite declining health and loss of income, capabilities, and friends. Because of this, 'happy life years' give more optimistic accounts of life than 'disability-adjusted' or 'active life years' or 'health-related quality of life' measures (Bowling, 2007, p 2; George, 2010, p 336).

But it may also be the case that in some ways bodily health and objective life conditions actually improve in old age: stresses are calmed, diets improve, and there is more time to enjoy friends and beautiful environments, even if we are left with fewer friends and are less able to travel and trudge the wilderness. In eastern meditative and ascetic traditions, control over the body, especially in older age, has for thousands of years been emphasised, and there is increasingly clear evidence of health and longevity benefits from some of these practices (Bushell et al, 2009).

Themes of bodily control and dignity are combined in Barbara Myerhoff's poignant ethnographic account of a personal rite invented and conducted by a Jewish American who chose to die (naturally, without medical assistance) in the company of 200 friends at his 95th birthday party (Myerhoff, 1984). This man showed that when failing health prevents happiness from being possible, it can still be possible to choose a eudaimonic finale, to die with dignity and in some degree of control of the moment without actively committing suicide. With ever more exciting and challenging possibilities in life extension, debates on happiness, choice, and quality of life in the final 'fourth age' will become increasingly clamorous.

Enjoyment of old age is now, for the first time in many cultures, something that has to be planned both individually and collectively (Thang, 2006). The 'third age' transition from the adulthood of parenting and work, and the 'fourth age' (the moribund years of old age), have also been among the more abundant sources of social science knowledge about happiness. Older people are everywhere important sources of knowledge about the world, but they are interesting for what they enjoy or suffer. The well-being of the young has been a focus, too, but children are also seen as proto-adults, so a lot of the childhood research is about processes of becoming. Adulthood has been the main focus of social science but there has been much more emphasis on what adults do and think than on how they feel. Regarding older people, there has been little interest in what they will become, and not even much interest in what they are or what they do. So when older people are in the viewfinder, the lens filter is more likely to experiential, hence gerontology's important influence on the 'quality of life' movement and happiness studies.

In old age, other life goals such as working and bringing up families may no longer be available, leaving happiness as a more explicit and central objective. In a 40-nation comparative study Diener and Suh (1999) showed that while older people tend to experience less pleasure, their life satisfaction and experience of adverse emotions remain similar to those of younger ages. They also argued that the decline in reported pleasure may in part be an artefact of measurement: most studies have asked about 'arousal' emotions, whereas if less-aroused emotions such as 'contentment' and 'affection' were explored, the reported age declines in pleasure might disappear. Yet in some parts of the world demographic transition and socio-economic changes are causing lots of worrying new sources of suffering in old age – particularly financial insecurity, powerlessness, isolation from family, and so on (Hermalin et al, 2002; Van der Geest, 2004).

Social and medical gerontologies, that is, studies of the later stages of people's lives, have made uniquely explicit contributions to our understanding of well-being and of the prospects for happiness policy. As a source of information and inspiration on happiness, old age is particularly interesting for many reasons, including:

- **Emphasis on happiness and savouring:** In old age, 'doing well' means 'enjoying life'. In relative freedom from the distractions of earlier life stages like success, productivity, reputation, and deferred enjoyment, older people are more likely to savour the small and calm pleasures that are within everyone's daily reach but tend to be ignored by younger generations (Baltes and Baltes, 1990). They also have more time to enjoy memories and to fabricate meaning through the narration of autobiographies. Assessment of their well-being requires respect for subjectivity, particularly because today's criteria and standards for 'objective' well-being may be less relevant to those who grew up in a different era (Bury and Holme, 2009, chapter 5).

- **Well-being focus in gerontological research:** Gerontologists have now built up several decades' worth of research on the well-being and life satisfaction of the elderly (see for example Neugarten, Havighurst and Tobin, 1961; Bowling, 2007; Fagerström et al, 2007), rejecting the previous dominance of pathological 'geriatric' approaches to old age and engaging with the challenge to 'add life to years, not just years to life'. Geronto-eudaimonic researchers accept that the elderly often suffer adverse health, social isolation, or poverty, but they also respect the fact that enjoyment and meaning are more obviously what matters in later life. But they do have to contend with the 'medicalisation' of old age and with policy concerns about the financial affordability of increased numbers and percentages of 'nonproductive' old people (George, 2010, p 336).

- **Demographic trends and evolutionary novelty:** As lengthy old age becomes normal worldwide, more policy attention will be given to its enjoyability, with spillover benefits in heightened awareness of happiness as a social policy concern. These trends carry major challenges for social innovation. The older we get, the less relevant our genetic heritage becomes: evolution favours survival only insofar as survival favours breeding, so, as Baltes bluntly puts it, 'evolution ignored old age' (2003, p 17). The 'greying' of whole populations also renders our cultural and social evolutionary heritage less relevant, demanding new creativity in the social construction of optimal experience.

- **Accessibility and transparency:** Older people tend to be less busy and less conscious of the opportunity cost of time, and so are more likely than middle-aged adults to welcome social researchers and be prepared to spend significant amounts of time with them. Old people are often described by researchers as more honest, less constrained in their information giving and in their opinions by personal considerations of status, embarrassment, or wishful thinking about the future. They may have more to hide, but have less reason for doing so.

- **Experience:** Old people have the most complete experience-based sense of the full life course, and so are able to give a more holistic and balanced perspective on the full range of factors that make a life go well or badly (Schaie and Carstensen, 2006). They can tell us not only what it feels like to be old, but what it feels like to be young or middle-aged, and how feelings at different life stages compare and interact.

- **Social orientation:** Old people may be as egocentric as any, but are probably more likely than people at other life stages to take a socio-centric rather than purely egocentric perspective on values, goods, and outcomes (Stirling, 2010, p 2). From this they derive resilience (Fry and Keyes, 2010). Though in very old age people's social networks inevitably dwindle, early old age is often a phase of 'social growth' (van Willigen, 1989, p 120). Old people's contributions to the social good are very significant, but go largely untracked by formal accounting systems like the GDP measure.
- **Temporal orientation:** Despite the advantages of the holistic life-course perspective, old people are interesting because of their unique time perspectives. Often seen as living in the past by thriving on memories, older people can also be presentist, and can have an interest in their future legacy and in other-worldly futures, but are unlikely to focus much on life plans for this-worldly futures.
- **Longitudinal studies:** Although still almost entirely North American and West European, life-course studies following people through many years of ageing are increasingly bringing to light uniquely helpful information on how people change through the life course, right through to old age, providing much stronger information on the processes of cause and effect through which happiness interacts with character, events, and environment

Old-age ethnography

Arguably the most important book written on ageing is George Vaillant's *Ageing well* (2002), which also happens to be one of the more important outputs from happiness studies and positive psychology. Derived from three extraordinary prospective life-course studies of individuals (one of men from privileged backgrounds, one of men from disadvantaged backgrounds, one of exceptionally gifted middle-class women) in the US aged between 60 and 80 years (collectively called the 'Study of Adult Development'), this book is unusual in its combination of survey responses with autobiographical information and biographical interpretation, and in its conscious efforts to complement pathological science with full investigation of the positive causes of good experiences at different stages through the life course. Dispelling pathological myths about decline and sadness in old age, Vaillant provides compelling statistical and case-study evidence to show how old age in the US normally is happier, healthier, and more playful and creative than is commonly assumed.

As well as the 'joy' and 'enjoyment' themes that dominate this book, there is a core argument about subjectivity as the key to not only experiencing events better but also making better things happen. *Feeling well* ('subjective good health') matters more to successful ageing than *being well* ('objective health'), not just because it is intrinsically good to feel well but also because feeling well makes you live longer and keep better health. The story is similar for the relationship between finance and enjoyment: successful ageing correlates with wealth, but 'financial success seemed much more a reflection of mental health than a consequence of social class or parental privilege':

> Even among the Inner City men the story was the same. Good mental health, good coping both as children and adults, warm friendships, admired fathers, and loving mothers predicted high income. In contrast, dysfunctional families and fathers on Welfare did not predict future income [...] *What goes right in childhood predicts the future far better than what goes wrong.* (Vaillant, 2002, p 95)

Fascinating and inspiring though all of this may be, there remains a crucial problem with Vaillant's account. Like so much of the psychological literature on happiness, it is unashamedly ethnocentric, generalising from North American experiences as if all readers were North Americans for whom the rest of the world were of no concern. Even in the US, the huge expense of long-term cohort studies make them a rarity, so it is unrealistic to expect much comparable research material from the rest of world. Nonetheless, it would be helpful to compare Vaillant's account with what is known about the objective facts and experiences of ageing in other parts of the world.

Anthropological and sociological writings on old age have tended to polarise between those who see modernity as good or bad for the well-being of older people. As part of anthropology's more general critiques of modern pathologies, many early anthropological texts on ageing tended to portray modern and individualistic western societies as peculiarly uncaring towards old people, in contrast to the respect and care given to old people in more traditional and collectivist societies. It is crucial, of course, to avoid naïve reproductions of rhetorical respect as if these are necessarily reflected in practice. Van der Geest notes that in rural Ghana, although respect for the elderly is a key moral concept, and although younger people say they particularly value the advice and folklore of older people, in practice they are 'not interested in their stories'. Old people get few visitors, are scared of loneliness and neglect, and are rarely asked for advice or invited out (Van der Geest, 1998, p 339; 2004). The overall conclusions to which he comes provide a devastating portrayal of the experience of social worthlessness and isolation among the housebound elderly, and a strong reminder of the need for cautious ethnographic investigation of whether people's actual experience matches cultural rhetoric:

> If wisdom is the epitome of old age and if respect for that wisdom [...] constitutes the essence of all respect, the absence of interest in that wisdom can only be an experience of losing what one believes one is most entitled to. This experience seems to be the Kwahu equivalent of what has been termed 'social death' in Western society ... Elderly people in Kwahu-Tafo [...] are denied what they regard as their deepest existential right: the listening ear of a younger person. (Van der Geest, 2004, p 95)

In contemporary accounts of old age among western or westernised people, a recurrent theme is the effusive denial of the idea of old age as a kind of decline. Sharon Kaufman's ethnography *The ageless self* (1986), based on interviews with 60 Californians over 70, uses her informants' lively denials of feeling 'old' as a platform to criticise gerontologists who assume that meaning in old age must be about being old (p 7). Still, Kaufman's vague advocacy in favour of 'positive roles' and 'meaningful institutions' for old people (p 4) does implicitly concede that old age is a distinctive life stage requiring specific kinds of rethinking at individual and societal levels. In any case, her informants' age denial reveals in the old people themselves a gerontophobia that Kaufman appears not to recognise. If old people say they don't 'feel old', they are, ironically, confirming old age as a denigrated life stage, even while claiming their own personal autonomy from it. The path of anti-ageism, like those of anti-racism and anti-sexism, is unavoidably plagued with ethical conundrums of this sort: claims that old age, or gender, or race isn't central to one's identity are claims to freedom that must be traded off against claims for social justice. Justice requires recognition that these social categories do matter a great deal.

One key area of policy-relevant debate concerns the temporal orientation of old people. For example, whereas a great deal of policy attention for other life stages relates to helping people plan for the future, in the later years of life, planning and future orientation don't feature, so that 'the future is not perceived as a source of meaning'

(Kaufmann, 1986, p 111). Others, however, deny that future orientation is insignificant in the lives and experiences of the elderly: Jennie Keith's review of anthropological writing on old age used the phrase 'The best is yet to be' in the title, indicating an assertive claim to a future (Keith, 1980).

A different and more strongly practice-oriented perspective on old age comes from Jeanie Kayser-Jones's two-location ethnographic study of age-care institutions: *Old, alone, and neglected: Care of the aged in the United States and Scotland* (1981). She compared long-term institutionalised care arrangements in those two countries, based on detailed participant observation and patient interviews covering all aspects of life in nursing homes. The Scottish elderly, she argued, enjoyed much more freedom and respect than the North American elderly, and their lives were allowed to resemble those of the mainstream population much more closely. North American institutionalised elderly, she claimed, tended to be infantilised, depersonalised, dehumanised, and even victimised by the staff. No one would deny that such fates commonly befall the institutionalised elderly in any society, however, so it remains far from clear whether the two-country contrast was broadly representative of better policies and conditions in Scottish institutions. In any case, it is vital to acknowledge that those many ethnographic studies that take advantage of the relatively easy-access communities and institutions of elderly people are a long way from being representative of mainstream old age in any society: in no country do most old people live in institutions for the elderly. Just as too much social psychology is based on surveys and experiments conducted on undergraduates, far too much gerontology is based on institutional studies. There remains a dire need for more 'natural habitat' ethnography of the elderly to inform policy (Keith, 1980, p 347).

Box 16.2: Social policies and practices for old-age happiness

The **World Health Organization Age-friendly Cities project** consulted with elderly people in 33 cities worldwide about the factors that influenced their well-being, and consolidated this information into a Guide promoting simple initiatives worldwide, such as facilitation of flexible work opportunities (paid and unpaid), affordable social activities, help with information services, and so on (World Health Organization, 2007).

Encore Careers (www.encore.org) was established by author Marc Freedman (see Freedman, 2008) to promote purpose-driven, fulfilling, later-life career shifts that will also help to resolve worries about both labour shortages and dependency ratios due to ageing populations.

Reminiscence therapy groups are springing up around the world, building on various research strands that have demonstrated the health and happiness benefits of encouraging older people to share memories as a way of reconstructing meaningful threads that have run through their lives (see for example www.uk-care.com/reminiscence-therapy.html).

Lifelong learning initiatives have been shown to be highly effective in improving the happiness of older people, both directly, through the intrinsic value of learning, and indirectly, through the social benefits of group learning and the economic benefits of improved employability (Field, 2009).

Madan Kataria's laughter yoga movement (www.laughteryoga.org) has spread rapidly from its Bangalore origins through the formation of hundreds of laughter clubs worldwide, which are always popular with older people. This and other laughter therapies have been found to be an effective form of group therapy in old age (Mathieu, 2008), linking the well-known health benefits of laughter with the social benefits of stress-free conviviality.

Discussion points

- Old age tends not to be associated with happiness, yet it is also the age at which other life goals, such as working and bringing up families, are no longer available, leaving happiness as a more explicit and central objective.
- The study of how old people manage to increase their happiness, despite their various sufferings, losses, and disempowerments, could hold useful lessons not just for good policies and practices to support old people, but also for the benefit of younger people.

Key readings

Baltes, P.B. and Baltes, M.M. (eds) (1990) *Successful aging*, Cambridge: Cambridge University Press.

Bowling, A. (2007) *Ageing well: quality of life in old age*, Maidenhead: Open University Press.

Bury, M. and Holme, A. (eds) (2009) *Life after ninety*, London: Routledge.

Bushell, W.C. et al (2009) *Longevity, regeneration, and optimal health: Integrating Eastern and Western perspectives*, Annals of the New York Academy of Sciences.

Fry, P.S. and Keyes, C.L.M. (eds) (2010) *New frontiers in resilient aging: Life-strengths and well-being in late life*, Cambridge: Cambridge University Press.

Mollenkopf, H. and Walker, A. (eds) (2007) *Quality of life in old age*, Dordrecht: Springer.

Schaie, K.W. and Carstensen, L. (eds) (2006) *Social structures, aging, and self-regulation in the elderly*, New York: Springer.

Stirling, E. (2010) *Valuing older people: The positive psychology of ageing*, London: John Wiley.

Vaillant, G.E. (2002) *Ageing well*, Melbourne: Scribe.

SEVENTEEN

Conclusions: review and prospects

Reviewing the benefits of the happiness lens

Not all readers, by this point, will be persuaded that a happiness lens implies a radical shake-up of social research or social policy. But I trust it will not have been possible to read these pages without being convinced, if you weren't already, of two things: that evaluative claims about ethics, progress, goodness, or altruism are all inadequate and potentially dangerous without some use of happiness criteria; and that happiness criteria have been curiously absent or downplayed in many of our treasured disciplines.

We have also seen that the deployment of happiness scholarship in policy and practice has two seemingly contradictory tendencies. On the one hand, it is about respecting people's own opinions on the qualities of their lives and experiences. On the other hand, it is about recognising the limits of people's ability to understand and/or act on what is good for them. Ironically, we need to assess happiness outcomes and develop and disseminate happiness scholarship precisely because people are so easily led astray and so readily make mistakes and mispredict what will make them or other people happy.

Perhaps the biggest single potential advantage of the happiness lens is that by respecting subjectivity we are promoting a way of evaluating lives and institutions that cuts through many of the problems of cultural and institutional bias. Particularly in cases where one set of people wants another to be happy but finds it hard to appreciate or understand their preferences, happiness information promotes empathic evaluation where the use of culture-specific evaluative criteria would promote misunderstanding and empathy barriers. For example, as is increasingly the case, if parents want to understand what is good for their children, it is often extremely hard for them to assess their children's cultural world, which is so different from the one they grew up in. However hard I try, aged over 50, I'm unlikely ever to be able to fully appreciate the goods and harms of my children's net-generation culture. But by enquiring into what brings them happiness and how, I can avoid the common mistake of misjudging their life quality by applying my generation's cultural values to theirs.

It is now several years since scholars in the vanguard of happiness scholarship began trying to develop recommendations for social policy, and longer since they began offering recommendations for personal self-help. If policy impact is assessed in terms of explicit public interest in the findings of happiness scholarship, then the achievements are already remarkable, with numerous heads of state, journalists, TV companies, and academics in a wide range of disciplines taking a substantial interest. Few people interested in policy trends can have failed to notice these developments, but they will also have noticed the sceptical backlash against the whole idea of measuring happiness and applying knowledge based on those measures.

If we judge impact in terms of real-world changes in practice, however, there is a long way to go. Even in countries like Bhutan that have foregrounded happiness rhetoric, it remains hard to identify specific areas of policy where insights from happiness policy have made a difference, let alone real changes in practices and outcomes. The promised benefits of happiness scholarship will doubtless take many years to achieve. Psychology has been producing knowledge for over a century, with little evidence of clear translation into benefits via psychotherapies and self-help advice. Even when these are evidence based, the line of influence from therapies and advice to personal practices and benefits is often hard to discern. So instead of expecting a logical progression from happiness studies to advice and thence to real-world changes, it is perhaps more realistic to hope instead for more subtle shifts of attention that we might attribute to a 'happiness lens' rather than to specific 'policies for happiness'.

I made five generalisations about the justifications and expected significance of the happiness lens: that it would promote empathic respect for subjectivity, positivity, holism, and a life-span perspective, and that it would make organisations more transparent about their beliefs concerning how specific kinds of change would make people's lives better. To avoid tediously over-determined analysis I haven't used this as an analytical framework for each of the policy domains I have explored in Part Two, but each chapter has shown the need for these qualities to improve policy processes. Though these expected benefits of the happiness lens may sound obvious, they do seem to require reiteration in the face of continued neglect of happiness. We have seen how this neglect manifests in empathy failures; in excessive pathologism and associated lack of ambition; in piecemeal approaches to people's lives; in inadequate attention to the life course; and in an overall lack of transparency regarding beliefs about progress – all of which could be redressed by attention to happiness.

Although all of these matter, it is this lack of transparency that I have found most compelling and damning: the more you think about what it means to neglect happiness, the more you become aware that our academic disciplines, our policy specialisms, and our most important social and cultural institutions and social reform movements alike suffer from fundamental weaknesses associated with inadequate clarity of purpose. This isn't too bothersome for those institutions whose contribution to happiness is very obvious because it is very specific (agriculture, fire fighting and road mending, for example), but it matters a great deal in the planning of multi-purpose institutions or of social movements. They need transparent purposes and explicit, evidence-based theories of how they take account of people's feelings and life plans and make their lives go better.

In an era of rapid change, debates about the purposes of our disciplines and institutions become all the more essential, and probably the most important contribution of the happiness lens is this diffuse reminder of the need to question our motives, purposes, and objectives. The priority functions of marriage and the family are in most countries utterly different from what they were in our grandparents' day, with much less need for emphasis on financial and physical security and much more on love, companionship, and socialisation. Schooling was designed for purposes that are much less relevant today, and throughout history national schooling systems have rarely paused to consider whether facilitating the happiness of children was an important function. If we believe that this ought to be an important function today, it should be obvious that in most countries the approaches to schooling need a radical overhaul. Profit-making businesses have nearly always been assumed to be adequately justified by their profit margin, which serves as a proxy for the quality and usefulness of their goods and services, but if business owners and managers agree that a substantial part of their purpose is to facilitate workers' happiness and public happiness, this necessitates major changes in ways of working and in criteria for performance assessment.

We have seen some similar patterns in social policies and cultural attitudes in all domains, but there have been some interesting differences. Systematic attention to happiness developed earliest in the policy domains of marriage, workplace, and gerontology, and in each domain the translation into policy and practice has been very different. Policies for happy workers and happy old people have been promoted in many countries for several decades. By contrast,

237

after nearly a century of research on marital happiness, most marital support policies emphasise mitigation and sometimes prevention of harmful relationships, rather than happiness. In marketing, there has always been substantial attention to customer satisfaction and to attracting customers with promises of happiness, but rarely has this been supported by serious research on whether products or services actually improve customers' lives. Disappointingly, the global 'corporate social responsibility' movement has failed to develop an evaluative interest in marketers' happiness promises, and has yet to extend adequately beyond commercial businesses to address the social responsibilities of the rest of our institutions.

Good prospects for a happiness focus in other themes and domains

Part Two explored a few of the most obvious themes and domains where more happiness-focused policies and practices might be expected to take root, but we can in the coming years expect to see increasingly radical rethinking of many more policy domains as people are invited to think more carefully about subjective experiences in these domains and about their relevance to the overall quality and meaning of life. I offer below some thumbnail sketches of other promising domains and themes worth exploring, but of course I hope that an interest in the happiness lens will be awakened in many more domains of policy and practice.

Health and social medicine

Research and policy in the health sector has already made important strides towards taking happiness seriously as part of the process of addressing patients holistically and respecting their feelings, and as part of actively promoting health rather than responding to illness. It is widely recognised that governments tend to spend too large a proportion of their 'health' budgets on medicine, and too little on promoting and supporting health-giving 'salutogenic' cultures and environments (Nordenfelt, 1993; Antonovsky, 1996; Hershberger, 2005; Mittelmark et al, 2005; Seligman 2008; Angner et al, 2010).

Further, although there is a trend towards greater respect of people's subjective health by medical professions, there is also recognition that people knowingly or unknowingly make bad decisions for their own health, yet may be 'nudged' towards better self-care (Thaler and Sunstein, 2008, part 3).

Sleep

Like work, sleep tends to be seen as a subtraction from the discretionary time we have for enjoyment. But getting enough good-quality sleep is one of the most significant influences on our happiness and health, and sleep disorders rob millions of happiness and are one of the world's most important causes of premature mortality (Dement, 2001; Martin, 2003). And if we manage to sleep regularly and well, we need less of it and so make a double gain. In the modern era, though some of us damage our well-being by not sleeping enough, in general our sleeping arrangements are so much better than in previous eras that we can afford to sleep fewer hours, and this constitutes an under-recognised form of life extension – we don't only get more years of life, we also get more wakeful hours per year, so arguably the 'happy life years' concept ought to be adapted to measure 'sleep-adjusted happy life years'.

Sleep is seen as largely a personal and biological matter rather than a social issue. Yet people learn to sleep in radically different ways in different cultures and families (Steger and Brunt, 2003). Our working habits, domestic arrangements, and cultural habits all affect our sleeping habits and attitudes to sleep. So this seems to be a most important and promising domain of happiness-relevant policy and practice (Batchelder, 2002; Ekirch, 2005; Williams, 2005).

Voluntary simplification and slow-down movements

People are becoming more conscious of the problems of runaway time pressure (that is, stressful speed and/or sense of shortage of time), even if the availability of leisure time is actually staying still or (at least over a lifetime) increasing (Robinson and Godbey, 1997; Levine, 1997/2006; Bertman, 1998; Gleick, 2000; Jacobs and Gerson, 2004). For a long time associated with countercultural separatist and utopian movements, the ideology of deliberately simplifying our lives and slowing down the speed at which we do things is now spreading into mainstream society. Instead of heading off to isolate themselves in rural communes, people are increasingly trying to enjoy the benefits of some degree of simplification while also living in cities and having professional jobs.

But it is far from self-evident that by earning less, we also work less, or that we can simply choose – as one book title would have us believe – to *Work less, live more* (Clyatt, 2007). So there is plenty of room for debates about the middle ground between full-time urban professionalism and opt-out frugality, and in any case the long-standing belief in 'work' as a discrete domain may be breaking down (Haworth and Veal, 2004; Kane, 2004; Bennett, 2006; Pinquart and Silbereisen, 2010).

Play, leisure, and sport

If research on domains such as health, education, family life, and work can often proceed as if satisfaction and happiness were irrelevant, the same is not true of the study of leisure, which is always understood as having the core function of helping people to enjoy their lives. As people become able to devote an increasing percentage of their lives to leisure activities (as least over the extended life course, even if not during mid-life) there will be increasing attention to the purposes of leisure, with some people favouring relaxation and others seeking new forms of fulfilment through 'serious leisure' (Stebbins, 2007; Rojek, 2010), and some deliberately promoting a 'fun' approach to sports, emphasising the intrinsic enjoyment in contrast to the perfectionist fanaticism and endless deferral of gratification that takes over as sports become dominated by elitist competition (Kimiecik, 2002; Wright, 2004).

Peace making, conflict management and post-conflict rehabilitation

Despite media portrayals and many people's beliefs, we live in an era of unprecedented peace and safety, which both facilitates happiness pursuits and also derives from increasingly empathetic and non-violent approaches to conflict resolution. At international and national levels, and also at the levels of local and family dramas, we are seeing efforts to respond to conflicts in a spirit of healing rather than punitive justice, and the growing discipline of Peace Studies echoes and overlaps with Happiness Studies in drawing inspiration from various disciplines such as Psychology, Anthropology, Sociology, Theology, Political Science and Legal Studies. This work is beginning to translate into real-world applicability (Bar-Siman-Tov, 2004; Kim et al, 2008; Hamber, 2009; Larson, 2009; Mayton, 2009; Montiel and Noor, 2009; Francis, 2010; Kalayjian and Paloutzian, 2010).

Responsible citizenship and prosocial behaviour

One of the more revolutionary themes in happiness studies has been the questioning of traditional beliefs that 'ethical' and 'self-interested' behaviour are distinct and even in opposition. There is now ample research demonstrating positive synergies and bidirectional causation between virtue, altruism, and prosocial behaviour on the one hand, and happiness on the other. Happiness is known to be contagious and to have generally good outcomes for society, while prosocial, 'altruistic' activities are known to be good for our happiness and health (Thoits and Hewitt, 2001; Schwartz et al, 2003; Post, 2005; Borgonovi, 2008).

Social capital, so often treated in the past by economists and planners as an instrumental good, is now seen to be intrinsically rewarding (Thin, 2002, chapter 4; Bartolini et al, 2009; Helliwell and Wang, 2011). In the business world, the new policy science of 'organisational citizenship' is blossoming (Glomb et al, 2011). So, as governments, community organisations, and schools try to develop policies and strategies to promote prosocial activities such as volunteering, they may change their strategies and put more emphasis on the joys and intrinsic rewards of this work, and less on the sense of duty or 'heavenly' (extrinsic and – frankly – implausible) rewards.

Legal reform and criminal justice

The legal profession is starting to learn about the implications of happiness science for legal practice. Though it will retain some degree of suspicion about the place of emotion and empathy in the law court, it will increasingly be required to understand and respond to people's subjective experiences. Crime fighters recognise now that they need to battle not only against 'objective' crime but also against fears and suspicions of crime. Judges offering compensation to victims may have to adjust their awards to recognise the evidence of hedonic adaptation. And more generally, happiness considerations are creeping into the debates about the purposes and outcomes of laws, crime fighting measures, and taxation (Griffith, 2004; Seligman, Verkuil and Kang, 2005; Angner, 2007; Bronsteen et al, 2009; Patmore, 2009; Sunstein and Posner, 2010).

Cybereudaimonics and the joys of the 'social web' (Web 2.0)

When hypothetically offered virtual happiness or pleasure via the 'experience machine' in Nozick's thought experiment (1974, p 44), most people may recognise this as somehow inauthentic and undesirable. But not everyone objects equally strongly, and many would rather like the idea of regular spells enjoying those 'unreal' pleasures. Many of the arguments about virtual experience, particularly concerning the internet, turn on similar lines, questioning the authenticity and ultimate desirability of the various surrogate experiences and multiple identities that people can now enjoy.

Critiques of the social web tend to focus on possible psychological harms at the individual level (overstimulation through multi-tasking, sleep deprivation, time pressure, identity confusion, and so on), or on possible new social pathologies such as the new kinds of exclusion and inequality brought about by the 'digital divide', online bullying, and loss of real social ties. It is also possible, however, to explore more positively the many kinds of radically new psychological and social benefit brought about by the social web, such as being able to reduce the limitations on our relationships imposed by our bodies, time availability, and places of residence (Obst and Stafurik, 2002; Sirgy et al, 2006; Al-Mutawa, 2009; Hoffman, 2011; Lee et al, 2011; Rainie et al, 2011).

Positive environmentalism, urban planning, and architecture

Architects and town planners have doubtless always been aware that their work influences people's happiness, but they have done little to engage with other disciplines to understand these influences. The importance of housing for well-being varies among cultures, ages, and environments. This depends on what people use houses for, how much time they spend in them, and how salient the house is as a status indicator. A World Bank evaluation study found that simply replacing dirt floors with cement floors in Mexico led to dramatic improvements in the health and happiness of children and adults, changes that more than justified the investment, despite nil effect on standard 'economic' indicators (Cattaneo et al, 2007). In Thailand researchers found that while some 'objective' indicators of housing quality had no relationship with health, there were significant relationships between health outcomes and people's *subjective* views on housing quality, which better reflected the factors that were locally important (Fuller et al, 1993).

This latter study implicitly makes the case for interpretive and ethnographic approaches to housing quality as a complement to more 'technical' (biophysical and objectivist) approaches. Although concepts such as 'feng shui' and 'biophilic architecture' have been justifiably criticised for naïvety and vagueness, there is ample research nowadays providing convincing evidence of the way plants, natural views, and access to nature influence things like obesity (Lake et al, 2010), academic performance (Han, 2009), worker performance and stress control (Lohr et al, 1996), mental health (Oliver, 2006), recovery from illness (Hansen-Ketchum and Halpenny, 2011), and crime rates (Kuo and Sullivan, 2001).

Research on the social ecology of office spaces and public buildings such as schools and hospitals has also begun paying more attention to subjective and social aspects, rather than seeing these issues primarily as questions of efficiency (Becker, 2004). Oldenburg's work on 'third places' (1999) has been influential in persuading planners to consider the importance of ensuring that people have places to socialise that are distinct from both home and work, and de Botton's *Architecture of happiness* (2006) similarly emphasises the need for social planning at levels between the private home and the town.

Religion, spirituality, and self-transcendence

Religions tend to justify their existence by reference to sacred traditions, deities, and expected afterlives, often with the promise that faith will be rewarded with other-worldly happiness or mystical union with the divine. Both of these promises exhibit the lack of transparency and the obfuscation of purpose that I have been arguing should be addressed with a happiness perspective. But religious traditions may also offer real and verifiable happiness prospects, such as encouragements to self-transcendence, the fun of festive singing and dancing, the calm of prayer and meditation, and other opportunities to explore a range of emotional experiences and make sense of mental threats (Corrigan, 2004; Koenig, 2005; Loewenthal, 2006).

Religions can also be happiness thieves, sowing guilt about the pleasures of sexuality and science, justifying the inequities and absurdities of hierarchy and fundamentalist dogma, generating worries about things that don't matter, and distracting attention from things that do matter (Samways, 1994; Dawkins, 2006). We will never be able to definitively judge one religious tradition or practice as better for our happiness, compared with another. Nor can happiness scholarship provide persuasive arguments for or against religiosity in general. A strong assumption that religion is pro-happiness has been identified among US youth (Smith, 2005, pp 162–3). Since a lot of happiness surveys have been conducted by and among religious North Americans there is some pro-religious bias in happiness research: perhaps religiosity correlates with happiness in North America, but not in the more secular parts of Europe. But religiosity–happiness correlations tend to prove insignificant once they are controlled for cultural context (Lewis and Cruise, 2006; Eichhorn, forthcoming).

We could clarify our understanding of the values, purposes, goods, and harms of religion by referring to happiness, thereby humanising our appreciation of religion. If promoters of religion were to justify their existence on happiness grounds, they might optimise the ways in which they promote this-worldly happiness. Though the benefits and costs of religiosity in general are all context-dependent, a rational follower would rightly be suspicious of any doctrine that relied mainly on promises of other-worldly rewards or that invited customers to pay for religious merit or divine forgiveness. A happiness lens could vastly improve the plausibility and value of religious institutions, and there is no evidence in support of the Archbishop of Wales' claim, in his 2010 Christmas sermon, that happiness surveys are bound to nudge people towards selfishness rather than altruism (Morgan, 2010).

Last word

In modern times, conversations about happiness have increased for both positive and negative reasons. We have very much more freedom and time to pursue our own happiness, but are also more worried about not being happy enough, about reaching our deathbeds with a sense of unfulfilment. Scholars tell us that we should worry about the loss of happiness (Scitovsky, 1976; Lane, 2000), but also about loss of sadness (Horwitz and Wakefield, 2007; van Deurzen, 2009). Approaching happiness as 'social policy' rather than as pure philosophy or as a self-help issue can help us to work through some of these doubts. We see selfish zero-sum competitions for scarce goods as socially destructive, and we recognise the imagined boundary between ourselves and the social environment as porous at best. The pursuit of personal well-being then becomes necessarily a social project, one of working with others to define common aims that would facilitate everyone's happiness.

Negative 'push factors' encouraging happiness conversations have developed from recognition of the various social ills, or social pollutions, that inhibit personal happiness. Modernity has almost certainly enabled people not only to live longer, but also on average to live more happily. But there are several important pathologies of modernity that threaten those happiness gains. Of these, the most worrisome seem to be:

- **Social fears:** In an era when on most counts other people are more trustworthy than ever before since the dawn of humanity, we suffer new kinds of mistrust in other people's goodwill towards us. Many of us are particularly bothered by *status anxiety*, the worry that other people won't recognise our value. At the same time, we also tend to be bothered by fear of inequality, by the irrational belief that society is becoming more unequal.

- **Unrealistic aspirations:** Just when we have every good reason to abandon fatalism and explore a massively increased range of options for self-realisation, many of us feel cheated by the false promises of the myths of self-esteem and self-help in a generally optimistic social environment. In thinking too much about our own happiness, and simultaneously being dazzled by the array of life choices, it can also happen that we allow ourselves to become perpetually tormented by both the variety and the sheer brilliance of our possible selves.
- **Love deficit:** Though our options for developing warmly affectionate and intellectually stimulating relationships with other people have multiplied rapidly, it is more than likely that our actual ability to sustain meaningful pair-bonding with other people has in many ways declined.
- **Time famine:** Although discretionary 'leisure' time may for many of us have actually increased, our perception of time pressure has increased still more steeply, with the result that more people in modern society feel rushed and worried about the passage of time than ever before.
- **Meaning deficit:** As social scientists have never tired of pointing out, we suffer a variety of uncertainties and sense of purposelessness deriving from secularisation, urbanisation, industrialisation, globalisation, schooling, and fragmentations of families and kin networks.
- **Fear of the future:** After a century of unprecedented progress in so many valued domains, we have developed a sense of guilt and vertigo, a reluctance to believe that things could go on getting better.
- **Fear of happiness itself:** Like sexuality and other privately powerful but self-transcendent experiences, happiness seems to engender in some people a fear of talking or perhaps even of thinking about it, and this phobia readily translates into dangerous forms of institutionalised neglect.

Let us hope that we will not only address those worries and doubts better, but also recognise and celebrate more the gains we have already made, if we develop more substantial engagements between happiness scholars and the people who try to make human lives go better.

References

Aburdene, P. (2005) *Megatrends 2010: The rise of conscious capitalism*, Newburyport, MA: Hampton Roads Publishing.

Ahmed, S. (2010) *The promise of happiness*, Durham, NC: Duke University Press.

Ainsworth, M.D.S. et al (1978) *Patterns of attachment: A psychological study of the strange situation*, Hillsdale, NJ: Lawrence Erlbaum.

Aknin, L.B. et al (2010) 'Prosocial spending and wellbeing: cross-cultural evidence for a psychological universal', Working Paper No 16415, Cambridge: National Bureau of Economic Research.

Albert, D.H. (1999) *And the skylark sings with me: Adventures in homeschooling and community-based education*, Gabriola Island, BC: New Society Publishers.

Albright, K. et al (2011) 'Moving beyond geography: health practices and outcomes across time and place', in L.M. Burton et al (eds), *Communities, neighborhoods, and health: Expanding the boundaries of place*, Dordrecht: Springer, pp 127–44.

Alesina, A.F., Glaeser, E.L. and Sacerdote, E.L. (2005) 'Work and leisure in the U.S. and Europe: why so different?', National Bureau of Economic Research Working Paper No 11278, www.nber.org/papers/w11278.

Alexander, M.G. and Wood, W. (2000) 'Women, men and positive emotions', in A. Fischer (ed), *Gender and emotion: Social psychological perspectives*, Cambridge: Cambridge University Press, pp 189–210.

Al-Mutawa, N. (2009) 'Positive social media', in S.J. Lopez (ed), *Encyclopedia of positive psychology*, San Francisco: Jossey-Bass, pp 752–4.

Amabile, T.M. et al (2005) 'Affect and creativity at work', *Administrative Science Quarterly*, vol 50, pp 367–403.

Amato, P.R. et al (2007) *Alone together: How marriage in America is changing*, Cambridge, MA: Harvard University Press.

Anderson, C. (2009) *Free: The future of a radical price*, New York: Hyperion.

Angner, E. (2004) 'Subjective measures of wellbeing: a philosophical examination', PhD thesis, University of Pittsburgh.

Angner, E. (2007) 'Natural law and the science of happiness', in H. James (ed), *Natural law and economics*, Princeton, NJ: Witherspoon Institute.

Angner, E. et al (2010) 'Health literacy and happiness: a community-based study', *Social Indicators Research*, vol 95, no 2, pp 325–38.

Anielski, M. (2007) *The economics of happiness: Building genuine wealth*, Gabriola Island, BC: New Society Publishers.

Annas, J. (1993) 'Women and the quality of life: two norms or one?' in M. Nussbaum and A. Sen (eds), *The quality of life*, Oxford: Clarendon Press, pp 279–301.

Antidote (1997) Conference report: 'Emotional development and the school curriculum', London: Antidote, www.antidote.org.uk

Antonovsky, A. (1996) 'The salutogenic model as a theory to guide health promotion', *Health Promotion International*, vol 11, pp 11–18.

Appadurai, A. (2004) 'The capacity to aspire: culture and the terms of recognition', in V. Rao and M. Walton (eds), *Culture and public action*, Washington, DC: World Bank, pp 59–84.

Appleton, J.J., Christenson, S.L., Kim, D. and Reschly A. (2006) 'Measuring cognitive and psychological engagement: validation of the student engagement instrument', *Journal of School Psychology*, vol 44, no 5, pp 427–45.

Aronowitz, S. (2008) *Against schooling: For an education that matters*, London: Pluto Press.

Aronson, E. (2004) 'Reducing hostility and building compassion: lessons from the jigsaw classroom', in A.G. Miller (ed), *The social psychology of good and evil*, New York: The Guilford Press, pp 469–88.

Aronson, E. and Patnoe, S. (1997) *Cooperation in the classroom: The jigsaw method*, New York: Longman.

Arrindell, W.A. and Veenhoven, R. (2002) 'Feminine values and happy life-expectancy in nations', *Personality and Individual Differences*, vol 33, no 5, pp 803–13 .

Australian Unity (2010) *What makes us happy? Ten years of the Australian Unity Wellbeing Index* (2nd edn), www.australianunitycorporate.com.au/Publications/Pages/Whatmakesushappy.aspx.

Bacon, N., et al (2010) 'The state of happiness: can public policy shape people's wellbeing and resilience?', London: Young Foundation/IdeA, www.youngfoundation.org/files/images/wellbeing_happiness_Final__2_.pdf.

Bagaric, M. and McConvill, J. (2005) 'Goodbye justice, hello happiness: welcoming positive psychology to the law', *Deakin Law Review*, vol 10, no 1, pp 1–26.

Baltes, P.B. (2003) 'Extending longevity: dignity gain – or dignity drain?' *MaxPlanckResearch*, vol 3, pp 15–19.

Baltes, P.B. and Baltes, M.M. (eds) (1990) *Successful aging*, Cambridge: Cambridge University Press.

Bandes, S.A. (ed) (2000) *The passions of law*, New York: New York University Press.

Barnett, C., Philip, C. and Newholm, T. (2005) 'Philosophy and ethical consumption', in R. Harrison, T. Newholm and D. Shaw (eds), *The ethical consumer*, London: Sage, pp 11–21.

Bar-Siman-Tov, Y. (2004) *From conflict resolution to reconciliation*, New York: Oxford University Press.

Bartolini, S., Bilancini, E., and Sarracino, F. (2009) 'Social capital predicts happiness: world-wide evidence from time series', www.econ-pol. unisi.it/bartolini/papers/BBS_1_dic_2009.pdf.

Batchelder, T. (2002) 'Medical anthropology: the cultural biology of sleep', *Townsend Letter for Doctors and Patients*, vol 28, pp 47-48.

Bauman, Z. (2004) *Work, consumerism and the new poor*, Maidenhead: Open University Press.

Beck, A.T. and Steer, R.A. (1988) *Beck Hopelessness Scale manual*, San Antonio: The Psychological Corporation.

Beck, U. (2000) *The brave new world of work*, Cambridge: Polity Press.

Beck, U. and Beck-Gernsheim, E. (2002) *Individualization: Institutionalized individualism and its social and political consequences*, London: Sage.

Becker, F. (2004) *Offices at work: Uncommon workspace strategies that add value and improve performance*, San Francisco: Jossey-Bass.

Belknap, J. and McDonald, C. (2010) 'Judges' attitudes about and experiences with sentencing circles in intimate-partner abuse cases', *Canadian Journal of Criminology & Criminal Justice*, vol 52, no 4, pp 369–95.

Belliotti, R. (2004) *Happiness is overrated*, Lanham, MD: Rowman and Littlefield.

Ben-Ami, D. (2010) *Ferraris for all: In defence of economic progress*, Bristol: The Policy Press.

Ben-Arieh, A. (2006) 'Measuring and monitoring the wellbeing of young children around the world', Paris: UNESCO unesdoc.unesco. org/images/0014/001474/147444e.pdf.

Benatar, D. (2006) *Better never to have been: The harm of coming into existence*, Oxford: Oxford University Press.

Bennett, J. and Grimley, L.K. (2000) 'Parenting in the global community: a cross-cultural/international perspective', in M.J. Fine and S.W. Lee (eds), *Handbook of diversity in parent education*, New York: Academic Press, pp 97–124.

Bennett, R. (2006) *The underachiever's manifesto: The guide to accomplishing little and feeling great*, San Francisco, CA: Chronicle Books.

Ben-Shahar, T. (2007) *Happier: Learn the secrets to daily joy and lasting fulfillment*, New York: McGraw-Hill.

Bentall, R. (1992) 'A proposal to classify happiness as a psychiatric disorder', *Journal of Medical Ethics*, vol 18, pp 94–98.

Bentall, R. (2009) *Doctoring the mind: Why psychiatric treatments fail*, Harmondsworth: Penguin.

Berger, L. and Berger, P. (2003) *The talent management handbook*, New York: McGraw-Hill.

Bertman, S. (1998) *Hyperculture: The human cost of speed*, Westport, CT: Praeger.

Best, J. (2004) *More damned lies and statistics: How numbers confuse public issues*, Berkeley, CA: University of California Press.

Bhattacharya, S. (2005) 'Happiness helps people stay healthy', *New Scientist*, 18 April.

Biswas-Diener, R. (ed) (2011) *Positive psychology as a mechanism for social change*, Dordrecht: Springer.

Biswas-Diener, R. and Dean, B. (2007) *Positive psychology coaching*, Hoboken, NJ: John Wiley.

Bjørnskov, C. (2005) 'Life satisfaction: is there a role for policy?' European Enterprise Institute Policy Paper, www.cepos.dk/uploads/media/Lifesatisfaction_Bjornskov.pdf.

Bjørnskov, C., Dreher, A. and Fischer, J.A.V. (2007a) 'The bigger the better? Evidence of the effect of government size on life satisfaction around the world', *Public Choice*, vol 130, nos 3–4, pp 267–92.

Bjørnskov, C., Dreher, A. and Fischer, J.A.V. (2007b) 'On decentralization and life satisfaction', *Economics Letters*, vol 99, no 1, pp 147–51.

Blanchflower, D.G. and Oswald, A.J. (2004) 'Money, sex and happiness: an empirical study', *Scandinavian Journal of Economics*, vol 106, no 3, pp 393–415.

Blustein, D.L. (2008) 'The role of work in psychological health and wellbeing: a conceptual, historical, and public policy perspective', *American Psychologist*, vol 63, no 4, pp 228–40.

Blustein, D.L. (2011) 'A relational theory of working', *Journal of Vocational Behavior*, vol 79, no 1, pp 1-17.

Boehm, J. and Lyubomirsky, S. (2008) 'Does happiness promote career success?', *Journal of Career Assessment*, vol 16, no 1, pp 101–16.

Boissiere, M. (2004) 'Determinants of primary education outcomes in developing countries', Washington, DC: World Bank Background Paper for the Evaluation of the World Bank's Support to Primary Education.

Bok, D. (2010) *The politics of happiness: What government can learn from the new research on well-being*, Princeton, NJ: Princeton University Press.

Bolton, S.C. (2000) 'Who cares? Offering emotion work as a "gift" in the nursing labour process', *Journal of Advanced Nursing*, vol 32, no 3, pp 580–6.

Booth, P.B. and Jernberg, A.M. (1979/2010) *Theraplay: Helping parents and children build better relationships through attachment-based play* (3rd edn), San Francisco: Jossey-Bass.

Borgonovi, F. (2008) 'Doing well by doing good: the relationship between formal, volunteering and self-reported health and happiness', *Social Science & Medicine*, vol 66, pp 2321–34.

Borooah, V.K. (2006) 'How much happiness is there in the world? A cross-country study', *Applied Economics Letters*, vol 13, no 8, pp 483–8.

Boulin, J., Messenger, J.C. and Lallement, M. (eds) (2006) *Decent working time: New trends, new issues*, Geneva: ILO.

Bowling, A. (1995) 'What things are important in people's lives? A survey of the public's judgements to inform scales of health related quality of life', *Social Science and Medicine*, vol 41, no 10, pp 1447–62.

Bowling, A. (2003) 'Current state of the art in quality of life measurement', in A.J. Carr, I.J. Higginson and P.G. Robinson (eds), *Quality of life*, London: BMJ Books, pp 1–8.

Bowling, A. (2007) *Ageing well: quality of life in old age*, Maidenhead: Open University Press.

Boyle, D. and Simms, A. (2009) *The new economics: A bigger picture*, London: Earthscan.

Bradshaw, J. (ed) (2002) *The wellbeing of children in the UK*, London: Save the Children.

Bragues, G. (2006) 'Seek the good life, not money: the Aristotelian approach to business ethics', *Journal of Business Ethics*, vol 67, pp 341–57.

Braithwaite, A. (2002) 'The personal, the political, third-wave and postfeminisms', *Feminist Theory*, vol 3, no 3, pp 335–44.

Breggin, P.R. (1998/2001) *Talking back to Ritalin: What doctors aren't telling you about stimulants and ADHD* (2nd edn), Cambridge, MA: Da Capo Press.

Brezovsky, S.H. (2002) 'School enjoyment: the impact of students', enjoyment of school on their perceptions of their school experience', Paper at annual conference of the New England Educational Research Organization, Northampton, Massachusetts, 24–26 April.

Brighouse, H. (2005) *On education*, London: Routledge.

Bronfenbrenner, U. (1977) 'Who needs parent education?' Position paper for the Working Conference on Parent Education, Charles Stewart Mott Foundation, Flint, Michigan.

Bronfenbrenner, U. (1979) *The ecology of human development: Experiments by nature and design*, Cambridge, MA: Harvard University Press.

Bronsteen, J., Buccafusco, C. and Masur, J. (2009) 'Happiness and punishment', *University of Chicago Law Review*, vol 76, no 3, pp 1037–82.

Bruni, L. (2006) *Civil happiness: Economics and human flourishing in historical perspective*, London: Routledge.

Brunwasser, S.M., Gillham, J.E. and Kim, E.S. (2009) 'A meta-analytic review of the Penn Resiliency Program's effect on depressive symptoms', *Journal of Consulting and Clinical Psychology*, vol 77, no 6, pp 1042–54.

Burnett, J. (1974) *Useful toil: Autobiographies of working people from the 1820s to the 1920s*, London: Routledge.

Burns, D.D. (1980) 'Perfectionists' script for self defeat', *Psychology Today*, November, pp 34–52.

Burns, T., and M.Firn (2002) *Assertive outreach in mental health*. Oxford: Oxford University Press.

Bury, M. and Holme, A. (eds) (2009) *Life after ninety*, London: Routledge.

Bushell, W.C. et al (2009) *Longevity, regeneration, and optimal health: Integrating Eastern and Western perspectives*, Annals of the New York Academy of Sciences.

Buys, L. and Miller, E. (2009) 'Enhancing social capital in children via schoolbased community cultural development projects: A pilot study', *International Journal of Education & the Arts*, vol 10, no 3, pp 1–19.

Cameron, K.S. and Lavine, M. (2006) *Making the impossible possible: Leading extraordinary performance: the Rocky Flats story*, San Francisco: Berrett-Koehler.

Cameron, K.S., Dutton, J.E. and Quinn, R.E. (2003) *Positive organisational scholarship*, San Francisco: Berrett-Koehler.

Camfield, L. (2006) 'The why and how of understanding "subjective" wellbeing: exploratory work by the WeD group in four developing countries', University of Bath: Wellbeing in Developing Countries Working Paper 25, www.welldev.org.uk/research/workingpaperpdf/wed26.pdf.

Camfield, L., Choudhury, K. and Devine, J. (2009) 'Well-being, happiness and why relationships matter: evidence from Bangladesh', *Journal of Happiness Studies*, vol 10, no 1, pp. 71–91.

Campbell, A., Converse, P.E., and Rogers, W.L. (1976) *The Quality of American Life*. New York: Russell Sage Foundation

Campis, L.K., Lyman, R.D. and Prentice-Dunn, S. (1986) 'The Parental Locus of Control Scale: development and validation', *Journal of Clinical Child Psychology*, vol 15, no 3, pp 260–7.

CareerBuilder (2011) 'Nearly one-in-five workers have dated co-workers at least twice during their career, finds annual CareerBuilder Valentine's Day Survey', www.careerbuilder.com, accessed March 2011.

Carey, S. (2003) *Whole child: Restoring wonder to the art of parenting*, Oxford: Rowman & Littlefield.

Carr, E.R. (2010) 'The place of stories in development: creating spaces for participation through narrative analysis', *Development in Practice*, vol 20, no 2 pp 219–26.

Carr, S., McAuliffe, E. and MacLachlan, M. (1998) *Psychology of aid*, London: Routledge.

Cattaneo, M.D. et al (2007) 'Housing, health and happiness', Washington, DC: World Bank Policy Research Working Paper 4214; Impact evaluation series no. 14.

Centre for Bhutan Studies (2008) 'Gross National Happiness Index', www.grossnationalhappiness.com//gnhIndex/intruductionGNH. aspx.

Chapman, E.N. (2009) 'From object to subject: young women's experience of sexuality education within sex-negative taboos', PhD dissertation, Iowa State University.

Charlton, B.G. (2001) 'What is the meaning of life? Animism, generalised anthropomorphism and social intelligence', www.hedweb. com/bgcharlton/meaning-of-life.html.

Charon, R. (2006) *Narrative medicine: Honoring the stories of illness*, New York: Oxford University Press.

Cheavens, J.S. and Gum, A.M. (2010) 'From here to where you want to be: building the bridges with hope therapy in a case of major depression', in G.W. Burns (ed), *Happiness, healing, enhancement*, Hoboken, NJ: John Wiley, pp 51–63.

Cherniss, C. and Goleman, D. (eds) (2001) *The emotionally intelligent workplace*, San Francisco, CA: Jossey-Bass.

Chida, Y. and Steptoe, A. (2008) 'Positive psychological wellbeing and mortality: a quantitative review of prospective observational studies', *Psychosomatic Medicine*, vol 70, pp 741–56.

Childstats.gov US Forum on Child and Family Statistics (2009) *America's Children: Key National Indicators of Wellbeing, 2009*, www. childstats.gov/americaschildren.

China Human Capital Projects (accessed 8 September 2011) 'Gansu Survey of Children and Families', http://china.pop.upenn.edu/ research-products.

Christakis, N.A. and Fowler, J.S. (2010) *Amazing power of social networks and how they shape our lives*, New York: HarperCollins.

Christie, I. and Nash, L. (eds) (1998) *The good life,* London: Demos

Christner, R.W. and Mennuti, R. (eds) (2008) *School-based mental health: A practitioner's guide to comparative practices*, London: Routledge.

Chua, A. (2011) *The battle hymn of the tiger mother*, New York: Penguin.

Ciaramicoli, A. (2004) *Performance addiction: The dangerous new syndrome and how to stop it from ruining your life*, Chichester: Wiley.

Clark, A.E. (1997) 'Job satisfaction and gender: why are women so happy at work?' *Labour Economics*, vol 4, no 4, pp 341–72.

Clark, A.G. and Oswald, A.J. (2002) 'A simple statistical method for measuring how life events affect happiness', *International Journal of Epidemiology*, vol 31, pp 1139–44.

Clark, D.A. (2002) 'Development ethics: a research agenda', *International Journal of Social Economics*, vol 29, no 11, pp 830–48.

Clark, M.S. et al (2011) 'Heightened interpersonal security diminishes the monetary value of possessions', *Journal of Experimental Social Psychology*, vol 47, no 2, pp 359–64.

Clauss-Ehlers, C.S. (ed) (2009) *Encyclopedia of cross-cultural school psychology*, New York: Springer.

Clyatt, B. (2007) *Work less, live more: The way to semi-retirement*, Berkeley, CA: Nolo.

Code, L. (1991) *What can she know? Feminist theory and the construction of knowledge*, Ithaca, NY: Cornell University Press.

Cohen, J.L. (2002) *Regulating intimacy: A new legal paradigm*, Princeton, NJ: Princeton University Press.

Cohen, S. and Pressman, S.H. (2006) 'Positive affect and health', *Current Directions in Psychological Science*, vol 15, no 2, pp 22–5.

Cohen, S. et al (2003) 'Emotional style and susceptibility to the common cold', *Psychosomatic Medicine*, vol 65, no 4, pp 652–7.

Colclough, C., Kingdon, G. and Patrinos, H.A. (2009) 'The pattern of returns to education and its implications', University of Cambridge: RECOUP Policy Brief no 4, http://recoup.educ.cam.ac.uk/publications/policybriefs.html.

Comim, F. (2008) 'Social capital and the capability approach', in D. Castiglione, J.W. van Deth and G. Wolleb (eds), *The handbook of social capital*, Oxford: Oxford University Press, pp 624–51.

Conoley, C.W. and Conoley, J.C. (2009) *Positive psychology and family therapy*, London: Wiley.

Cook, S. (2008) *The essential guide to employee engagement*, London: Kogan Page.

Cooperrider, D.L. and Sekerka, L.E. (2003) 'Toward a theory of positive organizational change', in K.S. Cameron, J.E. Dutton and R.E. Quinn (eds), *Positive organizational scholarship*, San Francisco: Berrett-Koehler, pp 225–40.

Corrigan, J. (2004) *Religion and emotion: Approaches and interpretations*, New York: Oxford University Press.

Coster, W. (2007) 'Childhood in crisis?' in P. Zwozdiak-Myers (ed) *Childhood and youth studies*, Exeter: Learning Matters, pp 25–34.

Courtenay, W.H. (2000) 'Constructions of masculinity and their influence on men's well-being: a theory of gender and health.' *Social Science and Medicine*, vol 50, no 10, pp 1385–1401.

Craig, C. (2009) 'Wellbeing in schools: The curious case of the tail wagging the dog?', Glasgow: Centre for Confidence and Wellbeing, www.centreforconfidence.co.uk/projects. php?p=cGlkPTU2JmlkPTYzMw==.

Crawford, M.B. (2009) *Shop class as soulcraft: An inquiry into the value of work*, Harmondsworth, UK: Penguin.

Crisp, R. (2001) 'Wellbeing', in *Stanford encyclopedia of philosophy*, www. seop.leeds.ac.uk/entries/wellbeing/.

Crumbaugh, J.C. and Maholick, L.T. (1964) 'An experimental study in existentialism: The psychometric approach to Frankl's concept of noogenic neurosis', *Journal of Clinical Psychology*, vol 20, pp 200–7.

Csikszentmihalyi, M. (1990) *Flow: The psychology of optimal experience*, New York: HarperCollins.

Csikszentmihalyi, M. (1997) *Finding flow: The psychology of engagement with everyday life*, New York: Basic Books.

Csikszentmihalyi, M. (2000) 'If we are so rich, why aren't we happy?', *American Psychologist*, vol 54, pp 821–7.

Csikszentmihalyi, M. (2003) *Good business: Leadership, flow, and the making of meaning*, Harmondsworth: Penguin.

Csikszentmihalyi, M. and Csikszentmihalyi, I.S. (eds) (2006) *A life worth living: Contributions to positive psychology*, New York: Oxford University Press.

Csikszentmihalyi, M. and Hermanson, K. (1995) 'Intrinsic motivation in museums: what makes visitors want to learn?', *Museum News*, vol 74, pp 34–61.

Daily Telegraph (2007) 'Happiness lessons to cost council £25,000', 10 May.

Dambrun, M. and Ricard, M. (2011) 'Self-centeredness and selflessness: a theory of self-based psychological functioning and its consequences for happiness', *Review of General Psychology*, vol 15, no 2, pp 138–57.

Danner, D.D., Snowdon, D.A. and Friesen, W.V. (2001) 'Positive emotions in early life and longevity: findings from the Nun Study', *Journal of Personality and Social Psychology*, vol 80, no 5, pp 804–13.

Darling, C.A. and Turkki, K. (2009) 'Global family concerns and the role of family life education: an ecosystemic analysis', *Family Relations*, vol 58, no 1, pp 14–27.

Dawkins, R. (2006) *The God delusion*, London: Bantam Press.

de Botton, A. (2006) *The architecture of happiness*, London: Hamish Hamilton.

De Shazer, S. (1985) *Keys to solution in brief therapy*, New York: W.W. Norton.

De Waal, F. (2009) *The age of empathy: Nature's lessons for a kinder society*, Toronto: McClelland & Stewart.

Dean, H. (2009) 'Critiquing capabilities: the distractions of a beguiling concept', *Critical Social Policy*, vol 29, no 2, pp 261–78.

Deater-Deckard, K. (2004) *Parenting stress*, New Haven: Yale University Press.

DeCato, L.A. et al (2002) 'Adolescents and their parents: a critical review of measures to assess their satisfaction with one another', *Clinical Psychology Review*, vol 22, pp 833–74.

Decety, J. and Ickes, W. (eds) (2009) *The social neuroscience of empathy*, Cambridge: MIT Press.

Deci, E.L. and Ryan, R.M. (1985) *Intrinsic motivation and self-determination in human behaviour*, New York: Plenum Press.

Dement, W.C., with Vaughan, W. (2001) *The promise of sleep: A pioneer in sleep medicine explores the vital connection between health, happiness, and a good night's sleep*, London: Macmillan Pan.

Department for Children, Schools, and Families (2005) *Social and emotional aspects of learning (SEAL): Improving behaviour, improving learning*, nationalstrategies.standards.dcsf.gov.uk/node/87009.

Department of Communities and Local Government (2007) 'New Performance Framework for Local Authorities and Local Authority Partnerships', www.communities.gov.uk/publications/localgovernment/nationalindicator.

Diener, E. (1984) 'Subjective wellbeing', *Psychological Bulletin*, vol 95, pp 542–75.

Diener, E. (2003) 'Subjective wellbeing is desirable, but not the summum bonum', Paper at the University of Minnesota Interdisciplinary Workshop on Wellbeing, 23–25 October, Minneapolis, www.tc.umn.edu/~tiberius/workshop_papers/Diener.pdf.

Diener, E. (2006) 'Guidelines for national indicators of subjective wellbeing and ill-being', *Journal of Happiness Studies*, vol 7, no 4, pp 397–404.

Diener, E. and Chan, M. (2011) 'Happy people live longer: subjective well-being contributes to health and longevity', *Applied Psychology: Health and Well-Being*, vol 3, no 1, pp 1–43.

Diener, E. and Suh, E. (1999) 'National differences in subjective wellbeing', in Kahnemann et al (eds), *Wellbeing: The foundations of hedonic psychology*, New York: Russell Sage, pp 434–50.

Diener, E., Kahneman, D. and Helliwell, J.F. (eds) (2010) *International differences in wellbeing*, Oxford: Oxford University Press.

Diener, E. et al (1999) 'Subjective well-being: three decades of progress', *Psychological Bulletin*, vol 125, no 2, pp 276–302.

Diener, E. et al (2002) 'Dispositional affect and job outcomes', *Social Indicators Research*, vol 59, pp 229–59.

Diener, E. et al (2009) *Wellbeing for public policy*, Oxford: Oxford University Press.

Diener, E. et al (2010) 'Wealth and happiness across the world: material prosperity predicts life evaluation, whereas psychosocial prosperity predicts positive feeling', *Journal of Personality & Social Psychology*, vol 99, no 1, pp 52–61.

Dijkstra, A.G. (2006) 'Towards a fresh start in measuring gender inequality: a contribution to the debate', *Journal of Human Development*, vol 7, no 2, pp 275–83.

Dolan, P., Peasgood, T. and White, M. (2006) *Review of research on the influences on personal wellbeing and application to policy making*, London: Defra.

Doll, B., with Brehm, K. (2010) *Resilient playgrounds*, London: Taylor & Francis.

Donner, H. (2002) '"One's own marriage": love marriages in a Calcutta neighbourhood', *South Asia Research*, vol 22, no 1, pp 79–94.

Donovan, N. and Halpern, D., with Sargeant, R. (2002) 'Life satisfaction: the state of knowledge and implications for government', London: UK Government Cabinet Office, www.cabinetoffice.gov.uk/media/cabinetoffice/strategy/assets/paper.pdf.

Drahos, P. (2004) 'Trading in public hope', *Annals of The American Academy of Political and Social Science*, vol 592, no 6, pp 18–38.

Drake, J.D. (2001) *Downshifting: How to work less and enjoy life more*, San Francisco, CA: Berrett-Koehler.

Duncan, G. (2010) 'Should happiness-maximization be the goal of government?', *Journal of Happiness Studies*, vol 11, no 2, pp 163–78.

Dundes, L., Cho, E. and Kwak, S. (2009) 'The duty to succeed: honor versus happiness in college and career choices of East Asian students in the United States', *Pastoral Care in Education*, vol 27, no 2, pp 135–56.

Durlak, J.A. et al (2011) 'The impact of enhancing students' social and emotional learning', *Child Development*, vol 82, no 1, pp 405–32.

Durre, L. (2010) *Surviving the toxic workplace*, New York: McGraw-Hill.

Duska, R.F. (1997) 'The whys of business revisited', *Journal of Business Ethics*, vol 16, pp 1401–9.

Dychtwald, K. and Kadlec, D.J. (eds) (2009) *With purpose: Going from success to significance in work and life*, New York: William Morrow.

Easterbrook, G. (2003) *The progress paradox: How life gets better while people feel worse*, New York: Random House.

Easton, M. (2006) 'Britain's happiness in decline', BBC online, 2 May, news.bbc.co.uk/1/hi/programmes/happiness_formula/4771908.stm.

Ecclestone, K. and Hayes, D. (2008), *The dangerous rise of therapeutic education*, London: Routledge.

Eckholm, E. (2002) 'A Chinese dad in defense of the average child', *New York Times,* 8 June.

Edgerton, R. (1992) *Sick societies: Challenging the myth of primitive harmony*, New York: Free Press.

Ehrenreich, B. (2002) *Nickel and dimed: On (not) getting by in America*, New York: Holt.

Ehrenreich, B. (2009) *Smile or die: How positive thinking fooled America and the world*, London: Granta.

Ehrenreich, J.T. et al (2009) 'Assessment of relevant parenting factors in families of clinically anxious children: the Family Assessment Clinician-Rated Interview', *Child Psychiatry and Human Development*, vol 40, no 3, pp 331–42.

Eichhorn, J. (forthcoming, online 2011) 'Happiness for believers? Contextualising the effects of religiosity on life-satisfaction', *European Sociological Review*.

Eisler, R.T. (2007) *The real wealth of nations: Creating a caring economics*, San Francisco: Berrett-Koehler.

Ekirch, R.A. (2005) *At a day's close: Night in times past*, New York: W.W. Norton.

Elias, M.J. (2010) 'Coordinating social-emotional and character development (SECD) initiatives improves school climate and student learning', *Middle School Journal*, vol 42, no 1, pp 30–37.

Elci, M. and Alpkan, L. (2009) 'The impact of perceived organizational ethical climate on work satisfaction', *Journal of Business Ethics*, vol 84, pp 297–311.

Emde, R.N., Wolf, D.P. and Oppenheim, D. (eds) (2003) *Revealing the inner worlds of young children: The Macarthur story stem battery and parent–child narratives*, Oxford: Oxford University Press.

Emmons, R.A. (1999) *The psychology of ultimate concerns*, New York: Guilford Press.

Engel, B. (2008) *The nice girl syndrome: Stop being manipulated and abused and start standing up for yourself*, Chichester: John Wiley.

Engels, N. et al (2004) 'Factors which influence the wellbeing of pupils in Flemish secondary schools', *Educational Studies*, vol 30, no 2, pp 127–43.

Etzioni, A. (1993) *The parenting deficit*, London: Demos.

Fagerström, C. et al (2007) 'Life satisfaction and associated factors among people aged 60 years and above in six European countries', *Applied Research in Quality of Life*, vol 2, pp 33–50.

Fahlberg, L.L. and Fahlberg, L.A. (1997) 'Wellness re-examined: a cross-cultural perspective', *American Journal of Health Studies*, vol 13, pp 8–17.

Falk, J.H. and Dierking, L.D. (2000) *Learning from museums: Visitor experiences and the making of meaning*, Lanham, MD: Rowman & Littlefield.

Faludi, S. (1991/2006) *Backlash: The undeclared war against American women*, New York: Random House.

Farrelly, E.M. (2008) *Blubberland: The dangers of happiness*, University of New South Wales Press.

Fava, G.A. and Ruini, C. (2009) 'Wellbeing therapy', in S.J. Lopez (ed), *Encyclopedia of positive psychology*, San Francisco: Jossey-Bass, pp 1034–6.

Fehr, B. and Sprecher, S. (2009) 'Compassionate love: conceptual, measurement, and relational issues', in B. Fehr, S. Sprecher and L.G. Underwood (eds), *The science of compassionate love*, Chichester: Wiley-Blackwell, pp 27–52.

Fehr, B., Sprecher, S. and Underwood, L.G. (2008) *The science of compassionate love*, Chichester: Wiley-Blackwell.

Feinstein, L. et al (2006) 'What are the effects of education on health?' in R. Desjardins and T. Schuller (eds), *Measuring the effects of education on health and civic/social engagement*, Paris: OECD.

Field, J. (2009) 'Good for your soul? Adult learning and mental wellbeing', *International Journal of Lifelong Education*, vol 28, no 2, pp 175–91.

Fine, B. (2010) *Theories of social capital*. London: Pluto Press

Fineman, S. (2003) *Understanding emotion at work*, London: Sage.

Fischer, A.H. and Manstead, A.S.R. (2000) 'The relationship between gender and emotions in different cultures', in A. Fischer (ed), *Gender and emotion: Social psychological perspectives,* Cambrdge: Cambridge University Press, pp 71–94.

Fletcher, G. (2002) *The new science of intimate relationships*, London: Wiley-Blackwell.

Folbre, N. (2001) *The invisible heart: Economics and family values*, New York: The New Press.

Fong, V.L. (2004) *Only hope: Coming of age under China's one-child policy*, Stanford, CA: Stanford University Press.

Fong, V.L. (2007) 'Parent–child communication problems and the perceived inadequacies of Chinese only children', *Ethos*, vol 35, no 1, pp 85–127.

Fordyce, M. (1987/2000) *Human happiness: Its nature and its attainment*, 2 vols, online publication, www.gethappy.net/freebook.htm.

Forrest, S., Strange, V. and Oakley, A. (2004) 'What do young people want from sex education? The results of a needs assessment from a peer-led sex education programme', *Culture, Health and Sexuality*, vol 6, no 4, pp 337–54.

Foster, G. (1965) 'Peasant society and the image of limited good', *American Anthropologist*, vol 67, pp 293–15.

Francis, D. (2010) *From pacification to peacebuilding: A call to global transformation. Does conflict transformation work?* London: Pluto Press.

Frank, J. (1968) 'The role of hope in psychotherapy', *International Journal of Psychiatry*, vol 5, pp 383–95.

Frank, R.H. (1999) *Luxury fever: Why money fails to satisfy in an era of excess*, New York: Free Press.

Franks, D.D. (2010) *Neurosociology: The nexus between neuroscience and social psychology*, Dordrecht: Springer.

Fredrickson, B.L. (1998) 'What good are positive emotions', *Review of General Psychology*, vol 2, no 3, pp 300–19.

Fredrickson, B.L. (2011) *Positivity*, Oxford: Oneworld.

Fredrickson, B.L. and Losada, M.F. (2005) 'Positive affect and the complex dynamics of human flourishing', *American Psychologist*, vol 60, no 7, pp 678–86.

Freedman, M. (2008) *Encore: Finding work that matters in the second half of life*, New York: PublicAffairs.

Freire, P. (1995) *Pedagogy of hope: Reliving pedagogy of the oppressed*, London: Continuum.

Freire, P. (1972) *Pedagogy of the oppressed*, Harmondsworth: Penguin.

Freire, P. (2000) *Pedagogy of the heart*, London: Continuum.

Freud, S. (1930) *Civilization and its discontents*, London: Hogarth Press.

Frey, B.S. and Stutzer, A. (2007) 'Should national happiness be maximized?', University of Zurich: Institute for Empirical Research in Economics, Working Paper No 306, www.iew.unizh.ch/wp/iewwp 306.pdf.

Frey, B.S., with Stutzer, A. and Benz, M. (2008) *Happiness: A revolution in economics*, Cambridge, MA: MIT Press.

Friedli, L. (2009) 'Mental health, resilience and inequalities', Geneva: WHO, www.euro.who.int/document/e92227.pdf.

Friedman, M.I. (1997) *Improving the quality of life: A holistic scientific strategy*, Westport, CT: Praeger.

Frisch, M.B. et al (2005) 'Predictive and treatment validity of life satisfaction and the Quality of Life Inventory', *Assessment*, vol 12, pp 66–78.

Fromm, E. (1968) *The revolution of hope*, New York: Bantam Books

Fry, P.S. and Keyes, C.L.M. (eds) (2010) *New frontiers in resilient aging: Life-strengths and well-being in late life*, Cambridge: Cambridge University Press.

Fukuyama, F. (1995) *Trust: The social virtues and the creation of prosperity*, New York: Free Press.

Fullbrook, E. (ed) (2003) *The crisis in economics: The post-autistic economics movement – the first 600 days*, London: Routledge.

Fuller, T.D. et al (1993) 'Housing, stress, and physical wellbeing: evidence from Thailand', *Social Science and Medicine*, vol 36, no 11, pp 1417–28.

Furedi, F (2001) *Paranoid parenting*. Harmondsworth, UK: Penguin

Furedi, F. (2004) *Paranoid parenting: Why ignoring the experts may be best for your child*, Atlanta, GA: A Capella Books.

Furedi, F. (2006a) 'We need teachers, not amateur therapists. Schools have no business teaching children how to be "happy"', Spiked online, 11 July, www.frankfuredi.com/articles/teachers-20060711.htm.

Furedi, F. (2006b) 'Why the 'politics of happiness' makes me mad: if you're unhappy with state-sponsored happiness programmes, clap your hands', Spiked online, www.spiked-online.com/index.php?/site/article/311/.

Furedi, F. and Bristow, J. (2008) *Licensed to hug: How child protection policies are poisoning the relationship between the generations and damaging the, voluntary sector*, London, Civitas.

Futris, T.G. et al (2011) 'The impact of PREPARE on engaged couples: variations by delivery format', *Journal of Couple & Relationship Therapy*, vol 10, no 1, pp 69–86.

Gabhainn, S.N. and Sixsmith, J. (2006) 'Children photographing wellbeing: facilitating participation in research', *Children and Society*, vol 20, no 4, pp 249–59.

Galinsky, E. (2005) 'Children's perspective of employed mothers and fathers: closing the gap between public debates and research findings', in D.F. Halpern and S.E. Murphy (eds), *From work–family balance to work–family interaction: Changing the metaphor*, London: Routledge, pp 219–36.

Gardner, J. and Oswald, A. (2002) 'How does education affect mental wellbeing and job satisfaction?', Conference paper, University of Birmingham, www2.warwick.ac.uk/fac/soc/economics/staff/faculty/oswald/reveducationgardneroswaldjune2002.pdf.

Garner, A.M. (2008) 'Music for the very young: how to use the Suzuki Method in the preschool classroom', *Teaching Music*, vol 16, no 2, pp 28–31.

George, L.K. (2010) 'Still happy after all these years: research frontiers on subjective well-being in later life', *Journal of Gerontology: Social Sciences*, vol 65B, no 3, pp 331–9.

Gerson, K. (2010) *The unfinished revolution: How a new generation is reshaping family, work, and gender in America*, New York: Oxford University Press.

Gibbs, P. (2004) 'Marketing and the notion of wellbeing', *Business Ethics*, vol 13, no 1, pp 5–13.

Giddens, A. (1992) *The transformation of intimacy*, Cambridge: Polity Press.

Gilbert, D. (2006) *Stumbling on happiness*, New York: Knopf.

Gill, E. (2008) 'The "hope" and the social construction of the future', *International Journal of the Humanities*, vol 6, no 3, pp 9–14.

Gillies, V. (2011) 'Social and emotional pedagogies: critiquing the new orthodoxy of emotion in classroom behaviour management', *British Journal of Sociology of Education*, vol 32, no 2, pp 185–202.

Gilman, R., Furlong, M. and Huebner, E.S. (eds) (2009) *Handbook of positive psychology in schools*, London: Routledge.

Gini, A. (2003) *The importance of being lazy: In praise of play, leisure, and vacation*, London: Routledge.

Glassner, B. (1999) *The culture of fear: Why Americans are afraid of the wrong things*, New York: Basic Books.

Gleick, J. (2000) *Faster: The acceleration of just about everything*, London: Abacus.

Glenn, N.D. and Weaver, C.N. (1981) 'The contribution of marital happiness to global happiness', *Journal of Marriage and Family*, vol 43, no 1, pp 161–8.

Glomb, T.M. et al (2011) 'Doing good, feeling good: examining the role of organizational citizenship behaviors in changing mood', *Personnel Psychology*, vol 64, no 1, pp 191–223.

Glover, R.A. (2003) *No more Mr Nice Guy!*, Philadelphia, PA: Running Press.

Gmelch, G. (2003) *Behind the smile: The working lives of Caribbean tourism*, Bloomington, IN: Indiana University Press.

Goleman, D. (1995) *Emotional intelligence*, New York: Bantam.

Goleman, D. (2007) *Social intelligence: The new science of human relationships*, London: Arrow Books.

Gonzales, M.J. and Jurado-Guerrero, T. (2006) 'Remaining childless in affluent economies: a comparison of France, West Germany, Italy and Spain (1994–2001)', *European Journal of Population*, vol 22, no 4, pp 317–52.

Goodin, R.E. et al (2008) *Discretionary time: A new measure of freedom*, Cambridge: Cambridge University Press.

Goodman, J.A. (2009) *Strategic customer service*, New York: AMACOM.

Gore, C. (1997) 'Irreducibly social goods and the informational basis of Amartya Sen's Capability Approach', *Journal of International Development*, vol 9, no 2, pp 235–50.

Gottman, J. (1999) *The seven principles for making marriage work*, New York: Crown.

Gould, S.J. (1983/1996) *Mismeasure of man* (2nd edn), London: W.W. Norton.

Government of Bhutan (2002) *Education policy and strategy 2002–2012: Realizing vision 2020*. Thimphu: Ministry of Education

Graham, C. (2010) *Happiness around the world: The paradox of happy peasants and miserable millionaires*, Oxford: Oxford University Press.

Graham, C. and Hoover, M. (2006) 'Optimism and poverty in Africa: adaptation or a means to survival?', Washington, DC: Brookings Institute.

Grant, R.O. (2003) *I thought I was the crazy one: 201 ways to identify and deal with toxic people*, Fawnskin, CA: Personhood Press.

Greve, B. (ed) (2010) *Happiness and social policy in Europe*, Cheltenham: Edward Elgar.

Griffith, T.D. (2004) 'Progressive taxation and happiness', *Boston College Law Review*, vol 45, no 5, pp 1363–99.

Grimm, G. and Boothe, B. (2007) 'Narratives of life: storytelling in the perspective of happiness and disaster', *Journal of Aging, Humanities, and the Arts*, vol 1, pp 137–46.

Grouzet, F. et al (2005) 'The structure of goal contents across 15 cultures', *Journal of Personality & Social Psychology*, vol 89, pp 800–16.

Grundy, E.M. and Tomassini, C. (2010) 'Marital history, health and mortality among older men and women in England and Wales', *BMC Public Health*, vol 15, no 10, p 554.

Grzyb, J.E. and Chandler, R. (2008) *The nice factor: The art of saying no*, London: Satin Publications.

Gutstein, S.E. and Sheely, R.K. (2002) *Relationship development intervention with children, adolescents and adults*, San Francisco, CA: Jessica Kingsley.

Guven, C. (2009) 'Are happier people better citizens?', Deakin University SOEP Paper No 199, papers.ssrn.com/sol3/papers. cfm?abstract_id=1422493.

Guven, C. and Saloumidis, R. (2009) 'Why is the world getting older? The influence of happiness on mortality', Berlin: DIW Socio-Economic Panel Paper No 198.

Hair, E.C. (2005) 'The Parent–Adolescent Relationship Scale', in K. Moore and L. Lippman (eds), *What do children need to flourish? Conceptualizing and measuring indicators of positive development*, New York: Springer, pp 183–202.

Halford, W.K., Petch, J. and Creedy, D.K. (2010) 'Promoting a positive transition to parenthood: a randomized clinical trial of couple relationship education', *Prevention Science*, vol 11, no 1, pp 89–100.

Halpern, D. (2010) *The hidden wealth of nations*, Cambridge: Polity.

Haltzman, S. (2009) *The secrets of happy families: Eight keys to building a lifetime of connection and contentment*, San Francisco, CA: Jossey-Bass.

Hamber, B. (2009) *Transforming societies after political violence: Truth, reconciliation, and mental health*, Dordrecht: Springer.

Hamilton, C. and Denniss, R. (2005) *Affluenza: When too much is never enough*, Crows Nest, NSW: Allen & Unwin.

Hammond, A. (2006) *Tolerance and empathy in today's classroom: Building positive relationships within the citizenship curriculum for 9- to 14-year-olds*, London: Paul Chapman.

Hammond, V.L., Watson, P.J. and O'Leary, B.J. (2009) 'Preliminary assessment of Apache hopefulness: relationships with hopelessness and with collective as well as personal self-esteem', *American Indian and Alaska Native Mental Health Research*, vol 16, no 3, pp 42–51.

Han, K.T. (2009) 'Influence of limitedly visible leafy indoor plants on the psychology, behavior, and health of students at a junior high school in Taiwan', *Environment and Behavior*, vol 41, pp 658–92.

Hansen-Ketchum, P.A. and Halpenny, E.A. (2011) 'Engaging with nature to promote health: bridging research silos to examine the evidence', *Health Promotion International*, vol 26, no 1, pp 100–9.

Hanushek, E. (2008) 'Schooling, gender equity, and economic outcomes', in M. Tembon and Lucia Fort (eds), *Girls' education in the 21st century: Gender equality, empowerment, and economic growth*, Washington, DC: World Bank, pp 23–41.

Harber, C. (2004) *Schooling as violence: How schools harm pupils and societies*, London: Routledge Falmer.

Harker, L. and Keltner D. (2001) 'Expressions of positive emotion in women's college yearbook pictures and their relationship to personality and life outcomes across adulthood', *Journal of Personality and Social Psychology*, vol 80, no 1, pp 112–24.

Harkness, S. et al (2007) 'Teachers' ethnotheories of the "ideal student" in five western cultures', *Comparative Education*, vol 43, no 1, pp 113–35.

Harris, S. (2010) *The moral landscape: How science can determine human values*, New York: Simon & Schuster.

Harsanyi, D. (2007) *Nanny state*, New York: Random House.

Harsanyi, J.C. (1996) 'Utilities, preferences, and substantive goods', *Social Choice and Welfare*, vol 14, no 1, pp 129–45.

Harter, J.K., Schmidt, F.L. and Keyes, C.L.M. (2002) 'Wellbeing in the workplace and its relationship to business outcomes', in C.L.M. Keyes and J. Haidt (eds), *Flourishing: Positive psychology and the life well-lived*, Washington, DC: American Psychological Association, pp 205–24.

Hartog, J. and Oosterbeek, H. (1998) 'Health, wealth and happiness: why pursue a higher education?', *Economics of Education Review*, vol 17, pp 245–56.

Hartung, D. and Hahlweg, K. (2011) 'Stress reduction at the work–family interface: positive parenting and self-efficacy as mechanisms of change in workplace Triple P', *Behavior Modification*, vol 35, no 1, pp 54–77.

Hatch, S. et al (2007) 'A life course approach to well-being', in J. Haworth and G. Hart (eds), *Well-being: Individual, community, and societal perspectives*, London: Palgrave McMillan, pp 187–205.

Hatfield, E. and Rapson, R.L. (1996) *Love and sex: Cross-cultural perspectives*, Needham Heights, MA: Allyn and Bacon.

Hatfield, E. and Sprecher, S. (1986) 'Measuring passionate love in intimate relations', *Journal of Adolescence*, vol 9, pp 383–410.

Hawkins, A.J. and Ooms, T. (2011) 'What works in marriage and relationship education? A review of lessons learned with a focus on low-income couples', USA Department of Health and Human Services, www.acf.hhs.gov/healthymarriage/pdf/whatworks_edae.pdf.

Haworth, J. (2010) 'Life, work, leisure, and enjoyment', Working paper, ESRC Wellbeing research project, www.wellbeing-esrc.com/downloads/LifeWorkLeisure&Enjoyment.pdf.

Haworth, J. and Hart, G. (eds) (2007) *Well-being: Individual, community, and societal perspectives*, London: Palgrave MacMillan.

Haworth, J. and Veal, A.J. (eds) (2004) *Work and leisure*, London: Routledge.

Haybron, D.M. (2007) 'Do we know how happy we are? On some limits of affective introspection and recall', *Noûs*, vol 41, no 3, pp 394–428

Hazleden, R. (2004) 'The pathology of love in contemporary relationship manuals', *Sociological Review*, vol 52, no 2, pp 201–17.

Healy, D. (2002) *The creation of psychopharmacology*, Cambridge, MA: Harvard University Press.

Hein, C. (2005) *Reconciling work and family responsibilities*, Geneva: ILO.

Heinze, K.L.W. (2005) 'In the mood to give: how and why positive affect increases the importance of CSR to prospective employees', Northwestern University, www.kellogg.northwestern.edu/research/ktag/images/KJOB05%20Kate.pdf.

Held, B.S. (2004) 'The negative side of positive psychology', *Journal of Humanistic Psychology*, vol 44, pp 9–46.

Held, V. (2005) *The ethics of care*, Oxford: Oxford University Press.

Helliwell, J.F. and Wang, S. (2011) 'Trust and wellbeing', *International Journal of Wellbeing*, vol 1, no 1, pp 42–78.

Helm, B.W. (2010) *Love, friendship, and the self: Intimacy, identification, and the social nature of persons*, New York: Oxford University Press.

Helminiak, D.A. (2010) '"Theistic psychology and psychotherapy": a theological and scientific critique', *Zygon*, vol 45, pp 47–74.

Henry, J. (2005) 'Government tells schools to focus on emotional development as parents cannot be trusted', *Daily Telegraph*, 26 November.

Hermalin, A.I. (2002) *The wellbeing of the elderly in Asia: A four-country comparative study*, Ann Arbor, MI: University of Michigan Press.

Hershberger P.J. (2005) 'Prescribing happiness: positive psychology and family medicine', *Family Medicine*, vol 37, no 9, pp 630–4.

Hewitt, J.P. (1998) *The myth of self-esteem: Finding happiness and solving problems in America*, New York: St. Martin's Press.

Hinchliffe, G. (2004) 'Work and human flourishing', *Educational Philosophy & Theory*, vol 36, no 5, pp 535–47.

Hochschild, A.R. (1983) *The managed heart: Commercialization of human feeling,* Berkeley, CA: University of California Press.

Hodges, S.D., Clark, B.A.M. and Myers, M.W. (2011) 'Better living through perspective taking', in R. Biswas-Diener (ed), *Positive psychology as a mechanism for social change*, Dordrecht: Springer, pp 193–218.

Hodson, R. (2001) *Dignity at work*, Cambridge: Cambridge University Press.

Hoffman, D.L. (2011) 'Internet indispensability, online social capital, and consumer wellbeing', in D.G. Mick et al (eds), *Transformative consumer research for personal and collective wellbeing*, London: Routledge.

Hofstede, G. (ed) (1999) *Masculinity and femininity: The taboo dimensions of national cultures,* Thousand Oaks, CA: Sage.

Holden, R. (2008) *Success intelligence: Essential lessons and practices from the world's leading coaching program on authentic success*, Carlsbad, CA: Hay House.

Holland, P. (1992) *What is a child? Popular images of childhood*, London: Virago Press.

Holman, T.B. (2000) *Premarital prediction of marital quality or breakup: Research, theory, and practice*, New York: Springer.

Honore, C. (2008) *Under pressure: Rescuing our children from the culture of hyper-parenting*, New York: HarperOne.

Hoppmann, C.A. et al (2011) 'Spousal interrelations in happiness in the Seattle longitudinal study: considerable similarities in levels and change over time', *Developmental Psychology*, vol 47, no 1, pp 1–8.

Horwitz, A.V. and Wakefield, J.C. (2007) *The loss of sadness: How psychiatry transformed normal sorrow into depressive disorder*, Oxford: Oxford University Press.

Hoskyn, M. (2009) 'The prevention science perspective: early intervention research on literacy, mathematics, and social competence', in S. Rosenfield and V. W. Berninger (eds), *Implementing evidence-based academic interventions in school settings*, New York: Oxford University Press, pp 165–212.

Howard, K.I. et al (1996) 'The evaluation of psychotherapy: efficacy, effectiveness, and patient progress', *American Psychologist*, vol 51, pp 1059–64.

Hsieh, T. (2010) *Delivering happiness: A path to profits, passion, and purpose*, New York: Business Plus.

Huang, W.-J. (2005) 'An Asian perspective on relationship and marriage education', *Family Process*, vol 44, no 2, pp 161–73.

Hudson, W.R. (1993) 'Index of Self-Esteem', www.walmyr.com/ISESAMPL.pdf.

Huebner, E.S. (1991) 'Initial development of the student's life satisfaction scale', *School Psychology International*, vol 12, pp 231–40.

Huebner, E.S. (1994) 'Preliminary development and validation of a multidimensional life satisfaction scale for children', *Psychological Assessment*, vol 6, pp 149–58.

Huebner, E.S. et al (2004) 'Life satisfaction in children and youth: empirical foundations and implications for school psychologists', *Psychology in the Schools*, vol 41, no 1, pp 81–93.

Huff, D.L. (1993) *How to lie with statistics*, New York: W.W. Norton.

Hughes, M. and Terrell, J.B. (2007) *The emotionally intelligent team*, San Francisco: Jossey-Bass.

Hulac, D. et al (2010) *Behavioral interventions in schools: A response to intervention guidebook*, London: Routledge.

Huppert, F.A. (2009) 'Psychological wellbeing: evidence regarding its causes and its consequences', *Applied Psychology: Health and Well-Being*, vol 1, no 2, pp 137–64.

Hutcheson, F. (1725) *Inquiry into the original of our ideas of beauty and virtue*, http://oll.libertyfund.org.

Huxley, A. (1932) *Brave new world*, London: Chatto and Windus.

Inglehart, R. (2002) 'Gender, aging, and subjective wellbeing', *International Journal of Comparative Sociology*, vol 43, no 3–5, pp 391–408.

Inglehart, R. (2006) 'Democracy and happiness: what causes what?', Conference paper, 'New Directions in the Study of Happiness', Notre Dame University, 22–24 October, www.nd.edu/~adutt/activities/program.htm.

Inglehart, R. and Klingemann, H.D. (2000) 'Genes, culture and happiness', in E. Diener and E.M. Suh (eds), *Culture and subjective wellbeing*, Cambridge, MA: MIT Press, pp 165–83.

Inkeles, A. and Smith, D.H. (1974) *Becoming modern: Individual change in six developing countries*, London: Heinemann.

Institute of Education (2011) 'Case study on the impact of IOE research: music education', www.ioe.ac.uk/Research_Expertise/IOE_RD_A4_ME_final_d.pdf.

Ironmonger, D.S. (1996) 'Counting outputs, capital inputs and caring labor: estimating gross household product', *Feminist Economics*, vol 2, no 3, pp 37–64.

Ishikawa, K. (1985) *What is total quality control? The Japanese way*, trans D.J. Lu, Englewood Cliffs, NJ: Prentice-Hall.

Iyengar, S.S. and Lepper, M.R. (1999) 'Rethinking the value of choice: a cultural perspective on intrinsic motivation', *Journal of Personality and Social Psychology*, vol 76, pp 349–66.

Jackson, T. (2009) *Prosperity without growth: Economics for a finite planet*, London: Earthscan.

Jacobs, J.A. and Gerson, K. (2004) *The time divide: Work, family, and gender inequality*, Cambridge, MA: Harvard University Press.

Jaggar, A.M. (1992/2001) 'Feminist ethics', in L. Becker and C. Becker (eds), *Encyclopedia of ethics* (2nd edn), London: Routledge, pp 528–39.

James, O. (2002) *They f*** you up: How to survive family life*, London: Bloomsbury.

James, O. (2007) *Affluenza: How to be successful and stay sane*, London: Vermilion.

James, O. (2010) *How not to f*** them up*, London: Vermilion.

Jamieson, L. (1999) 'Intimacy transformed? A critical look at the "pure relationship"', *Sociology*, vol 33, pp 477–94.

Jankowiak, W.R. (ed) (2008) *Intimacies: Love and sex across cultures*, New York: Columbia University Press.

Jeffres, L.W. et al (2009) 'The impact of third places on community quality of life', *Applied Research in Quality of Life*, vol 4, pp 333–45.

Jenkins, H. et al (2008) *Foresight Mental Capital and Wellbeing Project. Mental health: Future challenges*, London: The Government Office for Science.

Jevons, W.(1871) *The theory of political economy.* London: Macmillan

Joanning, H., Brewster, J. and Koval, J. (1984) 'The Communication Rapid Assessment Scale: development of a behavioral index of communication quality', *Journal of Marital & Family Therapy*, vol 10, no 1, pp 409–17.

Johnny, L. (2006) 'Reconceptualising childhood: children's rights and youth participation in schools', *International Education Journal*, vol 7, no 1, pp 17–25.

Johns, H. and Ormerod, P. (2007) *Happiness, economics and public policy*, London: Institute of Economic Affairs, www.iea.org.uk/sites/default/files/publications/files/upldbook416pdf.pdf

Johnson, J. (2002) *Getting by on the minimum: The lives of working-class women*, London: Routledge.

Jones, J. and Ghazi, P. (1997) *Getting a life: The downshifter's guide to happier, simpler living*, London: Hodder & Stoughton.

Jordan, B. (2007) *Social work and wellbeing*, Lyme Regis: Russell House.

Jordan, B. (2008) *Welfare and wellbeing: Social value in public policy*, Bristol: The Policy Press.

Juffer, F. et al (2007) *Promoting positive parenting: An attachment-based intervention*, Hoboken, NJ: Lawrence Erlbaum.

Juntunen, C.L. and Wettersten, K.B. (2006) 'Work hope: development and initial validation of a measure', *Journal of Counseling Psychology*, vol 53, no 1, pp 94–106.

Kacapyr, E. (2008) 'Cross-country determinants of satisfaction with life', *International Journal of Social Economics*, vol 35, no 6, pp 400–16.

Kahneman, D. (1999) 'Objective happiness', in D. Kahneman, E. Diener and N. Schwarz (eds), *Wellbeing: The foundations of hedonic psychology*, New York: Russell Sage Foundation, pp 3–25.

Kahneman, D. et al (2004) 'A survey method for characterizing daily life experience: the day reconstruction method', *Science*, vol 306, no 5702, pp 1776–80.

Kakabadse, A. and Kakabadse, N.K. (2004) *Intimacy: An international survey of the sex lives of people at work*, London: Palgrave Macmillan.

Kalayjian, A. and Paloutzian, R.F. (2010) *Forgiveness and reconciliation: Psychological pathways to conflict transformation*, Dordrecht: Springer.

Kane, P. (2004) *The play ethic: A manifesto for a different way of living*, London: Macmillan.

Karatzias, A., Power, K.G. and Swanson, V. (2001) 'Quality of school life: development and preliminary standardisation of an instrument based on performance indicators in Scottish secondary schools', *School Effectiveness and School Improvement*, vol 12, no 3, pp 265–84.

Kasser, T. (2002) *The high price of materialism*, Cambridge, MA and London: MIT Press.

Kasser, T. and Ryan, R.M. (2001) 'Be careful what you wish for: wellbeing and the attainment of intrinsic and extrinsic goals', in P. Schmuck and K.M. Sheldon (eds), *Life goals and wellbeing*, Seattle, WA: Hogrefe & Huber, pp 116–31.

Kaufman, S.R. (1986) *The ageless self: Sources of meaning in late life*, Madison, WI: University of Wisconsin Press.

Kay, J. (2010) *Obliquity: Why our goals are best achieved indirectly*, London: Profile Books.

Kayser-Jones, J.S. (1981) *Old, alone, and neglected: Care of the aged in the United States and Scotland*, Berkeley. CA: University of California Press.

Keith, J. (1980) '"The best is yet to be": toward an anthropology of age', *Annual Review of Anthropology*, vol 9, pp 339–6.

Keizer, R., Dykstra, P.R. and Poortman, A.-R. (2010) 'Life outcomes of childless men and fathers', *European Sociological Review*, vol 26, no 1, pp 1–15.

Kelly, J.R. and Hutson-Comeaux, S.L. (2000) 'Gender–emotion stereotypes are context specific', *Sex Roles*, vol 40, no 1–2, pp 107–20.

Kelly, M.S., Kim, J.S. and Franklin, C. (2008) *Solution focused brief therapy in schools*, Oxford: Oxford University Press.

Kelly, M.S. et al (2010) *School social work: An evidence-informed framework for practice*, New York: Oxford University Press.

Kenny, C. (1999) 'Does growth cause happiness or does happiness cause growth?', *Kyklos*, vol 52, pp 3–25.

Kesebir, P. and Diener, E. (2008) 'In defence of happiness: why policymakers should care about subjective wellbeing', *Perspectives on Psychological Science*, vol 3, no 2, pp 117–25.

Kidahashi, M. (2010) 'Positive life models after normative retirement age: toward a typology construction', in H. Blatterer and J. Glahn (eds), *Times of our lives: Making sense of growing up and growing old*, Oxford: Inter-Disciplinary Press, pp 161–80.

Kim, S.C.H., Kollontai, P. and Hoyland, G. (eds) (2008) *Peace and reconciliation*, London: Ashgate.

Kim, T. and Kim, H. (2004) *Reconciling work and family: issues and policies in the Republic of Korea*, Geneva: ILO.

Kimiecik, J. (2002) *The intrinsic exerciser: Discovering the joy of exercise*, Boston, MA: Houghton Mifflin.

Kirsch, I. (2009) *The emperor's new drugs: Exploding the antidepressant myth*, London: The Bodley Head.

Klein, M. (2006) *America's war on sex: The attack on law, lust and liberty*, Westport, CT: Praeger.

Kleinman, A. (2006) *What really matters: Living a moral life amidst uncertainty and danger*, Oxford: Oxford University Press.

Kline, K.K. (ed) (2007) *Authoritative communities: The scientific case for nurturing the whole child*, New York: Springer.

Koenig, H.G. (2005) *Faith and mental health: Religious resources for healing*, West Conshohocken, PA: Templeton Foundation Press.

Koenig, T. and Spano, R. (2007) 'The cultivation of social workers' hope in personal life and professional practice', *Journal of Religion & Spirituality in Social Work*, vol 26, no 3, pp 45–61.

Koivumaa-Honkanen, H. et al (2001) 'Life satisfaction and suicide: a 20-year follow-up study', *American Journal of Psychiatry*, vol 158, pp 433–9.

Konu, A.I. and Lintonen, T. (2006) 'School wellbeing in Grades 4–12', *Health Education Research*, vol 21, no 5, pp 633–42.

Koopmans, T.A. et al (2010) 'Effects of happiness on all-cause mortality during 15 years of follow-up: the Arnhem elderly study', *Journal of Happiness Studies*, vol 11, pp 113–24.

Kringelbach, M.L. and Berridge, K.C. (eds) (2010) *Pleasures of the brain*, Oxford: Oxford University Press.

Krishna Dutt, A. and Radcliff, B. (eds) (2009) *Happiness, economics and politics: Towards a multi-disciplinary approach*, Cheltenham: Edward Elgar.

Krueger, A.B. (2007) 'Are we having more fun yet? Categorizing and evaluating changes in time allocation', *Brookings Papers on Economic Activity*, vol 38, pp 193–218.

Krueger, A.B. (ed) (2009) *Measuring the subjective wellbeing of nations: National accounts of time use and wellbeing*, Chicago, IL: University of Chicago Press.

Kumar, R. and Hipwell, A.E. (1996) 'Development of a clinical rating scale to assess mother–infant interaction in a psychiatric mother and baby unit', *British Journal of Psychiatry*, vol 169, pp 18–26.

Kuo, F.E. and Sullivan, W.C. (2001) 'Environment and crime in the inner city: does vegetation reduce crime?', *Environment and Behaviour*, vol 33, no 3, pp 343–67.

Kusy, M. and Holloway, E. (2009) *Toxic workplace!*, San Francisco: Jossey-Bass.

Lake, A., Townshend, T.G. and Alvanides, S. (2010) *Obesogenic environments*, Oxford: Wiley-Blackwell.

Lamb, M. (ed) (1976/2010) *The role of the father in child development* (5th edn), New York: John Wiley.

Lane, R. (1991) *The market experience*. Cambridge: Cambridge University Press

Lane, R.E. (2000) *The loss of happiness in market democracies*, New Haven, CT: Yale University Press.

Lang, P.L.F., Katz, Y. and Menezes, I. (eds) (1998) *Affective education: A comparative perspective*, London: Cassell.

Lantieri, L. (ed) (2001) *Schools with spirit: Nurturing the inner lives of children and teachers*, Boston, MA: Beacon Press.

Larrimore, M. (2010) 'Religion and the promise of happiness', *Social Research*, vol 77, no 2, pp 569–94.

Larson, C.C. (2009) *As we forgive: Stories of reconciliation from Rwanda*, Grand Rapids, MI: Zondervan.

Larzelere, R.E. and Huston, T.L. (1980) 'The Dyadic Trust Scale: toward understanding interpersonal trust in close relationships', *Journal of Marriage and Family*, vol 42, no 3, pp 595–604.

Lasch, C. (1980) *The culture of narcissism: American life in an age of diminishing expectations*, London: Abacus Press.

Lawton, G. and Wilson, C. (2010) 'Mind-reading marketers have ways of making you buy', *New Scientist*, vol 2772.

Layard, R. (2005) *Happiness: Lessons from a new science*, Harmondsworth: Penguin.

Layard, R. and Dunne, J. (2009) *A good childhood: Searching for values in a competitive age*, London: Penguin.

Leary, M.R., Tipsord, J.M. and Tate, E.B. (2008) 'Allo-inclusive identity: incorporating the social and natural worlds into one's sense of self', in H.A. Wayment and J.J. Bauer (eds), *Transcending self-interest: Psychological explorations of the quiet ego*, Washington DC: American Psychological Association, pp 137–48.

Lee, P.S.N. et al (2011) 'Internet communication versus face-to-face interaction in quality of life', *Social Indicators Research*, vol 100, no 3, pp 375–89.

Lee, S., McCann, D., and Messenger, J.C. (2007) *Working time around the world*, London: Routledge

Lehtinen, V. et al (2005) 'The intrinsic value of mental health', in H. Herrman, S. Saxena and R. Moodie (eds), *Promoting mental health: Concepts, emerging evidence, practice*, Geneva: WHO, pp 45–58.

Levett, R. (2007) *Wellbeing: International policy interventions*, London: Report to Defra, archive.defra.gov.uk/sustainable/government/documents/SD12004_5233_FRP.pdf

Levine, E., Sizer, T. and Peters, T. (2001) *One kid at a time: Big lessons from a small school*, New York: Teachers College Press.

Levine, R.V. (1997/2006) *Geography of time: The temporal misadventures of a social psychologist, or how every culture keeps time just a little bit differently*, Oxford: Oneworld.

Levy, N. (2005) 'Downshifting and meaning in life', *Ratio*, vol 18, no 2, pp 176–89.

Lewis, C. and Cruise, S. (2006) 'Religion and happiness: consensus, contradictions, comments and concerns', *Mental Health, Religion & Culture*, vol 9, pp 213–25.

Lewis, C.S. (1960) *The four loves*, London: Geoffrey Bles.

Liedloff, J. (1975/1985) *The continuum concept: In search of happiness lost*, Cambridge, MA: Da Capo Press.

Lindner, E. (2010) *Gender, humiliation, and global security: Dignifying relationships from love, sex, and parenthood to world affairs*, Santa Barbara, CA: Praeger Security International.

Linley, P.A., Harrington, S. and Garcea, N. (eds) (2009) *Oxford handbook of positive psychology and work*, Oxford: Oxford University Press.

Littky, D. and Grabelle, S. (2004) *The big picture: Education is everyone's business*, Alexandria, VA: Association for Supervision & Curriculum Development.

Lloyd, P. (1979) *Slums of hope? Shanty towns of the third world*, Manchester: Manchester University Press.

Locke, H.J. and Wallace, K.M. (1959) 'Short marital adjustment and prediction tests: their reliability and validity', *Journal of Marriage and the Family*, vol 21, pp 251–5.

Loewenthal, K. (2006) *Religion, culture and mental health*, Cambridge: Cambridge University Press.

Lohr, V.I., Pearson-Mims, C.H. and Goodwin, G.K. (1996) 'Interior plants may improve worker productivity and reduce stress in a windowless environment', *Journal of Environmental Horticulture*, vol 14, no 2, pp 97–100.

Luhtanen, R. and Crocker, J. (1992) 'A collective self-esteem scale: self-evaluation of one's social identity', *Personality and Social Psychology Bulletin*, vol 18, no 3, pp 302–18.

Luthans, F., Youssef, C.M. and Avolio, B.J. (2007) *Psychological capital: Developing the human competitive edge*, New York: Oxford University Press.

Lykken, D. (2000) *Happiness: The nature and nurture of joy and contentment*, New York: St. Martin's Press.

Lynch, K., Baker, J. and Lyons, M. (2009) *Affective equality: Love, care and injustice*, London: Palgrave Macmillan

Lyubomirsky, S. (2008) *The how of happiness: A practical guide to getting the life you want*, New York: Penguin.

Lyubomirsky, S. and Dickerhoof, R. (2010) 'A construal approach to increasing happiness', in J.E. Maddux and J.P. Tangney (eds), *Social Psychological Foundations of Clinical Psychology*, New York: Guilford Press, pp 229–44.

Lyubomirsky, S., King, L. and Diener, E. (2005) 'The benefits of frequent positive affect: does happiness lead to success?' *Psychological Bulletin*, vol 131, pp 803–55.

McAdams, D.P. (2005) *The redemptive self: Stories Americans live by*, New York: Oxford University Press.

McAdams, D.P. (2009) 'Narrative identity', in S.J. Lopez (ed), *Encyclopedia of positive psychology*, San Francisco: Jossey-Bass, pp 638–42.

McDonald, L. (2001) *Florence Nightingale: An introduction to her life and family: Collected works of Florence Nightingale, volume 1*, Wilfrid Laurier University Press.

Macklem, G.L. (2011) *Evidence-based school mental health service*, Dordrecht: Springer.

MacLeod, J. (1987/2009) *Ain't no makin' it: Aspirations and attainment in a low-income neighborhood* (3rd edn), Boulder, CO: Westview Press.

McLelland, D.C. (1961) *The achieving society*, New Jersey: D. Van Nostrand.

McMahon, D.M. (2006) *Happiness: A history*, New York: Atlantic Monthly Press.

McMahon, D.M. (2007) 'The pursuit of happiness in perspective', *Cato Unbound*, 8 April, www.cato-unbound.org/2007/04/08/darrin-m-mcmahon/the-pursuit-of-happiness-in-perspective/.

Macmurray, J. (1957) *The self as agent*, London: Faber & Faber.

Mcness, E., Broadfoot, P. and M. Osbor (2003) 'Is the effective compromising the affective?' *British Educational Research Journal*, vol 29, no 2, pp 243–57.

Mainiero, L. and Sullivan, S. (2006) *The opt-out revolt: Why people are leaving companies to create kaleidoscope careers*, Mountain View, CA: Intercultural Press.

Malley-Morrison, K. (2004) *International perspectives on family violence and abuse: A cognitive ecological approach*, Hoboken, NJ: Lawrence Erlbaum.

Mangahas, M. and Guerrero, L.L.B. (2008) 'Two decades of social weather reporting in the Philippines', in V. Møller, D. Huschka and A. Michalos (eds), *Barometers of quality of life around the globe: How are we doing?*, Dordrecht: Springer, pp 23–36.

Manz, C.C. (ed) (2008) *The virtuous organization*, Hackensack, NJ: World Scientific.

Marar, Z. (2003) *The happiness paradox*, London: Reaktion Books.

Marchevsky, A. and Theoharis, J. (2006) *Not working: Latina immigrants, low-wage jobs, and the failure of welfare reform*, New York: NYU Press.

Markman, H.J. and Halford, W.K. (2005) 'International perspectives on couple relationship education', *Family Process*, vol 44, no 2, pp 139–46.

Marks, G.N. and Fleming, N. (1999) 'Influences and consequences of wellbeing among Australian young people: 1980–1995', *Social Indicators Research*, vol 46, pp 301–23.

Markus, H.R. and Hamedani, M.J. (2007) 'Sociocultural psychology: the dynamic interdependence among self systems and social systems', in S. Kitayama and D. Cohen (eds), *Handbook of cultural psychology*, New York: Guilford Press, pp 3–39.

Markus, H.R. and Kitayama, S. (1991) 'Culture and the self: implications for cognition, emotion and motivation', *Psychological Review*, vol 98, pp 224–53.

Marmarosh, C., Holtz, A. and Schottenbauer, M. (2005) 'Group cohesiveness, group-derived collective self-esteem, group-derived hope, and the well-being of group therapy members', *Group Dynamics*, vol 9, no 1, pp 32–44.

Marmot, M. et al (2010) *Fair society, healthy lives: The Marmot Review (Strategic Review of Health Inequalities in England post-2010)*, www.marmotreview.org.

Marques, S.C. et al (2010) '"Building hope for the future": a program to foster strengths in middle-school students', *Journal of Happiness Studies*, vol 12, no 1, pp 139–52.

Martin, M.W. (2000) *Meaningful work: Rethinking professional ethics*, Oxford: Oxford University Press.

Martin, P. (2003) *Counting sheep: The science and pleasures of sleep and dreams*, London: Flamingo.

Martin, P. (2005) *Making happy people: The nature of happiness and its origins in childhood*, London: Fourth Estate.

Mary, M. (2003) *Die Glücklüge: vom Glaube an die Machbarkeit des Lebens. [The happiness lie: On the belief in life improvement]*, Bergisch Gladbach, Germany: Gustav Lübbe Verlag.

Mathieu, S.I. (2008) 'Happiness and humor group promotes life satisfaction for senior center participants', *Activities, Adaptation & Aging*, vol 32, no 2, pp 134–48.

Matthews, B. (2006) *Engaging education: Developing emotional literacy, equity and co-education*, Maidenhead: Open University Press.

Maxcy, S.J. (1988) 'Happiness in education through the development of a school philosophy', *Education*, vol 105, no 4, pp 427–32.

May, E.T. (1997) *Barren in the promised land: Childless Americans and the pursuit of happiness*, Cambridge, MA: Harvard University Press.

Mayton, D. (2009) *Nonviolence and peace psychology*, Dordrecht: Springer.

Meinert, L. (2009) *Hopes in friction: Schooling, health, and everyday life in Uganda*, Charlotte, NC: Information Age Publishing.

Michalos, A.C. (2007) 'Education, happiness and wellbeing', *Social Indicators Research*, vol 87, no 3, pp 347–66.

Micheletti, M. (2003) *Political virtue and shopping*, London: Macmillan.

Mill, J.S. (1869) *The subjection of women*, www.constitution.org/jsm/women.htm.

Miller, B.C. (2010) *Nice teams finish last*, AMACOM.

Miller, D.N. et al (2008) 'Authentically happy school psychologists: applications of positive psychology for enhancing professional satisfaction and fulfillment', *Psychology in the Schools*, vol 45, no 8, pp 679–92.

Miller, G. (2000) 'Social policy implications of the new happiness research', *American Journal of Sociology*, vol 49, pp 165–80.

Mills, L.G. (2006) *Insult to injury: Rethinking our responses to intimate abuse*, Princeton, NJ: Princeton University Press.

Mittelmark, M.B. et al (2005) 'Health promotion: a sketch of the landscape', in H. Herrman, S. Saxena and R. Moodie (eds), *Promoting mental health: Concepts, emerging evidence, practice*, Geneva: WHO, pp 18–33.

Mittleman, A. (2009) *Hope in a democratic age*, Oxford: Oxford University Press.

Mody, P. (2008) *Intimate state: Love-marriage and the law in Delhi*, London: Taylor & Francis.

Moeran, B. (2007) 'Creativity at work: from participant observation to observant participation: anthropology, fieldwork and organizational ethnography', Copenhagen Business School: Creative Encounters Working Paper no 2.

Mohler, A. (2009) 'Feminism unfulfilled – why are so many women unhappy?', www.albertmohler.com/2009/10/23/feminism-unfulfilled-why-are-so-many-women-unhappy.

Mollenkopf, H. and Walker, A. (eds) (2007) *Quality of life in old age*, Dordrecht: Springer.

Møller, V., Huschka, D. and Michalos, A. (eds) (2008) *Barometers of quality of life around the globe: How are we doing?*, Dordrecht: Springer.

Montgomery, H. (2001) *Modern Babylon: Prostituting children in Thailand*, Oxford: Berghahn Books.

Montiel, C.J. and Noor, N.M. (eds) (2009) *Peace psychology in Asia*, Dordrecht: Springer.

Moore, K. and Lippman, L. (eds) (2005) *What do children need to flourish?*, New York: Springer.

Morgan, B. [Archbishop of Wales] (2010) 'Archbishop of Wales' concern over happiness index', www.bbc.co.uk/news/uk-wales-12074964.

Morrall, P. (2008) *The trouble with therapy*, Maidenhead: Open University Press.

Morris, I. (2009) *Teaching happiness and well-being in schools: Learning to ride elephants*, London: Network Continuum.

Mulgan, G. (1998) 'Timeless values', in I. Christie and L. Nash (eds), *The good life*, London: Demos, www.demos.co.uk/publications/goodlife.

Murphy, S.E. and Zagorski, D.A. (2004) 'Enhancing work–family and work–life interaction: the role of management', in D.F. Halpern and S.E. Murphy (eds), *From work–family balance to work–family interaction: Changing the metaphor*, London: Routledge, pp 27–48.

Myerhoff, B.G. (1984) 'A death in due time: construction of self and culture in ritual drama', in J.J. MacAloon (ed), *Rite, drama, festival, spectacle*, Philadelphia: Institute for the Study of Human Issues, pp 149–78.

Myers, D.G. (2005) 'Scientific pursuit of happiness', *Innovation*, vol 5, no 3, pp 32–33.

Nakamura, J. and Csikzentmihalyi, M. (2002) 'The construction of meaning through vital engagement', in C.L.M. Keyes and J. Haidt (eds), *Flourishing: Positive psychology and the life well-lived*, Washington, DC: American Psychological Association, pp 83–104.

Nelson, D.L. and Cooper, C.L.E. (eds) (2007) *Positive organisational behavior*, London: Sage.

Nesse, R.M. (1999) 'The evolution of hope and despair', *Journal of Social Issues*, vol 66, pp 429–46.

Neugarten, B.L., Havighurst, R.J. and Tobin, S.S. (1961) 'The measurement of life satisfaction', *Journal of Gerontology*, vol 16, pp 134–43.

Newell, R.J. and Van Ryzin, M.J. (2008) *Assessing what really matters in school*, Lanham, MD: Rowman & Littlefield.

Ng, Y.-K. and Ho, L.S. (2006) 'Introduction: happiness as the only ultimate objective of public policy', in Y.-K. Ng and L.S. Ho (eds), *Happiness and public policy*, Houndmills: Palgrave Macmillan, pp 1–16.

Nielsen Wire (2008) 'Women's happiness is more recession-proof than men's', *Nielsen Wire*, 26 November, http://blog.nielsen.com/nielsenwire/global/womens-happiness-more-recession-proof-than-mens/.

Niu, W. (2007) 'Western influences on Chinese educational testing', *Comparative Education*, vol 43, no 1, pp 71–91.

Noddings, N. (2003) *Happiness and education*, Cambridge: Cambridge University Press.

Nordenfelt, L. (1993) *Quality of life, health and happiness*, Aldershot: Avebury.

Norman, J. (2008) *Compassionate economics: Rebuilding the foundations of prosperity*, London: Policy Exchange.

Nozick, R. (1974) *Anarchy, state and utopia*, Oxford: Blackwell.

Nussbaum, M. (2000) *Women and human development*, Cambridge: Cambridge University Press.

Nyklícek, I., Vingerhoets, A. and Zeelenberg, M. (eds) (2010) *Emotion regulation and wellbeing*, Dordrecht: Springer.

Obst, P. and Stafurik, J. (2002) 'Online we are all able bodied', *Journal of Community & Applied Social Psychology*, vol 20, no 6, pp 525–31.

Offer, A. (1996) 'Advertising and the quality of life', in A. Offer (ed), *In pursuit of the quality of life*, New York: Oxford University Press, pp 211–55.

Ofsted (Office for Standards in Education, Children's Services and Skills, UK) (2005a), *Healthy minds: Promoting emotional health and wellbeing in schools*, London: Ofsted.

Ofsted (2005b) *Pupils' satisfaction with their school*, London: Ofsted.

Ofsted (2006) *Parents' satisfaction with schools*, London: Ofsted.

Ofsted (2007) 'Time for change? Personal, social and health education', London: Ofsted.

Ofsted (2009) 'Making more of music: an evaluation of music in schools 2005–08', London: Ofsted.

Oldenburg, R. (1999) *The great good place*, New York: Marlowe.

Oliver, E. (2006) 'Mental life and and the metropolis in suburban America: The psychological correlates of metropolital place characteristics', Paper for conference 'New Directions in the Study of Happiness', Notre Dame University, 22–24 October, www.nd.edu/~adutt/activities/program.htm.

Ormerod, P. and Johns, H. (2007) 'Against happiness', *Prospect*, April.

Osterberg, E. (2010) *Friendship and love, ethics and politics: Studies in medieval and early modern history*, Budapest: Central European University Press.

Pacek, A. and Radcliff, B. (2008) 'Assessing the welfare state: the politics of happiness', *Perspectives on Politics*, vol 6, pp 267–77.

Palmer, S. (2007) *Toxic childhood: How the modern world is damaging our children and what we can do about it*, London: Orion.

Parker, I. (2007) *Revolution in psychology: Alienation to emancipation*, London: Pluto Press.

Patel, P. et al (2009) 'Bringing "light, life and happiness": British American Tobacco and music sponsorship in sub-Saharan Africa', *Third World Quarterly*, vol 30, no 4, pp 685–700.

Patmore, G. (2009) 'Happiness as an objective of labour law', University of Melbourne, Centre for Employment and Labour Relations Law Working Paper No 48, http://celrl.law.unimelb. edu.au/download.cfm?DownloadFile=980B2269-078F-FA3B-C23BA9ED85E5DDE4.

Payton, J. et al (2008) *The positive impact of social and emotional learning for kindergarten to eighth-grade students*, Chicago, IL: Collaborative for Academic, Social and Emotional Learning, http://casel.org/.

Peacock, G. et al (2009) *Practical handbook of school psychology*, New York: Guilford Press.

Pellegrino, E.D. and Thomasma, D.C. (1993) *Virtues in medical practice*, New York: Oxford University Press.

Perelman, M. (2005) *Manufacturing discontent: The trap of individualism in corporate society*, London: Pluto Press.

Persaud, R. (2006) 'Does smarter mean happier?', in P. Miller and J. Wilsdon (eds), *Better humans: The politics of human enhancement and life extension*, London: Demos, pp 129–36, www.demos.co.uk/publications/betterhumanscollection.

Peterson, C.M. and Seligman, M.E.P. (2003) 'Positive organizational studies: lessons from positive psychology', in K.S. Cameron, J.E. Dutton and R.E. Quinn (eds), *Positive organizational scholarship*, San Francisco, CA: Berrett-Koehler.

Peterson, K.D. and Deal, T.E. (2009) *The shaping school culture fieldbook*, San Francisco, CA: Jossey-Bass.

Peterson, T.D. and Peterson, E.W. (2009) 'Stemming the tide of law student depression: what law schools need to learn from the science of positive psychology', *Yale Journal of Health Policy, Law, and Ethics*, vol 9, pp 357–434.

Phillips, A. (2005) *Going sane: Maps of happiness*, London: Fourth Estate.

Phillips, B.J. (1997) 'In defense of advertising: a social perspective', *Journal of Business Ethics*, vol 16, pp 109–18.

Pickhardt, C.E. (2008) *The future of your only child: How to guide your child to a happy and successful life*, London: Palgrave Macmillan.

Piggott, C. (2010) 'Love is in the air: managing relationships in the workplace', *Personnel Today*, 12 February.

Pinheiro, P.S. (2006) *World report on violence against children*, www.violencestudy.org/r25.

Pink, Daniel (2006) *A whole new mind: Why right-brainers will rule the future* (2nd edn), New York: Penguin.

Pinker, S. (2007) 'A history of violence: we're getting nicer every day', *The New Republic*, 19 March, vol 236, no 12, pp 18–21.

Pinquart, M. and Silbereisen, R.K. (2010) 'Patterns of fulfilment in the domains of work, intimate relationship, and leisure', *Applied Research in Quality of Life*, vol 5, pp 147–64.

Poelmans, S.A.Y. and Caligiuri, P. (2008) *Harmonizing work, family, and personal life: From policy to practice*, Cambridge: Cambridge University Press.

Polsky, A.J. (1991) *The rise of the therapeutic state*, Princeton, NJ: Princeton University Press.

Popper, K.R. (1962) *The open society and its enemies*, London: Routledge and Kegan Paul.

Porter, T.M. (1995) *Trust in numbers: The pursuit of objectivity in science*, Princeton, NJ: Princeton University Press.

Post, S.G. (2003) *Unlimited love: Altruism, compassion, and service*, West Conshohocken, PA: Templeton Foundation Press.

Post, S.G. (2005) 'Altruism, happiness, and health: it's good to be good', *International Journal of Behavioral Medicine*, vol 12, pp 66–77.

Post, S. et al (2003) *Research on altruism and love*, West Conshohocken, PA: Templeton Foundation Press.

Potkay, A. (2010) 'Narrative possibilities of happiness, unhappiness, and joy', *Social Research*, vol 77, no 2, pp 523–45.

Powdthavee, N. (2009) 'Think having children will make you happy?', *The Psychologist*, vol 22, pp 308–11.

Pressman, S.D. and Cohen, S. (2005) 'Does positive affect influence health?', *Psychological Bulletin*, vol 131: 925–71.

Prilleltensky, I. and Prilleltensky, O. (2006) *Promoting wellbeing: Linking personal, organizational, and community change*, Chichester: John Wiley.

Pringle, R. (2010) 'Finding pleasure in physical education: a critical examination of the educative value of positive movement affects', *Quest*, vol 62, no 2, pp 119–34.

Proctor, C., Linley, P. and Maltby, J. (2009) 'Youth life satisfaction: a review of the literature', *Journal of Happiness Studies*, vol 10, no 5, pp 583–630.

Pryce-Jones, J. (2010) *Happiness at work: Maximizing your psychological capital for success*, Chichester: Wiley.

Pumpian, I., Fisher, D. and Wachowiak, S. (2006) *Challenging the classroom standard through museum-based education: School in the park*, Hoboken, NJ: Lawrence Erlbaum.

Putnam, R.D., with Leonardi, R. and Nanetti, R.Y. (1993) *Making democracy work: Civic traditions in modern Italy*, Princeton, NJ: Princeton University Press.

Puurula, A. et al (2001) 'Teacher and student attitudes to affective education: a European collaborative research project', *Compare*, vol 31, no 2, pp 165–86.

Queen, C. and Comella, L. (2008) 'The necessary revolution: sex-positive feminism in the post-Barnard era', *The Communication Review*, vol 11, no 3, pp 274–91.

Quick, J.C. and Tetrick, L.E. (eds) (2002) *Handbook of occupational health psychology*, Washington, DC: American Psychological Association.

Quinn, R.W. and Quinn, R.E. (eds) (2009) *Lift: Becoming a positive force in any situation*, San Francisco: Berrett-Koehler.

Rader, M. (1981) *The right to hope: Crisis and community*, Seattle, WA: University of Washington Press.

Rainie, L., Purcell, K. and Smith, A. (2011) 'The social side of the internet', *Pew Internet and American Life Project*, www.pewinternet.org/Reports/2011/The-Social-Side-of-the-Internet.aspx.

Ram, R. (2009) 'Government spending and happiness of the population: additional evidence from large cross-country samples', *Public Choice*, vol 138, no 3-4, pp 483–90.

Raphael, D. et al (1996) 'The quality of life profile – adolescent version', *Journal of Adolescent Health*, vol 19, pp 366–75.

Rapson, J. and English, C. (2006) *Anxious to please: 7 revolutionary practices for the chronically nice*, Napierville, IL: Sourcebooks.

Rasmussen, D.C. (2006) 'Does "bettering our condition" really make us better off? Adam Smith on progress and happiness', *American Political Science Review*, vol 100, pp 309–18.

Rath, T. (2010) *Wellbeing: The five essential elements*, New York: Gallup Press.

Rathvon, N. (2008) *Effective school interventions* (2nd edn), New York: Guilford Press.

Redelmeier, D.A. and Singh, S.M. (2001) 'Survival in Academy Award-winning actors and actresses', *Annals of Internal Medicine*, vol 134, pp 955.

Reder, P., Duncan, S. and Lucey, C. (eds) (2003) *Studies in the assessment of parenting*, London: Brunner-Routledge.

Rees, G., Goswami, H. and Bradshaw, J. (2010) 'Developing an index of children's subjective well-being in England', London: Children's Society, www.childrenssociety.org.uk.

Reeves, R. (2001) *Happy Mondays: Putting the pleasure back into work*, New York: Basic Books.

Reeves, R. (2007) 'CoCo companies: work, happiness, and employee ownership', www.employeeownership.co.uk//coco-companies-work-happiness-and-employee-ownership.

Reynolds, R. (2009) *On guerrilla gardening: A handbook for gardening without boundaries*, London: Bloomsbury.

Ricard, M. (2007) *Happiness: A guide to developing life's most important skill*, London: Atlantic Books.

Richards, M. and Huppert, F. (2011) 'Do positive children become positive adults? Evidence from a longitudinal birth cohort study', *The Journal of Positive Psychology*, vol 6, no 1, pp 75–87.

Ridley, J. (2005) *Intimacy in crisis*, London: Wiley.

Rifkin, J. (2010) *The empathic civilization*, Cambridge: Polity Press.

Ripley, J.S. and Worthington, E.L. (2003) 'Hope-focused and forgiveness-based group interventions to promote marital enrichment', *Journal of Counseling & Development*, vol 80, no 4, pp 452–63.

Robertson, M. (1969) 'The pursuit of happiness at work', *Management Decision*, Autumn, pp 47–49.

Robinson, J.P. and Godbey, G. (1997) *Time for life: The surprising ways Americans use their time*, University Park, PA: Pennsylvania State University Press.

Rojek, C. (2005) *Leisure theory: Principles and practice*, London: Palgrave Macmillan.

Rojek, C. (2010) *The labour of leisure: The culture of free time*, London: Sage.

Rorty, R. (1999) *Philosophy and social hope*, Harmondsworth: Penguin.

Ross, C. and Van Willigen, M. (1997) 'Education and the subjective quality of life', *Journal of Health and Social Behavior*, vol 38, pp 275–97.

Ross, A. (2009) *Nice work if you can get it: Life and labor in precarious times*, New York: NYU Press.

Rothstein, B. (2010) 'Happiness and the welfare state', *Social Research*, vol 77, no 2, pp 1-28.

Rubin, Z. (1970) 'Measurement of romantic love', *Journal of Personality and Social Psychology*, vol 16, no 2, pp 265–73.

Russell, B. (1930/1975) *The conquest of happiness*, London: Unwin Books.

Ryan, A. (2010) 'Happiness and political theory', *Social Research*, vol 77, no 2, pp 421–39.

Ryff, C.D. (1989) 'Happiness is everything, or is it? Explorations on the meaning of psychological wellbeing', *Journal of Personality and Social Psychology*, vol 57, no 6, pp 1069–81.

Ryff, C.D. and Singer, B.H. (2008) 'Know thyself and become what you are: a eudaimonic approach to psychological wellbeing', *Journal of Happiness Studies*, vol 9, no 1, pp 13–39.

Sacks, D.W., Stevenson, B. and Wolfers, J. (2010) 'Subjective well-being, income, economic development and growth', Washington, DC: NBER Working Paper No 16441, www.nber.org/papers/w16441.

Sahlins, M.D. (1968/1974) 'The original affluent society', in *Stone Age economics*, London: Tavistock, pp 1–39.

Salerno, S. (2005) *SHAM: How the self-help movement made America helpless*, New York: Random House.

Samways, L. (1994) *Dangerous persuaders*, Harmondsworth: Penguin.

Sanders, M.R. (2008) 'Triple P-Positive Parenting Program as a public health approach to strengthening parenting', *Journal of Family Psychology*, vol 22, no 3, pp 506–17.

Sandhya, S. (2009) 'The social context of marital happiness in urban Indian couples: interplay of intimacy and conflict', *Journal of Marital and Family Therapy*, vol 35, no 1, pp 74–96.

Schaie, K.W. and Carstensen, L. (eds) (2006) *Social structures, aging, and self-regulation in the elderly*, New York: Springer.

Scheier, M.F., Carver, C.F. and Bridges, M.F. (1994) 'Distinguishing optimism from neuroticism (and trait anxiety, self-mastery, and self-esteem): a re-evaluation of the Life Orientation Test', *Journal of Personality and Social Psychology*, vol 67, pp 1063–78.

Schimmel, J. (2009) 'Development as happiness: the subjective perception of happiness and UNDP's analysis of poverty, wealth and development', *Journal of Happiness Studies*, vol 10, pp 93–111.

Schuller, T. et al (eds) (2004) *The benefits of learning: The impact of education on health, family life and social capital*, London: RoutledgeFalmer.

Schumacher, E.F. (1966/1973) 'Buddhist economics', in *Small is beautiful: Economics as if people mattered*, London: Blond and Briggs, pp 38–46.

Schwartz, B. (2004) *The paradox of choice: Why more is less*, New York: Ecco.

Schwartz, B. et al (2002) 'Maximizing versus satisficing: happiness is a matter of choice', *Journal of Personality and Social Psychology*, vol 83, no 5, pp 1178–97.

Schwartz, C. et al (2003) 'Altruistic social interest behaviors are associated with better mental health', *Psychosomatic Medicine*, vol 65, pp 778–85.

Schwartz, R.H., Tiamiyu, M. and Dwyer, D. (2007) 'Social worker hope and perceived burnout: the effects of age, years in practice, and setting', *Administration in Social Work*, vol 31, no 4, pp 103–19.

Schwarz, N. and Clore, G.L. (1983) 'Mood, misattribution, and judgments of well-being: informative and directive functions of affective states', *Journal of Personality and Social Psychology*, vol 45, no 4, pp 513–23.

Schwarz, N. and Strack, F, (1999) 'Reports of subjective well-being: judgmental processes and their methodological implications', in D. Kahneman et al, *Well-being: Foundations of hedonic psychology*, New York: Russell Sage, pp 61–84.

Scioli, A. and Biller, H.B. (2009) *Hope in the age of anxiety*, Oxford: Oxford University Press.

Scitovsky, T. (1976) *The joyless economy: An inquiry into human satisfaction and consumer dissatisfaction*, New York: Oxford University Press.

Scraton, P. (1997) *Childhood in crisis?*, London: UCL Press.

Scuka, R.F. (2005) *Relationship enhancement therapy: Healing through deep empathy and intimate dialogue*, London: Routledge.

Searle, B.A. (2008) *Well-being: In search of a good life?*, Bristol: The Policy Press.

Selekman, M.D. (2010) *Collaborative brief therapy with children*, New York: Guilford Press.

Seligman, M.E.P. (1990/2006) *Learned optimism: How to change your mind and your life*, New York: Vintage.

Seligman, M.E.P. (2003) *Authentic happiness*, London: Nicholas Brealey.

Seligman, M.E.P. (2008) 'Positive health', *Applied Psychology*, vol 57, pp 3–18.

Seligman, M.E.P. (2011) *Flourish: A visionary new understanding of happiness and well-being*, New York: Free Press.

Seligman, M.E.P., Verkuil, P.R. and Kang, T.H. (2005) 'Why lawyers are unhappy', *Deakin Law Review*, vol 10, no 1, pp 49–66.

Seligman, M.E.P. et al (2009) 'Positive education: positive psychology and classroom interventions', *Oxford Review of Education*, vol 35, no 3, pp 293–311.

Sen, A. (2009) *The idea of justice*, Cambridge, MA: Harvard University Press.

Shah, H. and Marks, N. (New Economics Foundation) (2004) *A wellbeing manifesto for a flourishing society*, www.neweconomics.org

Shaw, C. (2007) *The DNA of customer experience: How emotions drive value*, London: Palgrave Macmillan.

Sheldon, K.M. (2004) *Optimal human being: An integrated multi-level perspective*, New Jersey: Erlbaum.

Sheldon, K.M. et al (2010) 'Extrinsic value orientation and affective forecasting: overestimating the rewards, underestimating the costs', *Journal of Personality*, vol 78, no 1, pp 149–78.

Shirom, A. (2002) 'Job-related burnout: a review', in J.C. Quick and L.E. Tetrick (eds), *Handbook of occupational health psychology*, Washington, DC: American Psychological Association, pp 245–64.

Shoda, Y., Mischel, W. and Peake, P.K. (1990) 'Predicting adolescent cognitive and self-regulatory competencies from preschool delay of gratification: identifying diagnostic conditions', *Developmental Psychology*, vol 26, no 6, pp 978–86.

Shumway, D. (2003) *Modern love: Romance, intimacy, and the marriage crisis*, New York: NYU Press.

Sickler, J. and Fraser, J. (2009) 'Enjoyment in zoos', *Leisure Studies*, vol 28, no 3, pp 313–31.

Siegel, D. and Uviller, D. (eds) (2006) *Only child: Writers on the singular joys and solitary sorrows growing up solo*, New York: Harmony Books.

Simey, P. and Wellings, K. (2008) 'How do national newspapers report on sex and relationship education in England?', *Sex Education: Sexuality, Society and Learning*, vol 8, no 3, pp 357–70.

Simon, J. (2010) *Solution focused practice in end-of-life and grief counseling*, New York: Springer.

Sinclair, J. (1791–99) *Statistical account of Scotland*, http://edina.ac.uk/stat-acc-scot.

Sirgy, M.J., Lee, D.-J. and Bae, J. (2006) 'Developing a subjective measure of internet wellbeing: nomological (predictive) validation', *Social Indicators Research*, vol 78, no 2, pp 205–49.

Sirgy, M. J., Lee, D.-J. and Rahtz, D. (2007) 'Research in consumer wellbeing (CWB): an overview of the field and introduction to the special issue', *Journal of Macromarketing*, vol 27, no 4, pp 341–9.

Sirgy, M.J., Phillips, R. and Rahtz, D. (eds) (2011) *Community quality-of-life indicators: Best cases V*, Dordrecht: Springer.

Smart, R.N. (1958) 'Negative utilitarianism', *Mind*, vol 67, no 268, pp 542–3.

Smiles, S. (1859) *Self-help*, London: John Murray, www.emotionalliteracyeducation.com/classic_books_online/selfh10.htm.

Smith, C. (2005) *Soul searching: The religious and spiritual lives of American teenagers*, New York: Oxford University Press.

Snowdon, D. (2001) *Aging with grace: What the nun study teaches us about leading longer, healthier, and more meaningful lives*, London: Fourth Estate.

Snyder, C.R. (1994) *The psychology of hope*, New York: Free Press.

Snyder, C.R., Cheavens, J. and Sympson, S.C. (1997) 'Hope: an individual motive for social commerce', *Group Dynamics*, vol 1, no 2, pp 107–18.

Snyder, C.R. et al (1996) 'Development and validation of the State Hope Scale', *Journal of Personality and Social Psychology*, vol 70, pp 321–35.

Solnicka, S.J., Hong, L. and Hemenway, D. (2007) 'Positional goods in the United States and China', *Journal of Socio-Economics*, vol 36, no 4, pp 537–45.

Solomon, R.C. (ed) (2004) *Thinking about feeling: Contemporary philosophers on emotions*, New York: Oxford University Press.

Solomon, R.C. and Stone, L.D. (2002) 'On "positive" and "negative" emotions', *Journal for the Theory of Social Behavior*, vol 32, pp 417–43.

Soons, J.P.M., Liefbroer, A. and Kalmijn, M. (2009) 'The long-term consequences of relationship formation for subjective well-being', *Journal of Marriage & Family*, vol 71, no 5, pp 1254–70.

Sorensen, B. (2008) *Only-child experience and adulthood*, London: Palgrave Macmillan.

Soutter, A.K., Gilmore, A. and O'Steen, B. (2010) 'How do high school youths' educational experiences relate to well-being? Towards a trans-disciplinary conceptualization', *Journal of Happiness Studies*, vol 12, no 4, pp 591–631.

Sprecher, S. and Fehr, B. (2005) 'Compassionate love for close others and humanity', *Journal of Social and Personal Relationships*, vol 22, pp 629–52.

Spring, J.H. (2007) *A new paradigm for global school systems: Education for a long and happy life*, London: Routledge.

Stearns, P.N. (2001) *Consumerism in world history: The global transformation of desire*, London: Routledge.

Stearns, P.N. (2003) *Anxious parents: A history of modern childrearing in America*, New York: NYU Press.

Stearns, P.N. (2010) 'Defining happy childhoods assessing a recent change', *Journal of the History of Childhood and Youth*, vol 3, no 2, pp 165–86.

Stebbins, R.A. (2007) *Serious leisure: A perspective for our time*, Piscataway, NJ: Transaction.

Steger, B. and Brunt, L. (eds) (2003) *Night-time and sleep in Asia and the West*, London: RoutledgeCurzon.

Stein, L., and M.A. Test (1980) 'Alternative to mental hospital treatment.' *Archives of General Psychiatry* vol 37, pp 392-397

Steptoe, A., Wardle, J. and Marmot, M. (2005) 'Positive affect and health-related neuroendocrine, cardiovascular, and inflammatory processes, *Proceedings of the National Academic of Sciences of the USA*, vol 102, no 18, pp 6508–12.

Sternberg, R.J. (1997) 'Construct validation of a triangular love scale', *European Journal of Social Psychology*, vol 27, pp 313–35.

Sternberg, R.J. (1999) *Love is a story: A new theory of relationships*, New York: Oxford University Press.

Stevenson, B., and Wolfers, J. (2007) 'The paradox of declining female happiness', Universiy of Pennsylvania, http://bpp.wharton.upenn.edu/betseys/papers.asp#Paradox.

Stiglitz, J.E. et al (2009) *Report by the Commission on the Measurement of Economic Performance and Social Progress*, Paris: OECD, www.stiglitz-sen-fitoussi.fr/documents/rapport_anglais.pdf.

Stirling, E. (2010) *Valuing older people: The positive psychology of ageing*, London: John Wiley.

Stout, M. (2001) *The feel-good curriculum: The dumbing down of America's kids in the name of self-esteem*, Cambridge, MA: Da Capo Press.

Stradling, J. (2004) *Educating for the good life: Democratic schooling and its dilemmas*, Cresskill, NJ: Hampton.

Strang, H. and Braithwaite, J. (eds) (2002) *Restorative justice and family violence*, Cambridge: Cambridge University Press.

Stratton, A. (2010) 'Happiness index to gauge Britain's national mood', *Guardian*, www.guardian.co.uk/lifeandstyle/2010/nov/14/happiness-index-britain-national-mood.

Strauss, C. (2004) 'Is empathy gendered and if so, why? An approach from feminist psychological anthropology', *Ethos*, vol 32, pp 4432–57.

Sunstein, C. and Posner, E. (eds) (2010) *Law and happiness*, Chicago, IL: University of Chicago Press.

Sylvestre M., Huszti E. and Hanley, J.A. (2006) 'Do Oscar winners live longer than less successful peers? A reanalysis of the evidence', *Annals of Internal Medicine*, vol 145, no 5, pp 361–3.

Tannen, D. (1991) *You just don't understand: Women and men in conversation*, London: Virago.

Tanomsup, S. (2006) 'The 10th National Economic and Social Development Plan's Feedbacks', Bangkok: International Institute for Trade and Development.

Tatarkiewicz, W. (1976) *Analysis of happiness*, trans E. Rothert and D. Zielinskn, Warsaw: Polish Scientific Publishers.

Taylor, J. (2005) *Your children are under attack: How popular culture is destroying your kids' values, and how you can protect them*, Naperville, IL: Sourcebooks.

Taylor, J. et al (2009) 'Practitioner assessments of "good enough" parenting: factorial survey', *Journal of Clinical Nursing*, vol 18, no 8, pp 1180–9.

Terkel, S. (1974) *Working: People talk about what they do all day and how they feel about what they do*, New York: New Press.

Thaler, L.K. and Koval, R. (2006) *The power of nice: How to conquer the business world with kindness*, London: Allen and Unwin.

Thaler, R.H. and Sunstein, C.R. (2008) *Nudge: Improving decisions about health, wealth, and happiness*, New Haven, CT: Yale University Press.

Thang, L.L. (2006) 'Experiencing leisure in later life: a study of retirees and activity in Singapore', *Journal of Cross-Cultural Gerontology*, vol 20, pp 307–18.

Thin, N. (2002) *Social progress and sustainable development*, Rugby, UK: ITDG/West Hartford, CT: Kumarian.

Thin, N. (2005) 'Happiness and the sad topics of anthropology', University of Bath: Wellbeing in Developing Countries Working Paper no 10, www.welldev.org.uk/research/workingpaperpdf/wed10.pdf.

Thin, N. (2008) '"Realising the substance of their happiness": how anthropology forgot about *Homo Gauius*', in A. Corsin Jimenez (ed), *Culture and the politics of freedom: The anthropology of wellbeing*, London: Pluto Press, pp 134–55.

Thin, N. (2009a) 'Schoolchildren's wellbeing and life prospects: justifying the universal tax on childhood', University of Bath Wellbeing in Developing Countries Working Paper 09/46, www.bath.ac.uk/econ-dev/wellbeing/wedworkingpapers.htm.

Thin, N. (2009b) 'Good feelings and good lives: why anthropology can ill afford to ignore wellbeing', in G. Mathews and C. Izquierdo, *Pursuits of happiness: Wellbeing in anthropological perspective*, Oxford: Berghahn, pp 23–44.

Thin, N. (2011a) 'Socially responsible cheermongery: on the sociocultural contexts and levels of social happiness policies', in R. Biswas-Diener (ed), *Positive psychology as a mechanism for social change*, Dordrecht: Springer.

Thin, N. (2011b) '"No-one is unmusical". Elizabeth, everyday cheermongery, and active musical citizenship', *International Journal of Well-being*, July, pp 291–306.

Thoits, P.A. and Hewitt, L.N. (2001) 'Volunteer work and wellbeing', *Journal of Health and Social Behavior*, vol 42, no 2, pp 115–31.

Thomas, K. (1999) *The Oxford book of work*, Oxford: Oxford University Press.

Tolich, M.B. (1993) 'Alienating and liberating emotions at work: supermarket clerks' performance of customer service', *Journal of Contemporary Ethnography*, vol 22, no 3, pp 361–81.

Torras, M. (2008) 'The subjectivity inherent in objective measures of wellbeing', *Journal of Happiness Studies*, vol 9, pp 475–87.

Tracey, D. (2007) *Guerilla gardening: A manifesto*, Gabriola Island, BC: New Society.

Trawick, M. (1992) *Notes on love in a Tamil family*, Berkeley, CA: University of California Press.

Tremblay, D.-G. and Genin, E. (2008) 'Money, work–life balance and autonomy: why do IT professionals choose self-employment?', *Applied Research in Quality of Life*, vol 3, pp 161–79.

Trompenaars, F., and E. Voerman (2009) *Servant-leadership across cultures*, New York: McGraw-Hill

UNDP (2007) *Thailand Human Development Report 2007: Sufficiency Economy and Human Development Report*, http://hdr.undp.org/en/reports/nationalreports/asiathepacific/thailand/name,3418,en.html.

UNESCAP (2009a) 'Measuring the progress of societies: what is the relevance for Asia and the Pacific?' Bangkok: UNESCAP report of session 4–6 February.

UNESCAP (2009b) *Social services policies and family well-being in the Asian and Pacific region*, Bangkok: UNESCAP.

Unger, D. (2009) 'Sufficiency economy and the bourgeois virtues', *Asian Affairs*, vol 36, no 3, pp 139–56.

Unicef (2007) *Child poverty in perspective: An overview of child well-being in rich countries*, Florence: Unicef Innocenti Research Centre, www.unicef-icdc.org/publications.

Vaillant, G.E. (1990) 'Avoiding negative life outcomes', in P.B. Baltes and M.M. Baltes (eds), *Successful aging*, Cambridge: Cambridge University Press, pp 332–58.

Vaillant, G.E. (2002) *Ageing well: Surprising guideposts to a happier life from the landmark Harvard Study of Adult Development*, Melbourne: Scribe Publications.

Valenti, J. (2009) *The purity myth: How America's obsession with virginity is hurting young women*, Jackson, TN: Seal Press.

Van der Geest, S. (1998) 'Growing old and building a house in the Akan Culture of Ghana', *Journal of Cross-cultural Gerontology* vol 13, no 4, pp 333–59.

Van der Geest, S. (2004) '"They don't come to listen": the experience of loneliness among older people in Kwahu, Ghana', *Journal of Cross-cultural Gerontology*, vol 19, no 2, pp 77–96.

van Deurzen, E. (2009) *Psychotherapy and the quest for happiness*, London: Sage.

van Kempen, L. (2009) 'The "downside" of women's empowerment in India: an experimental inquiry into the role of expectations', *Social Indicators Research*, vol 94, pp 465–82.

van Willigen, J. (1989) *Gettin' some age on me: Social organization of older people in a rural American community*, Lexington, KY: University Press of Kentucky.

Veal, A.J. (2004) 'A brief history of work and its relationship to leisure', in J. Haworth and A.J.Veal (eds), *Work and leisure*, London: Routledge, pp 15–33.

Veenhoven, R. (1984) *Conditions of happiness*, Dordrecht: Kluwer Academic.

Veenhoven, R. (1996) 'Happy life-expectancy', *Social Indicators Research*, vol 39, pp 1–58.

Veenhoven, R. (2000) 'Wellbeing in the welfare state: level not higher, distribution not more equitable', *Journal of Comparative Policy Analysis*, vol 2, pp 91–125.

Veenhoven, R. (2002) 'Why social policy needs subjective indicators', *Social Indicators Research*, vol 58 no 1–3, 33–46.

Veenhoven, R. (2008a) 'Healthy happiness: effects of happiness on physical health and the consequences for preventive health care', *Journal of Happiness Studies*, vol 9, no 3, pp 449–69.

Veenhoven, R. (2008b) 'Sustainable consumption and happiness', in S. Reddy (ed), *Green consumerism: Approaches and country experiences*, Hyderabad: Icfai University Press, pp 39–68.

Veenhoven, R. (2009) 'How do we assess how happy we are? Tenets, implications and tenability of three theories', in A.K. Dutt and B. Radcliff (eds) *Happiness, economics and politics*, Cheltenham: Edward Elgar, pp 45–69.

Veenhoven, R. (2009) 'Wellbeing in nations and wellbeing of nations: is there a conflict between individual and society?', *Social Indicators Research*, vol 91, no 1, pp 5–21.

Veenhoven, R. (nd) 'Examples of measures of happiness', http://worlddatabaseofhappiness.eur.nl/hap_quer/hqi_fp.htm.

Veenhoven, R. and Hagenaars, A. (eds) (1989) *How harmful is happiness?*, Rotterdam: University Press Rotterdam.

Veenhoven, R. and Verkuyten, M. (1989) 'The well-being of only children', *Adolescence*, vol 24, no 93, pp 155–66.

Viswesvaran, C. and Deshpande, S.P. (1996) 'Ethics, success, and job satisfaction: a test of dissonance theory in India', *Journal of Business Ethics*, vol 1065–9.

Vitale, A. (2008) *City of disorder: How the quality of life campaign transformed New York politics*, New York: NYU Press.

Volling, B. and Blandon, A. (2005) 'Positive indicators of sibling relationship quality: the sibling inventory of behavior', in K. Moore and L. Lippman (eds), *What do children need to flourish?*, New York: Springer, pp 203–19.

Waddell, G. and Burton, K. (2006) *Is work good for your health and well-being?*, London: The Stationery Office.

Waite, L.J. and Gallagher, M. (2004) *The case for staying married*, Oxford: Oxford University Press.

Waite, L.J., Luo, Ye, and Lewin, A.C. (2009) 'Marital happiness and marital stability: consequences for psychological well-being', *Social Science Research*, vol 38, no 1, pp 201–12.

Walls, J.L. (2002) *Heaven: The logic of eternal joy*, Oxford: Oxford University Press.

Wangdi, K. (2008) 'Education indicators', Thimphu, Bhutan: Centre for Bhutan Studies, www.grossnationalhappiness.com/surveyReports/education/education_abs.aspx?d=edu&t=Education.

Warnick, B.R. (2009) 'Dilemmas of autonomy and happiness: Harry Brighouse on subjective wellbeing and education', *Theory and Research in Education*, vol 7, no 1, pp 89–111.

Warr, P.B. (2007) *Work, happiness, and unhappiness*, London: Routledge.

Warr, P.B. and Clapperton, G. (2010) *The joy of work? Jobs, happiness and you*, Hove, UK: Routledge.

Watson, G. (1930) 'Happiness among adult students of education', *Journal of Educational Psychology*, vol 21, pp 79–109.

Watten, R.G. et al (1997) 'Personality factors and somatic symptoms', *European Journal of Personality*, vol 11, no 1, pp 57–68.

Weingarten, K. (2010) 'Reasonable hope: construct, clinical applications, and supports', *Family Process*, vol 49, no 1, pp 5–25.

White, J. (1997) *Education and the end of work*, London: Cassell.

White, J. (2006) 'Autonomy, human flourishing and the curriculum', *Journal of Philosophy of Education*, vol 40, no 3, pp 381–90.

Wieck, A. et al (1989) 'A "strengths perspective for social work practice"', *Social Work*, vol 34, pp 350–4.

Wierzbicka, A. (2004) '"Happiness" in cross-linguistic and cross-cultural perspective', *Daedalus*, vol 133, no 2, pp 34–43.

Wilcox, W.B. and Nock, S.L. (2006) 'What's love got to do with it? Equality, equity, commitment and women's marital quality', *Social Forces*, vol 84, pp 1321–45.

Williams, R. (1976/1983) *Keywords: A vocabulary of culture and society* (rev edn), London: Fontana.

Williams, S. (2005) *Sleep and society: Sociological ventures into the (un)known*, New York: Routledge.

Wilson, E.G. (2008) *Against happiness: In praise of melancholy*, London: Sarah Crichton Books.

Wilson, W. (1967) 'Correlates of avowed happiness', *Psychological Bulletin*, vol 67, pp 294–306.

Winnicott, D.W. (1965) *The maturational process and the facilitating environment*, London: Hogarth Press.

Wirtz, D. et al (2009) 'What constitutes a good life?', *Journal of Personality*, vol 77, no 4, pp 1168–95.

World Health Organization (2007) *Global age-friendly cities: A guide*, Geneva: WHO.

Wright, L.J.M. (2004) 'Preserving the value of happiness in primary school physical education', *Physical Education & Sport Pedagogy*, vol 9, no 2, pp 149–63.

Wright, R. (2000) *Nonzero: The logic of human destiny*, New York: Pantheon Books.

Wrigley, T. (2003) *Schools of hope: A new agenda for school improvement*, Stoke-on-Trent: Trentham.

Xu, J. and Roberts, R.E. (2010) 'The power of positive emotions: it's a matter of life or death', *Health Psychology*, vol 29, pp 9–19.

Yalom, I.D. and Leszcz, M. (2005) *The theory and practice of group psychotherapy* (5th edn), New York: Basic Books.

Yazzie-Mintz, E. (2010) *Charting the path from engagement to achievement*, Indiana University, http://ceep.indiana.edu/hssse/images/HSSSE_2010_Report.pdf.

Zelenski, J.M., Murphy, S.A. and Jenkins, D.A. (2008) 'The happy-productive worker thesis revisited', *Journal of Happiness Studies*, vol 9, no 4, pp 521–37.

Zhang, W. and Liu, G. (2007) 'Childlessness, psychological well-being, and life satisfaction among the elderly in China', *Journal of Cross-cultural Gerontology*, vol 22, pp 185–203.

Zhang, Y. (2011) 'Educational expectations, school experiences, and academic achievements: a longitudinal examination', Gansu Survey of Children and Families, Working Paper, http://repository.upenn.edu/gansu_papers/22/.

Zimmerman, M.A. (1990) 'Toward a theory of learned hopefulness', *Journal of Research in Personality*, vol 24, pp 71–86.

Zins, J.E. et al (2004) *Building academic success on social and emotional learning*, New York: Teachers College Press.

Zlatev, J. et al (2008) *The shared mind: Perspectives on intersubjectivity*, John Benjamins.

Zuzanek, J. (2004) 'Work, leisure, time-pressure and stress', in J. Haworth and A.J. Veal (eds), *Work and leisure*, London: Routledge, pp 123–44.

Index